Rural Development in North East India

BY THE SAME AUTHOR

— Economy of a Premitive Tribal Village in Manipur

— Rural Development in India : Retrospect and Prospects

— Village Development in North East India: New Approaches

About the Editors

Komol Singha (1972) is a senior faculty in the Department of Economics, Royal University of Bhutan, Gaeddu College of Business Studies, Gedu, Bhutan. He specializes in Development Economics, and at present actively involved in rural development. Earlier, he has taught Development Economics at Don Bosco College, Manipur and St. Joseph's College, Nagaland for two and five years respectively. He has to his creadit a book entitled: *Village Development in North East India* (ed. 2009), besides a good number of research papers in the national and the international seminars, journals, and newspapers.

Gautam Patikar (1968) is a senior faculty in the Department of Commerce, Nagaland University, Kohima. He secured First Class First in M.Com. from the North Eastern Hill University, and obtained Ph.D. degree from Nagaland University. He is a life member of Indian Commerce Association. He has participated in several international and national seminars and conferences. He has also contributed a good number of papers in journals of repute and edited volumes.

Rural Development in North East India

Edited by

Komol Singha
Gautam Patikar

CONCEPT PUBLISHING COMPANY PVT. LTD.
NEW DELHI-59

ISBN-13-978-81-8069-668-8

First Published 2010

Published and Printed by

Concept Publishing Company Pvt. Ltd.
Regd. Office:
A/15-16, Commercial Block, Mohan Garden
New Delhi-110059 (India)
Phones : 25351460, 25351794, *Fax* : 091-11-25357109
Email : publishing@conceptpub.com,
Website: www.conceptpub.com

Editorial Office:
H-13, Bali Nagar, New Delhi-110 015, India.

Cataloging in Publication Data--*Courtesy:* D.K. Agencies (P) Ltd. <docinfo@dkagencies.com>

National Seminar on Rural Development in India : Prospects and Retrospect (2008 : Jakhama, India)

Rural development in North East India / edited by Komol Singha, Gautam Patikar.
p. cm.
Includes bibliographical references.
Includes index.
ISBN 13: 978-81-8069-668-8

1. Rural development--Government policy--India, Northeastern--Congresses. 2. Rural industries--India, Northeastern--Congresses. 3. Infrastructure (Economics)--India,Northeastern--Congresses. I. Singha, Komol, 1972- II. Patikar, Gautam, 1968- III. Title.

DDC 307.141209541 2

Preface

India's North-Eastern Region consists of eight States and is a 'mixed bag' of several ethnic groups. 200 out of 635 tribal groups of the country are found in this region. It covers an area of approximately 2,62,500 sq. km., *i.e.,* 8 per cent of the total area of the country. Its population is about 39 million, *i.e.,* 3.9 per cent of the country's total population. Around three-fourth of the North-East is covered by hilly terrain and majority of the people (around 85 per cent) live in villages, rural areas in poverty, in the midst of abundant resources.

Since independence, many initiatives on rural development have been taken up by the government and other institutions in the region. Still, it remains an illusive goal and became only an introductory speech of the politicians and the leaders in public platforms. So, the development of rural sector has become the need of the hour and requires re-look with different approaches in this region.

This volume contains nineteen (19) articles and most of them are contributed by the scholars at a National Seminar on *Rural Development in India: Prospects and Retrospect,* held on 21-22 November 2008 at St. Joseph's College, Jakhama, Nagaland with financial assistance from UGC (NERO), Guwahati. The volume tries to explore ways and means in remodelling the rural economy of North-Eastern Region. However, it focuses on infrastructure, finance, agriculture, social, political and other aspects of rural development in the region.

We are grateful to S.C. Ray, Deputy Secretary, University Grants Commission, NERO, Guwahati for the financial assistance in organizing this National Seminar. Our special thanks also go to Fr. Isaac Padinjarekuttu, the Principal of St. Joseph's College and the Management and staff of the College for their help in organizing the Seminar. We are also grateful and give our credit to valuable contributors. Last but not the least, we would like to thank Mr. Ashok Kumar Mittal of Concept Publishing Company Pvt. Ltd., New Delhi for taking keen interest in bringing out this volume.

22 March, 2009 **Komol Singha**
Gautam Patikar

Contents

SECTION III

INSTITUTIONS, AGENCIES AND PERFORMANCE

Keynote Address

S. K. Mishra

I am overwhelmed by the honour given to me by the organizer of this Seminar by reposing their confidence in me and entrusting me with the responsibility of delivering this keynote address for the Seminar. This seminar, as its title unambiguously declares, exhorts all of us to address to the very important problem of Rural Development in India.

India Lives in Villages

We all know that India lives in her villages. At the beginning of the 20th Century, about 90 per cent of her population lived in villages and at the beginning of the 21st Century about 72 per cent of her population still lives in the villages (Table 1). This is so far as the statistics go. But the truth is that most of the small towns in the country are not much different from the rural areas and even in the larger cities a great number of people are closely connected to their rural habitats. Much of India's urbanization is only an urban accretion. India's urbanization is often termed as over-urbanization, pseudo-urbanization. The big cities attained inordinately large population size leading to virtual collapse in the urban services and followed by basic problems in the field of housing, slum, water, infrastructure, quality of life etc. Urbanization is a product of demographic explosion and poverty induced rural-urban migration. Urbanization is occurring not due to urban pull but due to rural push. Globalization, liberalization, privatization are addressing negative process for urbanization in India (Datta, 2006).

But this is only that aspect which is reflected in the sheer number of people. Consider the sociological aspects; a large majority of people in the urban areas are still rural in customs, mores, interpersonal relations, values, etc. They have not been far from their rural roots. Indian villages and villagers only live in town that are only definition-wise urban areas.

Table 1: Growth of Population in India Since 1901

Census Year	*No. of Urban Agglomeration Town*	*Total Population*	*Urban Population*	*Rural Population*	*Rural Population as % to Total/ Population*
1901	1827	238396327	25851873	212544454	89.16
1911	1825	252093390	25941633	226151757	89.71
1921	1949	251321213	28086167	223235046	88.82
1931	2072	278977238	33455989	245521249	88.01
1941	2250	318660580	44153297	274507283	86.14
1951	2843	361088090	62443709	298644381	82.71
1961	2363	439234771	78936603	360298168	82.03
1971	2590	598159652	109113977	489045675	81.76
1981	3378	683329097	159462547	523866550	76.66
1991	3768	844324222	217177625	627146597	74.28
2001	5161	1027015247	285354954	741660293	72.22

Despite so many concerted efforts, the rural populace remains poor in the midst of abundant resources. The intention of the Government of India to assist the rural compartments cannot do much practically to alleviate the poor. The projects fell short of providing accessibility, infrastructures, electricity, telecommunication, water supply, employment, etc. to the rural areas in spite of the schemes' commendable objectives. Even the most flagship rural development programme of the UPA-led coalition government, NREGA (National Rural Employment Guarantee Act) has turned out to be an elite/urban bias programmes.

Therefore, the question arises: what went wrong in the planning for rural development and what have we undermined and even now continue to do so that rural areas remain underdeveloped and the rural people remain poor? This seminar poses this question in a bold relief.

The Urban-Rural Dualism

India is clearly divided into the dualism of rural and urban enclaves. As Boeke has put it, *"It is possible to characterize a society, in the economic sense, by the social spirit, the organizational forms and the technique dominating it. These three aspects are interdependent and in this connection typify a society, in this way that a prevailing social spirit and the prevailing forms of organization and of technique give a society its style, its appearance, so that in their interrelation they may be called the social system, the social style or the social atmosphere of that society."* Less developed economies, especially with a history of prolonged colonial rule, often exhibit a simultaneous existence of two (or more) enclaves of socio-economic systems, characteristically and conspicuously different from each other, and each dominating a part of the society, the economy and the polity. These enclaves markedly differ in matters of ownership of resources, production relations, the social spirit, institutions, customs, mores and attitudinal structure, socio-economic and political organization, technological know-how and its application and so on. Of course, among these enclaves there exists a gray zone where distinction may not easily be perceived. This gray zone might be the crucible for integration, but it is equally likely that a colloidal admixture of heterogeneous elements persists for long and camouflages integration process. In any case, the rate of integration is extremely slow such that these enclaves persist for long. The said enclaves often resist the functioning of each other. They function not in harmony but in conflict with each other. Frictional losses are significantly large. Such an economy has been nicknamed as a 'dualistic' or 'pluralistic' (depending on the number of enclaves coexisting) economy.

What makes an economist interested in studying such an economy is that explanation of the issues relating to operation, stability, growth and justice in such economies evade an application of a single theoretical framework. As one knows, much in economics, explicitly or tacitly, has been formulated on the basis of experiences in the Western developed economies. That is why some economists prefer to name such a body of economic theories as the "Establishment Economics." To explain the said issues in a dualistic economy, tools of the Establishment Economics fail. Nor the "economics of primitive societies" succeeds in the said explanation. So, the economics of such economies is in itself dualistic (pluralistic). A hybrid type of economics that one may venture upon to develop the internal contradictions and inconsistencies, and it cannot form a well-integrated body or a system of laws pertaining to the functioning of such an economy. So in the conceptual domain, one finds inconsistencies and in explaining the facts, one performs only poorly. This is the challenge that makes the study of such economies interesting.

The challenge that such an economy makes to the planners and policy makers is still more intriguing. In the absence of an understanding of the laws that govern such economies, planners and policy makers can only poorly succeed in controlling the policy instruments to achieve the desired goals. Cumulative experiences of failing in controlling the socio-economic forces for achieving the targets often induce decision makers to indulge in ad-hocism. Experiences of failure, aspirations of economic agents and ad-hocism in decision-making together invite opportunistic elements to operate that further complicate the management of such economies. The uncertainty and risk that brew in such an environment raise social and private cost of economic operation. Expensive production system limits the growth prospective of such an economy and it is caught in the *'low-level equilibrium'* characterizing poverty, inefficiency, unemployment of manpower together with under-utilization of available economic resources and so on.

The typology of dualism is primarily based on five basic, though often interrelated, criteria, namely, *societal, economic, political, spatial* (geographical) and *anthropological*. Societal criterion comprises value system, inter-familial and intra-familial relations forms of social organization and so on. Economic criterion covers ownership rules, production relations, forms of economic organization, the spirit of economic activities, etc. Political criterion mainly concerns with the conventions governing formation and functioning of, and changes in, political organizations. Spatial criteria relates to predominance of the socio-economic system as distributed over space. Anthropological criterion relates to cultural and racial attributes of the population.

Difficulties in Pin-Pointing the Factors of Development

What are the factors of development? Are factors of development a multitude of indicators of different facets of development such as measures (indicators) regarding per capita income, different heads or items of consumption, health, literacy, education, housing, space, transportation, recreational facilities, etc.? Or, are factors of development the multitude of determinant variables of development – infrastructure, physical and human capital with specifications, resources of various types, etc.? Development must accompany structural changes. Then are the structural relations the factors of development?

Several studies have been conducted on quantifying levels of economic development and searching for the determinants of levels of development. In the 1960s Irma Adelman and Cynthia Morris (1967) related growth and equity to interactions among changes in economic and social structure – political participation and income distribution. They found that the rate of improvement in human resources, direct government economic activity, socio-economic dualism, the potential for economic development, per capita GNP and the strength of the labour movement determine patterns of income distribution. Later, many studies appeared that measured levels of development using the quantitative approach of Adelman and Morris, but did not try to identify the determinants of development or differentials in the levels of development.

There are important issues related to quantifying relations among factors of development: (1) the issue of availability of data, (2) the issue of modelling the process or interrelation, (3) availability and use of suitable quantitative method(s) and finally, (4) identification and interpretation.

In most cases, data cannot be collected by individuals and therefore, secondary data must be relied upon. Secondary data are usually not cut and dried for the objectives of quantifying interrelations among factors of development. They have originally collected for some other purposes. They have their 'noise' and that may distort the findings. Next, assumptions regarding the relations are important. Whether relations are linear or non-linear, and if non-linear, then what is its specification? A mismatch of assumptions with the true nature of interrelations may seriously distort the findings. Nature of stochasticity and its specifications are important. We cannot always expect normally distributed errors with zero mean and so on. Thirdly, there are only a few methods available to us for doing a quantitative work and most of them are built on a multitude of assumptions.

Underdeveloped economies are often poorly integrated and therefore, factors of development are only poorly related. Moreover, empirical data on such variables contain large errors of observation as well as sizeable variability. Therefore, true relations are often hidden under the 'noise' and difficult to identify. Most statistical methods dealing with multivariate data are based on inter-correlation matrix or variance-covariance matrix. Poor integration among the factors of development makes sparse (statistically speaking) matrices with poor strength to meet the objectives of analysis.

Experiential Relevance of Economic Planning for Rural Development

Now economic Plans of the country do not generate much excitement – It was so with the VIII Plan, then IX Plan as well as the X Plan. Matters may not be very different with the XI

Plan too. If over the years successive plans have stirred less and less passion, the planners are to be blamed.

The II Plan showed comparative advantage in heavy and basic industries – all that begins from there and continued until 1991. The III Plan was multi-sector input-output system. The IV Plan was essentially based on the same logic but with an added consideration for material balances in the intermediate years too. The structure of imports was endogenous. The Fifth Plan recognized that private consumption must be consistent with the development of the economy and income, savings and consumption have a balance. It also had a consideration for resource mobilization. Poverty alleviation programe was added. The VI Plan integrated methodologies of III, IV and V Plans. It was technically much superior to its predecessors. The VII Plan was technically no improvement over the VI Plan, except some more details. So was the VIII Plan.

Before 1991 growth by import substitution was the major thrust, export promotion came much later. Industrialization policy was pro-heavy industries. Reduction in import content rather than domestic resource cost of production was stressed on. Heavy industries required lumpy investment, large capital/output ratio, long gestation lags, and large import of capital goods. Inadequate infrastructure, lack of experience, necessity to learn by doing lengthened the gestation period. Other problems are also due to many of such investments in the public sector.

Then we realized not only allocation, but use of resources too is important. Market mechanism can attain efficiency much better than central planning can do. After 1991, planning is still important. Why? Market may bring about equilibrium between demand and supply, but what about needs and its relations with the supply?

Poverty

The principal goal of development policy is to create sustainable improvement in the quality of life for all people (World Development Report, 1999-2000). Raising per capita income is only one objective. Others are education, health, participation in public life. Market mechanism may not attain all these if left free. So, Planning is needed.

Redistributive programmes – to lobby for the poor in economic policy making – to ensure that all markets function – to plan public action in areas where externalities create natural monopolies and where cost of public action is less than cost of regulation – to maintain macro-economic stability – Planning and policy analysis must be integrated – Policies must provide signals to the private economic agents. Will all these go in favour of the rural areas wherein the people living? It is a big question.

What Types of Models of Development?

Development models initially were begotten from growth models – the models that formalize how does a competitive economy expands, under what conditions will it best expand with minimal ups and downs and will not be subject to recessional forces. To begin with, therefore, some key variables were important – saving, investment, consumption, output, physical capital/output ratio, and physical capital/labour ratio and so on.

Raising per capita income was, therefore, the meaning of development, its trickle down was presupposed. But soon it was realized that there could be growth without development (Robert Clower, the case of Liberia). Development means structural changes – what is the structure of an economy and what is meant by structural changes? Is trickle down effect guaranteed?

Dudley Seers raised three basic questions: what is happening to poverty and the poor – what is happening with unemployment – what is happening to inequality – they are related to redistribution, resource utilization and welfare. Growth does not ensure welfare, but development does.

The World Development Report 1991 asserted that the challenge of development is to improve the quality of life – for the world's poor countries a better quality of life – beyond income it needs better education, higher standards of health and nutrition, less poverty, a cleaner environment, more equality of opportunities, greater individual freedom and a richer cultural life. Self-esteem and freedom from servitude are basic to development.

The World Development Report 1999-2000 emphasized on a comprehensive approach to development – sustainable development – justice and welfare over generations – enlargement of human capabilities.

Therefore, what was considered exogenous before, now, becomes endogenous in the development model. Health and education are endogenous now – growth of population must be brought inside the model – the objective function has changed – efficiency with justice and welfare. 'Land' is no longer 'the original and indestructible free gift of nature'.

Such a model would require immense wealth of information. Now, therefore, models cannot be expressed in a few equations or inequalities – How to specify the parameters so large in number – adequate information cannot be gathered and processed to make models formal. There is a tendency, therefore, not to build mathematical models of development any more.

Many more issues were raised in the process and factors of development – Myrdal spoke of 'modernization ideals' and their inculcation in the people by a design. David McClelland spoke of 'n-achievement' and its inculcation. Harvey Leibenstein said of creating pressures from above, pressures from below and pressures from sides. One may also think of generating pressure from within – what else 'n-achievement' means? One has to consider allocative efficiency, but one must think on X-efficiency– how market and even the Central Control build up X-efficiencies at different levels and in different sectors.

To begin with, capital and labour are basic ingredient variables of a development model, but capital is considered malleable and labour simply providing muscle power and possibly a little of what an 'automata' would provide. But when technology comes in, complications arise. The assumption of malleable capital gives rise to putty – clay models; labour is skilled and differentiated vertically and horizontally. Machines of different vintages function together. Knowledge and information come in. These are not exogenous factors in the process of development and must be included in the model.

At a technical level also, development models cannot be single objective function optimization models – multi-criteria decision-making is necessary – Goal programming in a dynamic framework is needed and the resulting solutions are 'satisfiying solutions' as visualized by Herbert A. Simon. Uncertainty replaces certainty, especially due to incomplete knowledge or large transaction costs.

Development Strategy in India in Retrospect

The period of 1947 to 1991 characterized protectionism, quota-permit-licence in the industrial policy. Was it a part of India's international politics not to join any bloc (capitalist or socialist) explicitly and wait and watch for some time? Or, as Pranab Bardhan has put it – Indian politics is essentially the interplay of three proprietorial classes, the big business class, rich farmers and a white collar educated middle class and the political leaders, who came in a tacit agreement to reap the fruits of Independence – based on Marx-Olson model – and it shaped the economic policy of India ?

Serious problems of stability and development – ultimately Balance of Payment Crisis in 1991 – the crisis was in making since 1980s – excess domestic expenditure over income – fiscal deficit soared to over 11 per cent – great inflow of foreign borrowings – public debt as a proportion of GNP went up to 60 per cent – foreign currency reserves depleted – 2-digit inflation – international credit rating of India got downgraded – borrowing against the gold reserve – measures such as devaluation of rupee – partial and then full convertibility of rupee on trade account were taken.

Among many, some important reasons were failure of the public sector to generate investible resources and the explosive growth of governmental current spending leading to deficit – was it due to micro-economic inefficiencies? Inefficiency of public sector enterprise – they dominated the provision of infrastructure and critical intermediates – their inefficiency had a multiplier effect on other industries – restrictive trade policies reduced scale of output, efficiency, bottlenecks – reduced rate of return on investment – revenue could not grow – tax base did not grow – ever-increasing expansion of employment in the public sector was also responsible.

Macro-economic Reforms

Trade policy reforms – import licensing system dismantled – all non-tariff barriers phased out from all tradables except consumer goods – the peak tariff from 55 per cent to 50 per cent – commitment with WTO to liberalize India's trade. Industrial policy reforms – New Industrial Policy – except in 14 select industries related with environmental hazards, national security and social well-being, licensing system abolished – foreign direct investment – disinvestments of public ownership in public sector corporations in steps – Exchange rate reforms – Capital Market reforms – Foreign Institutional Investors welcome – Multinational corporations welcome to joint ventures.

Major Issues

A soft state – what happened to the scams of the financial market? People lost their trust in all financial institutions – how the disinvestment programme is going on? – What was achieved by privatization of banks and such financial institutions? Is foreign direct investment increasing substantially in capital sector? Governance is important. Rationality, not rationalization, is needed.

Taking all these issues and many more into consideration, this seminar has come up with four issues of these for discussion. These are:

1. The role of institutions and people's participation for rural development in India,
2. The role of physical infrastructure and social sector for rural development, which includes Health, Education, Communication etc.,
3. Changing policies, strategies, poverty alleviation and employment generation programmes for rural India, and
4. Trade, industry and other primary sectors which include Agriculture, Forest and Environment, etc.

I am quite optimistic that scholars participating in this seminar will discuss all these matters and many more and finally, come to conclude a feasible solution to the problems of rural development. And finally, grant me to become a little emotional. I have seen the vast fields stretched between my stand and the blue canopy meeting the ground only to limit my farther vision; I have seen the mountainous, tar-black, clouds covering the sky, then pouring mightily on the ground; I have seen the roaring rivers hastily going to meet the unfathomable; and I have seen men tilling the land under the scorching sun and women under the torrents of rain transplanting the seedlings in the fields filled with knee-deep waters. The core economy that I saw is the economy of the majority of population. The greater part of cultivated tracks of land continues to be rain-fed; the wages of labourers in rural India or in the informal sector of urban India continue to be at the subsistence level; more than one-third of the total population – roughly about 370 millions in number – remains below poverty line; in spite of government declaration of primary education as 'compulsory', millions of children go to work than to school and so on. On the other hand, billions are spent overnight on mirth and merriment in the marriage parties of the children of some public figures. In spite of elaborate planning for development well over a span of fifty years my core economy remains unchanged. This is what I saw when I was an optimistic child; this is what I see when I have become an old and disillusioned man. I also wish that many of you turn emotional to the plight of the people in the rural areas.

References

Datta, P. (2006): "Urbanisation in India", Population Studies Unit, Indian Statistical Institute, Kolkata at *http://epc2006.princeton.edu/download.aspx?submissionId=60134*

Adelman, I. and Morris, C. (1967) : *Society, Politics and Economic Development: A Quantitative Approach*, John Hopkins Press, Baltimore.

Introduction

Komol Singha and **Gautam Patikar**

Development economics concerns with poor region, community or sector. It involves growth in income or output along with structural changes. In reality, the question of development arises only when the system/sector misses its basic necessary component(s). Within the State, perfect balance of development initiatives between the regions, the rural and the urban cannot be maintained. Very often the rural sector is missed out or considered as secondary by the planners and leaders. Plethoras of literature, theses and theories on rural development have been studied. A number of projects, schemes for rural development have been initiated in the country as well as in the North Eastern Region (NER). Still, the goal remains an illusive, particularly in the NER. It indicates that the initiatives or attempts have missed out some of the core issues, and this experience invites serious introspection on the part of the policy makers and the planners.

When we talk about North Eastern Region, definitely, it is the land of eight states, *i.e.* Assam, Arunachal Pradesh, Manipur, Meghalaya, Mizoram, Nagaland, Sikkim, and Tripura. It covers an area of approximately 2,62,500 sq. km., *i.e.,* 8 per cent of the total area of the country. The region has the longest international border among the States stretching over 5000 km. with as many as five foreign countries, namely, Myanmar, Bhutan, China, Nepal, and Bangladesh which comprises 98 per cent of the region's boundary leaving only two per cent being share with the mainland of our country. Its population is about 39 million, *i.e.,* 3.9 per cent of the country's total population. Around three-fourth of the region is covered by hilly terrain, and majority of the people (around 85 per cent) live in villages, rural areas. Their problems are multiple, which include social, political, and economy, that its leaders hardly register.

For rural development to succeed in a global environment, three things are essential: human capital, physical infrastructure, and adequate financing. Human capital and infrastructure (public capital) are critical components of sustainable rural development and the third element should be social capital. Communities/rural sector that have thriving social networks and institutions and good human capital will have adequate financing as well. Importance of infrastructure in the development of rural economy is accepted by everyone, but the equally important factor which is not noticed by everyone is the human capital. So, the education sector is one of the most important instruments for rural development. But, for the NE region, it is a quite complex phenomenon that whether the chick comes first or the egg. Whether the emphasis of the region needs to be given for human capital or physical infrastructure or institutional networks is the question that arises in front of us. The essays of this volume try to explore the ways and means of the dilemmas mentioned above.

Chapter Scheme

The primary objective of this volume is to provide readers with case studies and empirical insights into the structure of rural economy. This volume is broadly divided into three sections and contains nineteen (19) essays on various aspects of rural development in the North-East India. In his Keynote address by S. K. Mishra, said despite so many concerted efforts, the rural populace remains poor in the midst of abundant resources. The intention of the Government of India to assist the rural compartments cannot do much practically to alleviate the poor. The projects fell short of providing accessibility, infrastructures, electricity, telecommunication, water supply, employment, etc. to the rural areas in spite of the schemes' commendable objectives. For this, he suggested, Governance is important. Rationality, not rationalization, is needed. The role of institutions and people's participation is very significant. Infrastructure and social sector for rural development are to be made streamlined first.

Section One consists of five essays relating to empowerment and participation of the people in the rural development and the section is named as '*New Approaches, Empowerment and Participation*'. The first essay of the volume is jointly contributed by E. Haridev Singh, K. Muktasana Singh and E. Bijoy Kumar Singh entitled '*Business Linkage in Marketing Rural Industrial Products: A Study of Handicraft in Manipur*'. The essay tries to highlight the importance of handicraft industry as a source of employment for rural Manipur and India. But this industry has a big issue of sustainability in the present competitive market environment. To sustain in the present competitive environment, business linkage has to be adopted as a strategy to make the industry competitive in terms of productivity and help better marketing. The second essay of this volume is contributed jointly by Keisham Suresh Singh and Damodar Nepram entitled '*Taxation of Agricultural Income in Manipur*'. The essay tries to highlight the importance of agricultural income tax in the country as well as in Manipur. How to enhance the proceeds of land revenue in the State and the need for taxing agricultural income are also emphasized. Dani Chobin also, in his paper, '*Herbs in Aruncahal Pradesh: An Exploration for Economic Viability and Sustainability*' explores the potentials of medicinal herbs in the State. More than 80 per cent of the world's medicinal flora is found in the Himalayan ranges of India. Arunachal Pradesh is a state which lies within the Himalayan belt. Since the State has remained a generally inaccessible area with scarce means of communication and transport, very little is known about medicinal flora of the State. In his opinion, there is a positive correlation between economic development and deforestation. Further, he raises a question that, can the rich biodiversity of the State continues to be protected, as development comes?

The fourth essay of the volume contributed by Ritu Hazarika entitled '*SHGs and Women Empowerment: A Preliminary Investigation*' tries to highlight the role of women in rural development. In order to understand the role of women in rural development, two SHGs of Telahi Block of Lakhimpur district, Assam have been selected and analysed their activities in detail. The paper is a preliminary enquiry to understand the decision making power of the women forming into SHGs. Similarly, Komol Singha tries to portray the role of community in rural development in Nagaland. The paper entitled '*Communitisation in Nagaland: An Overview*' is the fifth essay of the volume and discusses role of a new community development programme 'Communitisation' which bagged coveted award United Nations Award for Public Services from the Asia and Pacific Region. Community has become a powerful capital for rural development, which we do not realize as a factor in economic development, especially for rural development.

Section Two deals with six essays on infrastructure including financial infrastructure and the section is subtitled as '*Physical Infrastructure and Finance*'. The first essay of this section and sixth of this volume is contributed by P. C. Dutta entitled '*Role of Infrastructure in Rural Development in North Eastern Region of India*'. Infrastructures are the basic essential services that should be put in place to enable development to occur. Socio-economic development of a region, especially the rural sector can be facilitated and accelerated by the presence of social and economic infrastructures. Similar points are also given by three more papers, like the seventh essay of the volume entitled '*Role of Infrastructural Facilities in Rural Development: Problems and Prospects*' contributed by K. H. Nakhro; the eighth essay entitled '*Infrastructure Development in Nagaland: An Overview*' contributed by Pradip Brahmachary, and the eleventh essay of the volume entitled '*Infrastructure Facilities and Economic Development in Nagaland*' jointly contributed by Pranab Baishya and P. K. Deka. All these essays discuss the existing scenario of physical infrastructure of Nagaland. Further, they emphasize the role of government for basic infrastructural development in the region. Without government's initiatives, further development of the region is a hard task. Coming to financial infrastructure, ninth essay of the volume contributed jointly by Jagadish Nath and Basabi Deb entitled '*Microfinance and Poverty Alleviation: A Study of RGVN-CSP*' tries to discuss the evolution of micro-finance as a tool for eradicating poverty. It also discusses the general model of operations of micro-finance in India with specific reference to Rashtriya Gramin Vikash Nidhi-Credit Savings Programme (RGVN-CSP). There is no denying fact that micro-finance is affecting a significant development in poverty eradication and rural development, especially the North-East India. The tenth paper of the volume entitled '*Indebtedness in Nagaland: A Cursory Look*' is contributed by Subhendu Dutta. It tries to make an attempt to examine the problem of rural indebtedness in Nagaland. It is found that about 32 per cent of the rural households in Kohima district were under debt and showed that on an average a sample household has debt burden of Rs. 12,450.00, but most of the loan amounts are put to non-productive purpose, which lead to accumulation and non-payment of loans.

Section Three covers the issues on institutions and its performance in rural development and this section is named as '*Institutions, Agencies and Performance*'. It contains eight essays based on the theme. The first essay of this section and twelfth of the volume is contributed by Elangbam Nixon Singh. In his essay entitled '*Entrepreneurship in SMEs: A Study of Rural Manipur*' discusses the role of Small and Medium Enterprises to uplift the rural sector of Manipur. Since the State is industrially weak, basically due to the paucity of investment in the big industries and business, the contribution of SMEs is very significant and relevant. Quite similarly, L. Rome Singh also highlights the importance of Small Scale industries in his paper '*Small-Scale Industries: A Boon of Economic Development*'. Apart from having small investment which can be started by any villager, it has also been becoming a means to preserve the inherited skills of our artisans; otherwise it would be frustrated and disappeared. The fourteen essay of the volume entitled *'People's Participation in Rural Development: Some Issues'* is contributed by Manoj Kumar Singh and tries to portray some modalities of people's participation in rural development.

To evaluate the performance of public policies, the seventeen paper of the volume jointly contributed by Rajmani Singh, Ksh. Ranjan Singh and Th. Surjit Singh entitled *'Performance Evaluation of NREGS in North East India: A Study of Manipur'* analyses the performance of the flagship national programme called National Rural Employment Guarantee Schemes (NREGS) launched in 2006. They suggest that the success of the project lies on the hand of the rural people. Slightly similar to this, the fifteen essay of the volume entitled *'Impact of SGRY on Socio-Economic Development of Rural Community: A Study of Nagaland'* jointly contributed by M. Yangar; K.K. Jha and Amod Sharma also tries to evaluate central government sponsored scheme called Sampoorna Grameen Rozgar Yojana (SGRY) which was launched on 25th September 2001 to provide food security through wage employment and building durable assets and infrastructure for the rural communities. It is also cleared that the success of this scheme requires some other supporting variables in the rural areas. The education, utilization of mass media sources and family size were found useful in influencing the level of impact of SGRY on the selected beneficiaries. The seventeenth essay of this volume entitled *'Rural Development in Nagaland: A Study of KOMUL'* is contributed jointly by Abhijit Chakraborty and Pranay Jyoti Goswami. They also try to explore the potentials of dairy farms in Nagaland and show that the State can be a developed one if it adopts AMUL model cooperative. The State has also initiated a cooperative society, called KOMUL; it is expected to grow faster and helps in rural employment in the State. If not exactly the same, Ram Krishna Mandal also in his essay, eighteen in number of the volume entitled *'Khadi and Village Industries in Arunachal Pradesh: Its Impact on Socio-Economic Development'* tries to explore the potentials of Khadi and Village Industries in providing income and employment in the rural sector, especially in Arunachal Pradesh. He further exposes the defects of the functionaries of the sector. If the officials and functionaries are sincere, the KVI could become a job creator and provider in rural masses. The last and Nineteenth essay of the volume '*Structure and Scinario of Agriculture in Nagaland*' contributed by Raju Das portrays the glimse of agricultural sector in Nagaland. He also highlights the need of the basic infrastructures in developing agriculture, and predicts bright future of agriculture in the State.

Thus, this volume has touched upon almost all the components needed for the development of rural sector in NER. Though the contributors have given insights and their approaches differently, all of them have highlighted the role of physical infrastructure with institutional support, the people's support or people's involvement in the development process of rural sector with the support of the government. It is also hoped that this volume will contribute positively to plan and execute projects and programmes for the development of North-East Region, especially in the rural sector, one of the resource-rich but underdeveloped region of the country.

List of Tables and Figures

Figures

List of the Contributors

Baishya, Pranab : Faculty, Department of Economics, S.D. Jain Girls' College, Dimapur, Nagaland

Brahmachary, Pradip : Faculty and Head, Department of Economics, S. D. Jain Girls' College, Dimapur, Nagaland

Chakraborty, Abhijit : Faculty and Acting Principal, Public College of Commerce, Dimapur, Nagaland

Chobin, Dani: Faculty, Department of Economics, D. N. Govt. College, Itanagar, Arunachal Pradesh

Deb, Basabi : Faculty, Department of Economics, ICFAI National College, Guwahati, Assam

Dutta, Subhendu : Faculty, Department of Economics, Public College of Commerce, Dimapur, Nagaland

Dutta, P. C. : Faculty and Head, Department of Statistics, S.S. College, Hailakandi, Assam

Das, Raju : Faculty, Department of Commerce, Baptist College, Kohima, Nagland

Deka, P. K. : Faculty and Head, Department of Commerce, Nagaland University, Kohima, Nagaland

Goswami, Pranay Jyoti : Faculty, Department of Commerce, Assam University, Silchar, Assam

Hazarika, Ritu : Faculty, Department of Home Science, N. L. College, Lakhimpur, Assam

Jha, K. K. : Faculty, Department of Rural Development and Planning, Nagaland University, Medziphema, Nagaland

Mishra, S. K.: Faculty, Department of Economics, North-Eastern Hill University, Shillong, Meghalaya

Mandal, Ram Krishna : Faculty, Department of Economics, DN Govt. College, Itanagar, Arunachal Pradesh

Nath, Jagadish : Faculty, Department of Marketing, ICFAI National College, Guwahati, Assam

Nakhro, K. H. : Faculty, Department of Rural Development and Planning, Nagaland University, Medziphema, Nagaland

Nepram, Damodar : Faculty, Department of Economics, Churachandpur College, Churachandpur, Manipur

Singh, Elangbam Nixon : Faculty, Department of Management, Mizoram University, Aizawl, Mizoram

Singh, Keisham Suresh : Mezhur Higher Secondary School, Kohima, Nagaland

Singh, L. Rome : Asst. Finance Manager, State Health Missiont. Manipur, NRHM, Imphal, Manipur

Singh, E. Haridev : Research Scholar, Department of Economics, Manipur University, Imphal, Manipur

Singh, K. Muktasana : Research Scholar, Department of Economics, Manipur University, Imphal, Manipur

Singh, E. Bijoykumar : Faculty, Department of Economics, Manipur University, Imphal, Manipur

Singh, Manoj Kumar : Faculty and Head, Department of Economics, People's College, Mokokchung, Nagaland

Singh, Rajmani : Faculty, Department of Commerce, Manipur Unversity, Imphal, Manipur

Singh, Ksh. Ranjan : Research Scholar, Department of Commerce, Manipur University, Imphal, Manipur

Singh, Th. Surjit : Research Scholar, Department of Commerce, Manipur University, Imphal, Manipur

Singha, Komol : Faculty, Department of Economics, Royal University Bhutan, GCBS, Gedu, Bhutan

Sharma, Amod : Faculty, School of Agricultural Science and Rural Development, Nagaland University, Medziphema, Nagaland

Yangar, M. : State Department of Agriculture, Govt. of Nagaland, Kohima, Nagaland

SECTION - I

NEW APPROACHES, EMPOWERMENT AND PARTICIPATION

1 Business Linkage in Marketing Rural Industrial Products

A Study of Handicraft in Manipur

E. Haridev Singh, K. Muktasana Singh and
E. Bijoy Kumar Singh

Introduction

In order to overcome the problems of rural unemployment and poverty in a higher incidence of migration of active population, the diversification of economy from subsistence to commercialized production of farm and non-farm products has been recognized as one of the most important alternative options and a necessary policy. But the scope for large scale diversification of non-farm economic activities is severely limited because of the number of factors. Problems in promoting non-farm activities in the rural sector are: lack of knowledge, lack of proper marketing facility, lack of finance, lack of raw material, lack of demand, lack of proper communication, competition from organized sector, lack of time, lack of technology, lack of common facility and lack of training, etc.

Among the non-farm sectors, handicraft sector is a major industry which is promoting employment to rural masses. The Khadi and Village Industry Commission (KVIC) is a main organization which undertakes the initiative of promoting rural industrialization in India. According to the KVIC sources, there are about 4.1 lakh of handicraft workers in Manipur and the annual sale of this sector was about Rs. 142 crore. As a rural industrialization strategy in India, handicraft cluster centre has been jointly initiated by United Nations Industrial Development

Organization (UNIDO) and Government of India in different parts of the rural India.

Definition of Handicraft Industry

Handicrafts are mostly defined as the items made by hand, often with the use of simple tools, and are generally artistic and/or traditional in nature. They are also objects of utility and objects of decoration.

Characteristics of Handicraft Industry

Some of the important characteristics of handicraft industry are:

1. Most of the craftsmen in this industry are women, children and uneducated man and who stay in rural and semi-urban area.
2. They work in the lean season.
3. Raw materials are available locally.
4. Indigenousness of the product.
5. Sustainable of product.
6. It represents the authentic creative form of the state or community.

Problems of Handicraft Industry

Presently, India's share in the global market stands at 2 per cent and valued at US$ 400 billion. However, the handicraft industries in rural Indian economy registered an annual growth rate of 15 per cent consistently over the last decade and it is estimated to grow at the rate of 42 per cent over the next five years annually.

Although, the handicraft industries in rural India is witnessing steady growth over the last five years but its growth is hampered by certain bottlenecks, like the following:

- The manufacturing process does not compliment with orders of such products

- Use of primitive techniques
- High manufacturing cost
- Poor quality of products
- Product design and development to be aligned with the background and history of the craft, the producer and the market requirements
- Poor standard of raw materials
- Lack of standardized vendor and suppliers
- Lack of standardized raw materials
- Improper pricing of finished products
- Absence of proper incentives and schemes by the Government of India
- Unorganized investment patterns and lack of regular investors
- Lack of proper marketing channels
- Poor access to urban markets

In response to this situation, Governments and other national and international organizations have understood for some time that if handicraft industry organizes their production, information gathering, and marketing efforts they can reduce these individual risks. Specifically, by organizing into group or cluster, handicraft firms will able to:

- improve their access to and reduce the cost of procuring raw materials through bulk-purchasing;
- increase their efficiency by sharing production skills and resources;
- enhance their product's quality and marketability through common production standards and market driven product specifications;
- increase access to available financing;
- obtain business development services (BDS) through embedded or fee-for-service mechanisms or institutional support for time-to-time scheme of government's policy and programme; and

- improve their market position by having the quality, quantity, and types of products that multiple buyers demand.

Although the benefits are many, craftsmen are sometimes risk averse and suspicious of any activity that may encroach upon the sovereignty or internal operations of their business. This is particularly evident in saturated markets, where intense competition for limited contracts drives prices down and inhibits growth. Craftsmen with limited economic options often develop a predatory/opportunistic competitive behaviour, whereby any activity that remotely implies a limitation on their ownership rights is ill received.

To overcome the suspicion, risks, and potential pitfalls, the Government agencies like, KVIC, NABARD, NEDFI and NGOs have been increasingly active in designing interventions that focus on bottom-line results, and activities that serve to diversify product-marketing channels through better linkage policy and programme between the firms and various other stake-holders. The effort is same in Manipur too.

The Objective of the Study

1. To explore the kind of inter-firm linkage or network that exists between handicraft firm, buyer and other stake-holders in rural handicraft industry in Manipur.
2. To study the impact of business-linkage on the performance of rural handicraft industry.

Business-linkage in Manipur

The term Business-linkage encompasses production linkage, micro-macro policy linkage, international or Trans-National Corporation linkage, institutional linkage. We again say business linkage as an integrated approach, which consists of the above four linkages for sustainable growth of Micro Small and Medium

Enterprise in developing world. The term production linkage means production linkages include forward and backward linkages. Forward linkages are created as a consequence of the supply of products of Small and Medium Enterprises (SMEs) to other sectors and backward linkages are created due to the demand from the SME sector for intermediate or capital goods. Macro-micro policy Linkage is termed as, the linkages relate to the multitude of effects that governmental policies (macro level policies such as fiscal policy, monetary policy and exchange rate policy) have on small enterprise operations. And on the other hand, an International Linkage is defined as the linkages that deal with the 'interdependencies' of national and international markets in which the small enterprises function. Lastly, Institutional Linkages is termed as, the relationships among the different types of individuals and organizations that operate and interact with small enterprises. So, in the broader sense, Business Linkage includes all strategies, efforts, and facilities that extended by government agencies, international organizations, institutions, large and small enterprises, private bodies, etc. for the sustainable growth of the MSMEs. Inter-organizational linkage works within the domain of business linkage and is important means of increasing the productivity. It is again necessary for better linkage to market for MSMEs. A linkage is defined as any transaction, which takes place between two or more firms. It usually expresses a continual relationship involving recurrent transactions. The term 'Inter–firm Linkage' is traditionally used to cover all possible forms of economic relationships between firms operating within an economy (Wong 1991, 1992).

After reviewing the type of inter-organizational linkage, we will study its relevant in the context of marketing of rural handicraft products of Manipur. The main problems of handicraft industry in Manipur are: *lack of productivity and marketing capabilities*. We assume that the issues of productivity can be addressed by using horizontal networks of handicraft firms giving necessary support by government department, agencies, and other stake-holders. At the operational level, we find that some handicraft firms in Manipur have collaboration with each other for (i) fulfilling the order, (ii) sharing knowledge (iii) sharing of resources, (iv) sharing of manpower, (v) sharing of expertise, etc. The NGOs and government agencies in Manipur are helping handicraft firms to make Self-Help Groups and other groups, effort to increase the production capacity in Manipur.

Figure 1.1 shows us the model of the horizontal network of the handicraft industry in Manipur. In the figure we assume that there are A, B, C, D...... , firms which are having cooperative linkage among themselves and are getting the help from government agencies, NGOs, in terms of value addition of product, training, finance, capacity building, documentation, etc. It is evident from the literature that vertical network like subcontracting has been used by several developing countries, to increase the marketing capabilities of the respective industry.

As an example: (i) The Nike/Reebok and Asian footwear producers subcontracting network (Rosenzweig, 1994); (ii) The Brazilian Sinos Valley and Mexican footwear subcontracting network (Ceiglie and Dini, 1999); (iii)The lightening subcontracting network (Sarathy, 1996).

In our case, we do not find manufacturing subcontracting linkages, like the example given above, but we do find commercial subcontracting in Manipur. The source of vertical linkage for our handicraft firms are:

1. Large exporter in metros like Delhi, Bombay, Goa, Kolkata, etc.
2. Alternative trade organizations like NGOs, SHGs.
3. Direct to independent retailers and whole sellers.
4. Direct to Government showrooms like Panthoibi showrooms at Delhi, Manipur handloom and handicraft emporium, etc.
5. The Government agencies are helping the entrepreneurs in making the linkage by organizing trade fair, seminars, *mela*, exhibition, buyer-seller meets, etc.

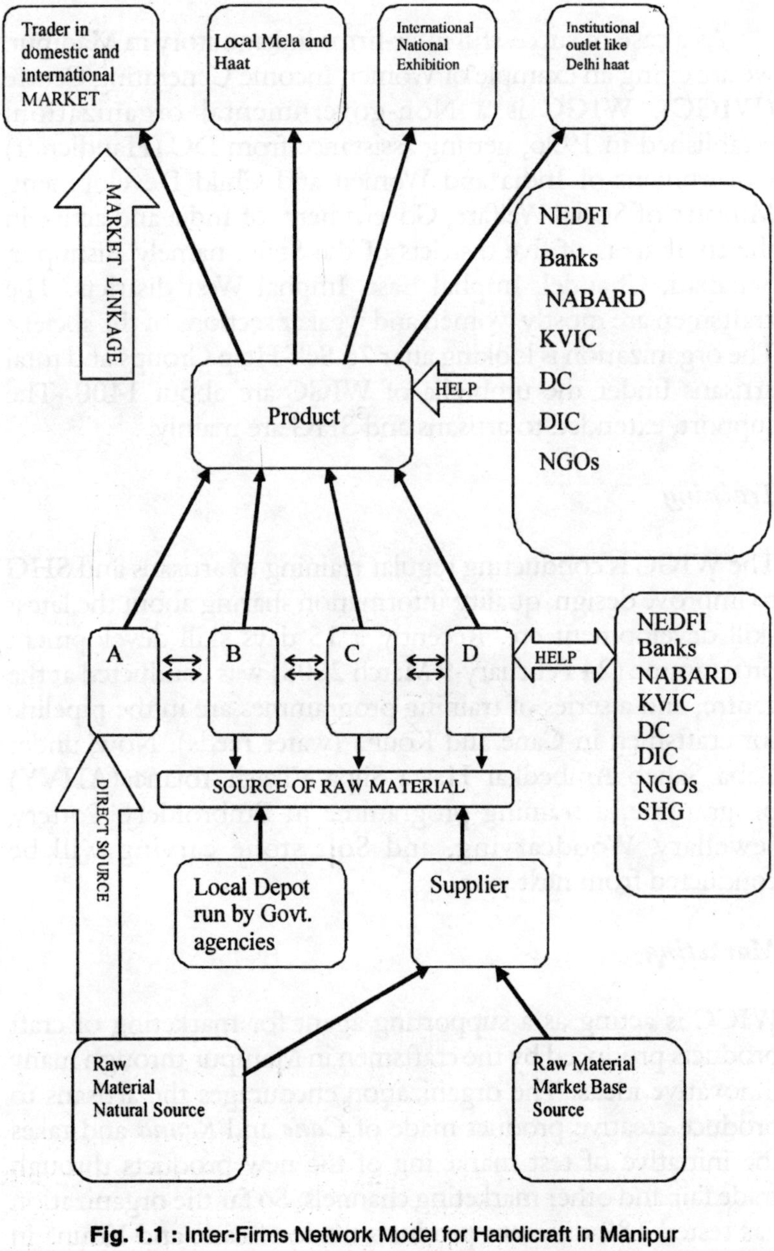

Fig. 1.1 : Inter-Firms Network Model for Handicraft in Manipur

As a case of successful inter-firms linkage story in Manipur, we are citing an example of Women Income Generating Centre (WIGC). WIGC is a Non-governmental organization, established in 1996, getting assistance from DC (Handicraft) Government of India and Women and Child Development, Ministry of Social Welfare, Government. of India and active in the rural areas of five districts of the State, namely Bisnupur, Senapati, Chandel, Imphal East, Imphal West districts. The craftsmen are mostly women and weaker sections of the society. The organization is looking after 75 Self-Help Groups and total artisans under the umbrella of WIGC are about 1400. The support, extended to artisans and SHG are mainly:

Training

The WIGC is conducting regular training to artisans and SHG to improve design, quality, information sharing about the latest skill development etc. Recently, a 15 days skill development programme (24 February-9 March 2008) was conducted at the centre, and a series of training programmes are in the pipeline for craftsmen in Cane and Kouna (water reeds). Now, under Baba Saheb Ambedkar Hasta Silpa Vikash Yojana (AHVY) programme, a training programme in Embroidery, Pottery, Jewellary, Woodcarving, and Soft stone carving will be conducted from next year.

Marketing

WIGC is acting as a supporting agent for marketing of craft products produced by the craftsmen in Manipur through many innovative ideas. The organization encourages the artisans to produce creative product made of *Cane* and *Kouna* and takes the initiative of test marketing of the new products through trade fair and other marketing channels. So far the organization has tested 180 different products made of cane and Kouna in the market, out of which 4 (Ladies bag, marketing bag, file cover, carry bag) products are successfully exploited commercially. WIGC is participating in many national and international fairs and buyer-seller meets, acting as a representative of 75 artisans and SHGs. The organization is also going for joint design development programmes with other creative firms for joint production. Recently, the organization was organizing a craft bazaar at Wangjing Mela ground, generating sales revenue of about Rs. 90 lakh. Now, they have received an order of 50 thick '*Kouna Mats*' from Brazil, worth few lakh of Indian rupees.

Buyback

WIGC is supporting the artisans by buying back the product made by the artisans. By buying back the products, the artisans are getting continuous source of income and motivated to adopt handicraft as a full time profession.

Micro-finance

The organization is having its own Micro-finance service centre, which extends financial support to craftsmen and Self-Help Group centres. The mode of operation is arranged as payback in product, i.e. the loanee will borrow money and repayment will be made in the form of product. By doing this, the repayment is absolute and the relation between the client and server is in perfect harmony. As an example, the organization is doing a contract farming of Kouna at Nongpok Sekmai, where the farmer is taking credit for farming and the organization is counter-guaranteed buyback of the product, thus benefiting both the parties.

Constant Feedback for Improvement

The management of the organization realizes that the success of the business depends upon the interaction between the parties. So, in order to know the problems and continuous improvement of the process, the management, craftsmen, and SHG members are regular meeting by conducting meetings, seminars, workshop, etc.

So, the success of this organization in marketing the products made by rural artisan in the State is the result of series of innovative techniques used by the management, for continuous supply of product by backward and forward integration of operation to local and international markets. And for our analytical purpose we assume that the handicraft firms in Manipur are having commercial subcontracting, buyback, arms length market transaction, liecencing, and joint venture.

Analytical Framework

Sample

A survey was conducted during 2005-07 to find the Entrepreneurs' personal profile, General profile of the enterprises, Entrepreneurial networks: networking, use of networking, network benefits, Subcontracting linkages, Performance of the firms of handicraft industry (Cane and bamboo and Kouna), etc. The number of enterprises taken for the study (n) is 200, spread over all the 9 districts (both hills and plain) of the State.

Growth of the Firms

The performance of the firm is measured on the basis of sales growth and increase in profitability over a three-year period (Donckels and Lambrecht, 1995; Hansen, 1995; Ostgaard and Birley, 1996).

Growth of Sale = Having growth in sales from 2005 to 2007
Growth of Profit = Having growth in profit from 2005 to 2007

Dependent Variables

Growth of Sales	Yes / No
Growth of Profit	Yes/ No

Independent Variables

Commercial subcontracting	Yes/No
Joint Venture	Yes/No
Licensing	Yes/No
Buyback	Yes/No
Arms length Market relationship	Yes/No

Model

Logistic regression is useful for the situation, in which we can predict the presence or absence of a characteristic or outcome based on values of a set of predictor variables. It is similar to a linear regression model and suited to models where the dependent variable is dichotomous.

The *logit model*, which is based on the cumulative logistic probability function (*F*), can be specified as follows :

$$P_i = F(\alpha + \beta X) = \frac{e^{(\alpha+\beta X_i)}}{1 + e^{(\alpha+\beta X_i)}}$$

Here *e* represents the base of natural logarithms, and α and α are the coefficients. *X* is the model matrix consisting of values of explanatory variables. *Pi* is the probability that an individual makes a certain choice, given *Xi*. For example, if an individual has external actors, the probability of having external actors is as:

$$P(External\ Actors,\ Yes) = \frac{e^{(\alpha+\beta X_i)}}{1 + e^{(\alpha+\beta X_i)}}$$

on the other hand, the probability that an individual does not have external actors is as :

$$P(External\ Actors, No) = 1 - P(External\ Actors,\ Yes) = \frac{1}{1+e^{(\alpha+\beta X_i)}}$$

The likelihood function then becomes:

$$L = \prod_{0} \frac{e^{(\alpha + \beta X_i)}}{1 + e^{(\alpha + \beta X_i)}} \prod_{1} \frac{1}{1 + e^{(\alpha + \beta X_i)}}$$

The procedure for obtaining estimates of α and α coefficients is to maximize L with respect to the parameters. This is called the ***maximum likelihood method*** (Agresti, 1990; DeMaris, 1992; Maddala, 1983; Pindyck and Rubinfeld, 1991).

Logistic regression coefficients can be used to estimate odds ratios for each of the independent variables in the model.

$$\text{Log}(p_i/1-p_i) = B_1 + B_2X + B_3X_2 + B_4X_3 + B_5X_4 + B_6X_5 + u_i \text{.....}\textbf{(M1)}$$

Where p_i is the probability of growth and 1 - p_i probability of no growth and B_i where i= 1, 2, 3, 4.......... are the coefficient independent terms, U_i an error. $(p_i/1-p_i)$ is known as the odds ratio is simply the odds in favor of getting a growth. The natural log of this odds ratio is called the *Logit*, and the model (1) is called the *Logit* model.

However, it is hard to interpret the logit coefficients. Therefore, most people work out odds ratios and probabilities (Mukherjee *et al.*, 1998; Norusis, 1997). A zero coefficient in a *logit* regression implies that an odd ratio is equal to 1 ($e^0 = 1$), corresponding to a unit change in the variable concerned. An odd ratio equals to 1 means that the corresponding probability is 0.5 [$e^0/(1+e^0) = 0.5$]. This indicates that minus coefficient in a *logit* regression predicts less probability than 0.5 (1/2), which implies that changes in the independent variable will have its less effect on the probability of choosing a given option at the mid-point of the cumulative logistic distribution. Therefore, corresponding probabilities can be calculated at the mid-point of the cumulative logistic distribution.

Statistical Analysis

Table 1.1 : Statistical Analysis

Variable	*Yes/No*	*Frequency*	*Percentage*
Pofit	0	83	41.5
	1	117	58.5
Sales	0	68	34
	1	132	66
Commercial subcontrating	0	62	31
	1	138	69
Licensing	0	145	72.5
	1	55	27.5
Buyback	0	59	29.5
	1	141	70.5
Arms lenght	0	8	4
	1	192	96
Joint Venture	0	193	96.5
	1	7	3.5

The data available from the survey (see Table 1.1) say that 69 per cent of the respondent goes for commercial sub-contracting, 27.5 per cent for lincensing, 70.5 per cent for buyback, 96 per cent for arms length and 3.5 per cent for Joint Venture.

Impact of Five Variables on Profit

We study the impact of these variables (as seen in the following *Box 1*) using SPSS10.0, and the model is found to be statistically significant and with a moderate goodness of fit as indicated by the model value of chi-square (p-value <.001, Nagelkerte $R^2 = 0.646$). Even though the model is significant, the contribution made by the variables to the profit of the firm is in different degree. The odd ratio of each of the variable Joint venture (216.842 at p-value<.793), Commercial subcontracting (COMSUB) (26.656 at p-value<.000), Lincensing (LINCEN) (13 at p-value<.015), Buyback (13.225 at p-value<.00), arms length transaction (.179 at p-value<.075). The result of the above analysis shows us that joint venture and arms length transaction is not significant, this may be due to the number of respondent in Joint venture is too small (*i.e.* 7 only), and in case of Arms length transaction the number of respondent is too large (*i.e.*192). In case of buyback, for 1 degree increase (*i.e.* addition of one respondent) will increase the odd of profitability by 13.225, likewise 26.265 for subcontracting, and 13 for lincesing. We can conclude that subcontracting, lincising, and buyback have positive impact on the profitability and joint venture, where as, the arms length transaction has no significant impact on the profit of the firms.

Box 1

Variables in the Equation

		B	*S.E.*	*Wald*	*df*	*Sig.*	*Exp(B)*
Step 1[a]	JOIVEN	5.379	20.544	.069	1	.793	216.842
	COMSUB	3.283	.541	36.857	1	.000	26.656
	LINCEN	2.592	1.106	5.495	1	.019	13.355
	BUYBACK	2.582	.520	24.696	1	.000	13.225
	ARMENGHT	-1.720	.966	3.174	1	.075	.179
	Constant	-2.267	.966	5.508	1	.019	.104

a. Variable(s) entered on step 1: JOIVEN, COMSUB, LINCEN, BUYBACK, ARMENGHT.

Impact of Five Variables on the Sales

We study the impact of these variables on sales (as seen in the following *Box 2*) using SPSS10.0, and the model is found to be statistically significant and with a moderate goodness of fit as indicated by the model value of chi-square (p-value <.001, Nagelkerte $R^2 = 0.630$). Even though the model is significant, the contribution made by the variables to the profit of the firm is in different degree. The odd ratio of each of the variable Joint venture (254.9 at p-value<.911), Commercial subcontracting (COMSUB) (6.656 at p-value<.001), Lincensing (LINCEN) (2793.922 at p-value<.711), Buyback (30.033 at p-value<.00), arms length transaction(.919 at p-value<.933). The result of the above result shows us that joint venture, LINCEN and arms length transaction is not significant. In case of buyback, for 1 degree increase (*i.e.* addition of one respondent) will increase the odd of increase in sales by 3.402 likewise 1.827 for subcontracting, and 13. We conclude that Subcontracting, and buyback have positive impact on the sales and joint venture, arms length transaction and LINCEN has no significant impact on the sales of the firms.

Box 2

Variables in the Equation

		B	S.E.	Wald	df	Sig.	Exp(B)
Step 1	JOIVEN	5.541	49.809	.012	1	.911	254.963
	COMSUB	1.827	.543	11.312	1	.001	6.216
	LINCEN	7.935	21.418	.137	1	.711	2793.922
	BUYBACK	3.402	.558	37.176	1	.000	30.033
	ARMENGHT	-.085	1.012	.007	1	.933	.919
	Constant	-2.866	1.052	7.417	1	.006	.057

Conclusion

We came to know from the above fact that business linkage is an important factor for the sustainable growth of handicraft industry in Manipur. We are taking the case of WIGC, to show that good inter-organizational linkage or relationship among craftsmen, government agencies, supplier, exporter, retailer, and whole seller, etc. have able to sustain competitive pressure from other states. We have defined the problems of handicraft industry, its characteristics, and importance in the rural development of India and Manipur in particular. Business linkage has been reviewed in detail, and we take five inter-firm linkage types, which are relevant to the handicraft industry in Manipur and applied statistical tools (Logistic regression) to test the significant of these five variables on the profit and sale of the handicraft firms in Manipur. We found that the maximum of the firms in Manipur are going for 'Arms-length Market transaction'. The effective types of inter-firm linkage for profitability and sales are buyback and subcontracting (Commercial subcontracting). Encouraging the handicraft firms in Manipur to go for commercial subcontracting or buyback with big show rooms, design house, exporter, NGOs, etc. would be a right direction for the handicraft industry.

References

Aldrich, H. *et al.* (1986), 'Social Behavior and Entrepreneurial Networks', Summarized in *Frontiers of Entrepreneurship Research*, Wellesley, MA, Center for Entrepreneurship Studies Babson College, pp. 239-40.

Anat BarNir and Ken S. Smith (2002): 'Inter-Firm Alliance in the Small Business', *Journal of Small Business Management*, 40(3), pp. 219-232.

Casson, M. and Cox H., (1997): 'An Economic Model of Inter- Firm Networks', in Ebers Mark, (ed.) *The Formation of Inter-Organizational Networks*, Oxford University Press, Oxford.

Donckels, R. and Hoebeke, K. (1992): 'SME-led Growth of the Belgian Economy: Fact or Fiction?' *Entrepreneurship and Regional Development*, Vol. 4 (2), 155–164.

Donckels, R. and Lambrecht, J. (1995): 'Networks and Small Business Growth: An Explanatory Model', *Small Business Economics*, Vol. 7, pp. 273-89.

Donckels, R. and Lambrecht, J. (1996), 'A Holistic Approach to the Expansion Decision of Small and Medium-sized Enterprises in a Metropolitan Area: The Case of Brussels', *Entrepreneurship and Regional Development*, Vol.8, pp.19-36.

Donckels, R. and Lambrecht, J. (1997): 'The Network Position of Small Businesses: An Explanatory Model', *Journal of Small Business Management*, Vol. 35, No. 2, pp. 13-25

Johanson, J. and Mattsson, L. G. (1993): 'Internationalization in Industrial Systems: A Network Approach', in Buckley P. J. and Ghuri P. (Eds.), *The Internationalization of the Firm: A Reader*, Academic Press, Harcourt.

Mukherjee, C. *et al.* (1998): *'Econometrics and Data Analysis for Developing Countries, Priorities for Development Economics'*, Series Editor: Paul Mosley, University of Reading, Routledge: London

Pfeffer, J. and Nowak P. (1976): 'Joint-Ventures and Inter-Organizational Interdependence'. *Ad-min. Sci. Q.* 21:398-418

Premaratne, S. P. (2003): "Entrepreneurial Networks and Small Business Development: The Case of Small Enterprises in Sri Lanka" Unpublished PhD. thesis, pp. 161-65.

UNIDO (1974): 'Subcontracting for Modernizing Economies', United Nations Industrial Development Organization, Vienna: New York.

Uzzi, B.(1997): 'Social Structure and Competition in Inter-firm Networks: The Paradox of Embeddedness', *Administrative Science Quarterly*, Vol. 42 (1), pp. 35-67.

Williamson, O.E (1975a): 'Market and Hierarchies', New York: Free Press.

Wong (1991): 'Technological Development Through Sub-contracting Linkages: A Case Study', Asian Productivity Organization, Faculty of Business Administration, National University of Singapore.

Wong, P.K., (1992): 'Technological Development through Sub-contracting Linkages: Evidence from Singapore', *Scandinavian International Business Review*, Vol. 1, pp. 28-40.

UNCTAD(2006) "Business Linkages Programme Guidelines", New York and Geneva.

Web resource

1. http://luna.cas.usf.edu/~mbrannic/files/regression/Logistic.html(12-06-08)
2. http://www.ats.ucla.edu/stat/dae/(15-06-08)

2 Taxation of Agricultural Income in Manipur

Keisham Suresh Singh and Damodar Nepram

I. Introduction

Land revenue and agricultural income tax are two taxes belonging to the states though many of them including Manipur levy only the former. The revenue generated from the tax in the state has been small and its contribution to the state's own tax revenues has gone down over the years. In the light of these findings, this paper examines how far the tax potential has been exploited and suggests measures needed for improving land revenue collections. It is divided into five sections. Section II illustrates a picture of land revenue collections of the state, possible reasons for low tax receipts and compares the tax potential with the actual proceeds. Section III gives certain recommendations for improving land revenue collections while the following Section IV argues for taxing agricultural income. Section V is the conclusion.

II. Land Revenue in Manipur

Land revenue in Manipur is levied on both agricultural and homestead land and the aggregate proceeds of the tax stood at Rs. 100.63 lakhs in 2006-07 as against Rs. 16.96 lakhs in 1960-61. Although the percentage increase in the tax revenue looks appreciable, actual tax collections rose by a little less than one crore rupees only over a period of 46 years. As a percentage of the total tax collections of the state, its contribution has gradually declined to just 0.83 per cent in 2006-07 as against 2.1 per cent in 1990-91 revealing the insignificance of the tax as a source of revenue. Land revenue collections have shown very little buoyancy and also witnessed wide fluctuations from year to year as seen in Fig. 2.1.

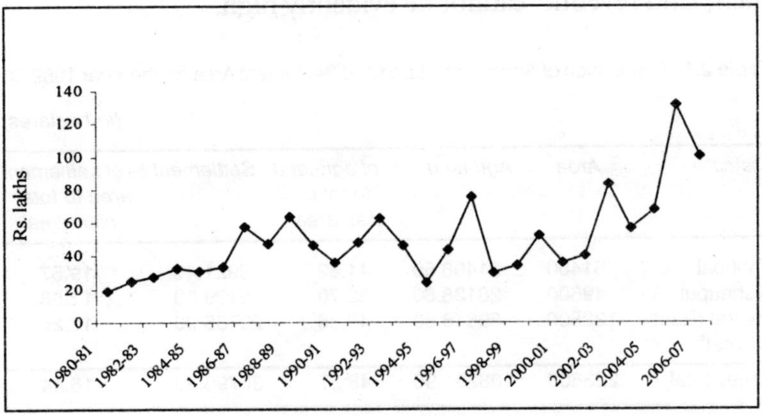

Fig. 2.1 : Land Revenue in Manipur

The reasons for the low tax collections can be attributed mainly to two factors, *viz*. small tax base and poor performance of the collection machinery. The overall geographical area of the state is small and agricultural land area constitutes roughly 6.65 per cent of it only due to the mountainous terrain of the region making the tax base extremely small. In the hill districts of Manipur, out of the total geographical area (TGA) of 20,089 sq. km only about 2 per cent is agricultural land (Table 2.1). The percentage of agricultural land to TGA ranges from 1.42 per cent in Ukhrul district to 3.39 per cent in Senapati district. On the other hand, agricultural land is 48.37 per cent of the TGA of the valley districts. Bishnupur district has the largest area under agricultural land (52.70 per cent) while that of Imphal East and West combined together occupies 49.36 per cent of their TGA. As regards non-agricultural land also, the tax base is mostly confined to the valley districts as there is community ownership of land in the hill districts excepting certain pockets of areas. In the hill districts there is hills house tax instead of revenue which currently stands at Rs. 15 per house per annum.

Thus, small geographical area of the state, mountainous terrain of the region and levying of hills house tax in place of land revenue have rendered the tax base extremely small and, as such, land revenue cannot be evidently high.

Table 2.1 : Distribution of Agricultural Land and Settlement Area for the Year 1989-90

(in hectares)

District	*Area*	*Agri-land*	*% of agri-land to total dist. area*	*Settlement*	*% of settlement area to total dist. area*
Thoubal	51400	21496.50	41.82	9921.40	19.57
Bishnupur	49600	26138.60	52.70	6139.00	11.58
Imphal (East & West)	122800	60616.80	49.36	20735.90	17.26
Valley total	223800	108251.90	48.37	36796.30	16.44
Senapati	327100	11101.82	3.39	2526.10	0.77
Tamenglong	439100	6907.89	1.57	4225.00	0.96
Churachandpur	457000	9675.02	2.12	6569.10	1.44
Chandel	331300	6192.82	1.87	1160.90	0.35
Ukhrul	454400	6442.92	1.42	3242.70	0.71
Hill total	**2008900**	**40320.47**	**2.01**	**17723.80**	**0.88**
Manipur	**2232700**	**148572.62**	**6.65**	**54520.10**	**2.44**

Source: Manipur Remote Sensing Application Centre (As quoted in GOM, *State of Environment Report*).

The performance of the collection machinery of the state cannot be considered as satisfactory either. The CAG reports from time-to-time analyses the revenue generated and cost incurred in collecting land revenue which normally reflects the poor performance of the collection machinery. Often, the costs incurred in collecting land revenues are higher than the actual revenues generated resulting in under exploitation of the tax potential. For example, between 1983-84 and 1988-89, the land revenue generated was almost equal to or less than the costs incurred. As such, an argument can be put for abolishing land revenue if such a trend continues in future. In order to generate more revenues from this source, there is an urgent need to improve the quality of the machinery as taxable land size of the state is very small and tax rates cannot be fixed at high rates due to economic and political reasons.

Table 2.2 : Costs Incurred and Revenue Generated from Land Revenue

Year	*Budget estimate* (*Rs. Lakhs*)	*Actual collection* (*Rs. Lakhs*)	*Collection charges* (*Rs. Lakhs*)	*Collection charges as a percentage of revenue generated* (*p.c.*)
1983-84	30.00	33.04	25.36	76.76
1984-85	45.00	31.31	32.63	104.22
1985-86	35.00	33.91	43.11	127.13
1986-87	40.00	57.40	41.56	72.40
1987-88	42.00	46.94	44.95	95.76
1988-89	49.00	63.34	75.25	118.80

Source : Report of the Comptroller and Auditor General of India 1988-89 (Manipur).

Tax Rates

Land in the state for taxation purposes is classified into four classes, *viz.* Phourel, Anganphou, Taothabi and Inkhol (homestead land). Phourel and Anganphou are generally considered to be good quality agricultural land while Taothabi is taken as inferior land. The current tax rates which has been effective from 1st January, 2003 as per the government order given in the Manipur Gazette dated 8th August, 2003 are Rs. 77.40, Rs. 69.60, Rs.61.90 and Rs. 84.40 per hectare for Phourel, Anganphou, Taothabi and Inkhol respectively (Table 2.3).

The tax rate is also a factor affecting the yield of the tax, but whether the rate prevalent in the State is high or low can only be ascertained by comparing with the rates existing in other states of the country. Examining the land revenue rates of the states given in Rajaraman (2003: 99-102), it seems that the tax rates in Manipur is not low. Meanwhile, how the state government fixes the tax rates and after what intervals they are revised are not known. A team of experts should be formed to decide this taking into consideration factors like inflation rate, productivity of the farm sector, tax rates prevailing in other states, etc.

Table 2.3 : Land Tax Rates in Manipur

Class of land	*Existing rate per hectare (Rs.)*	*Revised rate per hectare (Rs.)*
Phourel	38.70	77.40
Anganphou	34.80	69.60
Taothabi	30.95	61.90
Inkhol	42.20	84.40

Estimating the Tax Potential

As the various government publications did not give any data on the composition of land revenue a modest attempt is being made to estimate the revenue originating from both agricultural and homestead land by multiplying land size with the prevailing tax rates. The tax rate for Anganphou is taken as the representative tax rate of agricultural land as it is between that of Phourel and Taothabi classes of land. Agricultural and homestead land area in valley districts only are considered for estimation of potential land revenue as the size of taxable land in the hill areas is not known. Further, as data of net agricultural area in the valley districts is not available from the year 2000-01 onwards, it is taken to remain constant afterwards while settlement area given in Table 2.1 is taken as a proxy measure of homestead land. It is also assumed to remain constant due to the unavailability of data.

It is seen from Table 2.4 that total receipts from land revenue collected in the state both from agricultural as well as homestead land were even lower than the potential land revenue originating from agricultural land in the valley areas only. This shows that the state has not been able to collect the tax properly indicating the need for strengthening the tax collection machinery. Addition of the proceeds from land revenue originating from other taxable land to land revenue originating in the valley districts should have generated much more revenues than the actual collections. Although the estimated land area indicated in the table might be much more than actual area from where taxes were collected, the margin of difference between potential and actual collection was so high that there seems to be of little doubt that there was under exploitation of the base of land revenue in the state.

Table 2.4 : Land Revenue Originating from Agricultural and Homestead Land

Year	*Net agricultural area*	*Homestead area*	*Land revenue potential*			*Actual collections*
			Agri-land	*Homestead area*	*Total*	
	(hectare)	*(hectare)*		*(Rs. lakhs)*		*(Rs. lakhs)*
(1)	(2)	(3)	(4)	(5)	(6=4+5)	(7)
1996-97	154966	36796	53.93	15.53	69.46	76
1997-98	154981	36796	53.93	15.53	69.46	30
1998-99	155136	36796	53.99	15.53	69.52	34
1999-00	155232	36796	54.02	15.53	69.55	52
2000-01	155287	36796	54.04	15.53	69.57	36
2001-02	155287	36796	54.04	15.53	69.57	40
2002-03	155287	36796	54.04	15.53	69.57	83
2003-04	155287	36796	108.08	31.06	139.14	57
2004-05	155287	36796	108.08	31.06	139.14	67
2005-06	155287	36796	108.08	31.06	139.14	132
2006-07	155287	36796	108.08	31.06	139.14	101

Note: Land revenue potential is obtained by multiplying land area with prevailing tax rates.

Source : GOM (2008), *Statistical Abstract: Manipur 2007,* DES (for data on net agricultural area).

III. Measures for Enhancing Land Revenue

After examining some of the issues pertaining to land taxation in Manipur, some recommendations can be suggested to remove the defects in the system as well as to enhance the tax collections:

1. Agricultural land taxation is regressive as it is levied at a flat rate. There should be progressivity in the rate as taxation should be based on the principle of ability to pay.

2. Land revenue collection machinery is weak as revenues have been lower than costs incurred for many years. There is a valid argument for abolishing land revenue if this continues in future as well. Remedy lies in devising a new mechanism which can collect the tax at a much cheaper cost.
3. Jhum cultivation is an age old system of cultivation in the hill areas which leads to serious environmental problems. Introduction of private property system in land will not only improve land in the hill areas but also broaden the tax base. Hills house tax can then be replaced by more progressive land revenue. However, this should be done in consultation with the local population and in a manner suitable to them.
4. Land records should be updated constantly. Areas under agriculture in Manipur are being converted into homestead land, but the tax continues to be levied on rates applicable to agricultural land as per records. It results in loss of revenue to the government.
5. The Panchayats or village authorities should be allowed to collect and retain land revenues in rural areas. This will not only help in improving the financial health of the Panchayats or local bodies, but will also increase tax collections. The idea was also suggested by Rajaraman (2003) and the Twelfth Finance Commission.
6. Creation of a data base on land records in the state needs to be speeded up as it will simplify tax administration.

Arguments for Taxing more of the Agriculture Sector in the State

Agricultural sector in the state is poor and needs to be lightly taxed. In 2001 it employed about 52 per cent of the workforce (main and marginal workers) but contributed only about 30 per cent of the gross state domestic product. This would mean that 48 per cent of the workers were in the secondary and tertiary sectors enjoying 70 per cent of the state income. This reveals that the fruit of economic development is slow to trickle down to the agricultural sector.

The main argument being raised for taxing this sector is the amount of investments made for the development of agriculture. Besides direct investment on the sector, the state government has allocated large sums of money for providing irrigation facilities, flood control, etc. But the bulk of state's own tax receipts comes from a very few taxes like sales tax, professional tax, etc. and as a result there is a valid reason for making the sector contribute more to the state's revenues.

There also exists inequalities in the distribution of land in this sector. Area under marginal holdings (holdings less than 1 hectare) account for 50.36 per cent of the total holdings in 2000-01 but area operated under it was only 23.26 per cent of the total agricultural area. On the other hand, area under semi-medium (2-4 hectares) and medium holdings (4-10 hectares) together account for 16.78 per cent of the total holdings but total cultivated area extends to 40.12 per cent of the total agricultural area. The expenditures of the government are mostly benefiting the rich farmers and as a result there is a need for the land tax rates to be fixed in a progressive manner and at the same time levy some kind of tax from agricultural income. Levying of land revenue only and also at a flat rate would lead to under exploitation of the tax base in the agricultural sector.

The need for making the agricultural sector bear more tax burden also equally applies to other states and the Sixth Five Year Plan stated that "Direct taxes on agriculture at present constitutes less than 1 per cent of the total agricultural income. Land revenue, which is the principal direct tax on agriculture, is generally at a flat levy and consequently, regressive in character. Fixation of minimum support and procurement prices for major agricultural crops and provision of various inputs such as fertilizers, irrigation, and electricity at subsidised and concessional rates have helped raise agricultural incomes particularly large farmers. It is, therefore, necessary to consider for measures for raising additional sources from the agricultural sector and introducing a measure of progressivity in agricultural taxation. Care should, however, be taken to ensure that this does not in anyway help affect the incentives to increase production and productivity" (GOI,1981:77). The Central Government had also formed a committee known as the Raj Committee which recommended the introduction of Agricultural Holding Tax. The Raj Committee Report said that AHT should be levied from agriculturalists having no other assessable income and in case they have non-agricultural income in addition, income from agriculture should be included in the total income for the purpose of calculating income tax. Even though the report was considered a big attempt in taxing the rich in the agricultural sector, it was not implemented in the states. It is doubtful that the state government in Manipur will take a bold step and introduce such a reform measure in the near future.

V. Conclusion

Land revenue tax is levied on both agricultural as well as homestead land in the state. Revenue from it has shown little buoyancy and as a percentage of the total tax collections of the state, it has almost become negligible. Small tax base, poor performance of the collection machinery, failure to update land records, etc. are some of the important reasons for low tax collections. To revamp the tax system an expert committee needs to be formed to look into various aspects of land taxation in the state. The present policies not only lead to loss in revenue of the government but also the welfare of the people as the rich are not effectively taxed. A number of measures have been suggested including taxation of agricultural income. What is necessary is genuine interest on the part of the government to introduce reform measures.

References

Bhatia, H.L (1994): *Public Finance*, Vikas Publishing House Pvt. Ltd., New Delhi.

Devi, P. Binodini (2006): *Tribal Land System of Manipur*, Centre for Manipur Studies, Manipur University and Akansha Publishers, New Delhi.

Dantwala, M.L. (1972): "Agricultural taxation: Travails of tax designers", *Economic and Political Weekly*, Dec. 30.

Datt, Ruddar and K.P.M. Sundharam (2006): *Indian Economy*, S. Chand & Co. Pvt. Ltd., New Delhi.

Gailangam, Kamei (2004): "Agrarian problems in the hill areas of Manipur during the first half of 20th century" in N. Lokendra Singh (ed), *Land Use System in Manipur*, Rajesh Publications, New Delhi.

Gangmei, Thuanliang (2004): "Socio-economic impacts of the existing land use system in Manipur hills" in N. Lokendra Singh (ed), *Land Use System in Manipur*, Rajesh Publications, New Delhi.

GOI (2000): *Report of the Eleventh Finance Commission 2000-05.*

GOI (2005): *Report of the Twelfth Finance Commission 2005-10.*

GOI(1981): *Sixth Five Year Plan 1980-85*, Planning Commission.

GOI: *Report of the Comptroller and Auditor General of India (Manipur)*, various issues.

GOM: *Economic Survey: Manipur 2007-08*, DES.

GOM: *Statistical Handbook of Manipur*, DES, various issues.

GOM: *Statistical Abstract: Manipur* 2004, 2007, DES.

GOM: *State of environment report, Manipur.* (http://*www.manenvis.nic.in/soer.htm,* accessed on 12.8.2008).

Guite, K.C.(2004): "MLR & LR Act, 1960 and Sixth Schedule in relation to Manipur hill areas" in N. Lokendra Singh (ed), *Land Use System in Manipur*, Rajesh Publications, New Delhi.

Kurian, "If only Panchayats had the right to tax", http://www.financialexpress.com/news/If-Only-Panchayats-Had-The-Right-To-Tax/42361/0.

Rajaraman, Indira (2003): *A Fiscal Domain of the Panchayats*, Oxford University Press.

Rajaraman, Indira, O.P. Bohra and V.S. Renganathan (1996): "Augmentation of Panchayat Resources", *Economic and Political Weekly*, May 4.

Rao, C.H. Hanumantha (1972): "Agricultural taxation: Raj Committee's Report", *Economic and Political Weekly*, November 25.

Ranga Swamy, S. (2006): "Indian agricultural and rural sector – Application of accounting and audit concept", *The Chartered Accountant*, February.

Sharma, H.R. (1994): "Distribution of land holdings in rural India, 1953-54 to 1981-82: Implications for Land reforms", *Economic and Political Weekly*, September 24.

Singh, K. Suresh (2008): "Agricultural Land Taxation in Manipur", M.Phil thesis submitted to Manipur University.

Surrey, M.M. (1997): *The Indian Tax System*, Indian Tax Institute, New Delhi.

3 Herbs in Arunachal Pradesh

An Exploration for Economic Viability and Sustainability

Dani Chobin

Introduction

The use of herbs and drugs for treatment of ailments and injuries in the country dates back as early as 4500 B.C., mention of which is found in scriptures (*Rig Veda*). More than 2000 herb items are reportedly used for medicine out of which 200 are of minerals origin and the remaining are of vegetative nature. Forest wealth is one of the important natural aids to mankind which should be utilized judiciously. The forests in Arunachal Pradesh are primarily very large and there is vast wealth of plants, grasses, herbs, orchids and others of immense economic, commercial and medicinal values which may not be available in other parts of the country.

In recent years, there has been great demand for plant-derived products in developed countries. These products are increasingly being sought out as medicinal products, nutraceuticals and cosmetics. The World Health Organization (WHO) estimated that about three quarters of the world's population currently use herbs and other forms of traditional medicines to treat their diseases. The European market for phyto-pharmaceuticals in 1995 was reported to be US $ 1,098 million and to US $ 1,375 million in the year 2001 (Fahishi, 1996). The market for botanical health care remedies in the USA was reportedly US $ 3.24 billion in 1996 with some 60 million people using herbs to treat minor ailments such as allergies, burns, colds, depression, headache, insomnia, premenstrual syndrome and rashes (Johnston, 1997). Surveys carried out in the USA (Eisenberg *et al.,* 1993) and Australia (Maclennan *et al.,* 1997) indicates that substantial number of people are using complementary health treatments including herbs and herbal products. However, inspite of the popularity of the herbal drugs, several questions have been raised in the recent years regarding their efficacy and safety. There is only limited information available in the literature concerning the interaction of herbal and conventional medicines (Anderson *et al.,* 1985; D'Arcy, 1993). Herbal drugs have been found to report toxic effects as well as show interactions with food and other drugs. The first report of herb-drugs interaction published in 1970s stated that consumption of cruciferous vegetables resulted in lower plasma level of analgesic drug phenacetin. It was suggested that indoles, which are present in such vegetables enormously, could be responsible for interaction (Pantuck, 1996). In this study, herb-drug interactions have been reviewed. The rationale for such interactions is often difficult to explain if knowledge regarding the phytochemical constituents of the herbal products understood. It is well established that patients taking herbal drugs along with prescription medicines can experience drug interactions, which may be detrimental to their health (Mehta, 1998).

Arunachal Pradesh is very rich in medicinal flora. In the absence of any sophisticated system of medicine, the indigenous village elders have been claiming the presence of numerous life saving herbs. Simultaneously there are numerous known herbs with deadly poisons which when processed become very potent curing medicines.

As per the State Forest Report-1999, published by the Forest Survey of India, forest cover of Arunachal Pradesh is 68951 sq. km. accounting 82.21 per cent of its total geographical area. The recorded forest area of the state is 51540 sq. km. which is about 61.5 per cent of its total geographical area. Thus, the State is fortunate to have such high percentage of its area under valuable forest cover against the national percentage of 23.28.

Good agricultural and collection practices of Herbs can also be potential source of economic development and ecologically safer too to the State. It may also open up a new avenue in commercial cultivation for large production, processing and packaging, marketing and industrial application. The important types of forests found in the State are Tropical Ever Green, Semi Green, Wet Ever Green, Wet Temperate, Deciduous Mixed Coniferous, Alpine, Bamboo brakes, etc. The flora of this remote hill State has medicinal values which are utilized by indigenous people to cure their ailment without any side effect like modern medicines.

This paper attempts an in-depth study about the Herbs. It is divided into three sections. Section I has dealt with the investigation and survey done by certain botanists, naturalists, foresters and agricultural scientists in the State in regard to plants to identify the economic value or medicinal use in other parts of the country. Section II examines the sustainability of herbs due to environmental degradation caused by shifting cultivation, growth of urbanization, growth of population, growth of transportation and growth of industrialization in the State and Section III deals with suggestions and conclusion.

SECTION I

This section seeks to identify the existence of *Herbs* and its economic value in the State. It is well known fact that more than 80 per cent of the world's medicinal flora is found in the Himalayan ranges of India. Arunachal Pradesh is such type of State which is lying within the Himalayan belt. Since the State has remained a generally inaccessible area with scarce means of communication and transport, very little written record is available about medicinal flora. Mostly the knowledge and information were passed from generation to generation by word of mouth and through folklores. However, under Monasteries of Monpa (Buddhist), there were monks who had expertise and who trained some selected persons in the area of identification, collection and processing, and use of various active parts of the herbs. It is a common knowledge that only certain plants and certain parts of plants like flower, leaf, bark, root are of medicinal use.

The Department of Agriculture of Arunachal Pradesh during seventies made a positive effort to collect and circulate information on plants of medicinal and economic importance. In pursuance of this, an integrated scheme was also submitted to North Eastern Council for gainful utilization of the medicinal herbs and drugs. Dr. Rajendra Gupta, All India Co-ordinator of Medicinal and Aromatic Plants, Pusa, New Delhi, showed active interest and made some valuable suggestions. Dr. A. S. Rao, Deputy Director, Botanical Survey of India, Shillong, had also undertaken studies of certain plants and orchids of medicinal importance.

In 1976, the upper reaches of Lohit district were explored and the Herbs were listed. The main interest in Dibang Valley came on account of this area being the natural habitat of the prised roots of *mishmi teeta* (coptis), which is a rich source of berberin. For the purpose, Dr. Bordoloi of Regional Research Laboratory (R.R.L.), Jorhat, Assam toured different districts of Arunachal Pradesh extensively. During 1976, a team headed by Dr. Jamuwal from RRL, Srinagar visited West Kameng District in an expedition to explore the *Herbs* around Tawang. A valuable inventory of medicinal herbs and drugs were prepared by them in collaboration with the RRL, Jorhat and the Department of Agriculture of Arunachal Pradesh. During the course of their visit, the expedition came across the patches of lemon grass, growing naturally in hill slopes between Pamaghar and Lumla, beyond West Siang District. The grass has high lemon oil content and rich in vitamin 'A' which the knowledgeable Monpas claim to be a cure for malignant skin diseases including leprosy. Lemon grass oil is of considerable economic significance besides medicinal value.

RRL subsequently surveyed Wangchu area of Tirap district and conducted trials for cultivation of *mentha piperantha* and also undertook multiplication trial for the *solanum khasyanum* (yellow berries). Manthan yellow berries are the source of solicigin-steroid used as oral contraceptive. This berry was successfully grown in Seneua Farm. There were further trials for diascoreas particularly *D.Floribunda*, *D.Deltoiti*, etc. which also is a source for steroids. The department of agriculture screened large number of orchids, *Herbs* and other plants of economic significance. Ethno-botanical study is an important part of modern plant science, which will get a unique dimension in India in the exploration process of the ethno botanical wealth of different regions among various ethnic groups. The local tribes of Arunachal Pradesh still prefer to rely on the traditional methods of health care. These people are very familiar with the herbal medicines that are abundantly available from the surroundings. Vast climate variations in the region have resulted in existence of almost all types of *Herbs* and timber wealth ranging from tropical teak in foothill jungles to coniferous and alpine of high mountains. The State has very rich flora. It has about 4500 species of flowering plants, 400 species of pleridophytes, 23 species of coniferous, 35 species of bamboos, 20 species of canes, 25 Rhododendron species. Overall, Arunachal Pradesh is, as if, a natural garden of more than 20,000 identified species of medicinal plants and so many still remain unidentified. About 300 plant species out of native flora in North-Eastern India are used for edible purpose. Of these, over 25 provide tubers/rhizomes etc., which are eaten raw or boiled. Over 50 are consumed as green with their leaves/tender shoots cooked as vegetable; about 170 ripe fruits, which are pulpy and sweet/sub-sweet are eaten raw and many of these are used for pickles/vegetables when unripe; about 15 have edible seeds which are eaten raw or roasted.

No doubt, Arunachal Pradesh offers an ideal agro climate with vast potentials for growing varieties of orchids round the year. Out of about 1150 species of orchids known in India, about 550 species occur only in Arunachal Pradesh. These species occur in varying climatic and habitat conditions in varying concentration from the warm foothills to the cool temperate hills in Arunachal Pradesh. Such a diverse climatic situation has favoured the occurrence of about 550 species of orchids in the State which is a highest number for any state in India thus making it an "Orchid Paradise" of our country. There are over 500 Herbs recorded from Arunachal Pradesh of which 250 are used in various Ayurvedic formulations. Some important Herbs in the State with their application are shown below and listed in Annexure I.

Aromatic Oil Yielding Plants

1. *Java-Citronella*: This grass grows luxuriantly all along the foothill area of the territory. It is cultivated by planting two to three slips in a hole three feet apart. The oil is extracted through a distillation of plant by direct distillation method. The recovery of oil is between 0.8 to 1.0 per cent from fresh leaves of citronella. The prices are not much less than the other aromatic oil.
2. *Lemon Grass:* Lemon grass grows in deep clumps in high hills. Natural patches of these have been found in West Kameng in exploitable quantities. Effort is now being made to grow this grass under cultivated conditions for extraction of lemon oil. Lemon oil, besides being a base for perfumery, has been found to be very effective cure for persistent skin diseases and leprosy. Vitamin 'A' contained in lemon grass is said to have strong healing effects on skin and wounds.
3. *Mentha Piperanta:* Mentha oil is of medicinal importance and M/s Glaxo Laboratories have been organizing certain farms and extraction in certain States. For medicinal use menthol has considerable importance.
4. *Musk Dana:* There is a plant similar to Bhindi (Okra) plant of *malvacceae* family which produces musk scented seed known as musk dana. The oils of musk dana is used in high grade perfumery.

5. *Oleoresin Yielding Plants :* Ginger, turmeric and chillies grow widely under varying conditions of soil and agro-climate within the territory. Because of communication and transport limitation these bulky crops hardly attract any significant status. Once oleoresin is extracted from any of these three crops it becomes a low volume high value product and is of great demand in pharmacological industry and for cosmetics. Oleoresin plants will serve as an incentive for extensive cultivation of these crops for economic betterment of the rural communities. Basar, Along, Mebo, Roing, Chowkham, Miao and Bordumsa are potential areas for initiating such extraction plants.

Berberin Yielding Plants

1. *Coptis Teeta (locally known as Mishmi Teeta):* This is a widely known herb growing just below the snow line as small herb, at altitude between 9,999 to 12,000 ft. altitude MSL. The cultivation of Mishmi Teeta in Dang Valley around Anini was successfully demonstrated during 1975-76. Presently, it is being cultivated by a number of enthusiastic cultivators in Dibang Valley. Seeing the successful cultivation of Mishmi Teeta the Adis-Miniyong in Boleng circle of East Siang district have undertaken successful cultivation of coptis teeta locally known as 'Rinko' by the Adis. In Tuting Singa and Gelling Hills, coptis teeta grows naturally in the wild and is being utilized locally for medicinal purposes. It has considerable potential for providing a definite impact on the economy of the people of high hills and also to support a sizeable industry for extraction of berberin for medicinal purpose. Coptis teeta is considered as a vital drug by the village medicine men not only as debility tonic, cure for all kinds of stomach disorder, but also as an eye salve (*surma*). The use of coptis teeta (*memeera*) for eye salve is mainly known in J&K Hills of the Western Himalayas.

2. *Tupistra Aurantiasa:* Dipo Tale (Rinte) scientifically known as Tupistra Aurantiasa is another medicinal herb which grows in similar surroundings as coptis teeta but is more hardy with wider adaptations from elevations between 8000 ft. to 12500 ft. altitude MSL. Its leaves are long, fleshy, smooth and provide luxuriant foliage to the plant with characteristic creeping rhizomes. The creeping rhyzome is long fleshy with long internodes, having active bitter berberine content. The village medicine men use small pieces of the rhyzome also as debility tonic and for curing various kinds of stomach disorders and ailments.
3. *Apatani Ricoh:* In the higher hills of Apatani plateau there is a climber, the stem of which is widely used as a cure against all stomach ailments and as debility tonic. The plant is known as Ricoh by the Apatanies. The dry stem is equally bitter as the Mishmi Teeta and has medicinal use. Among the Nishyis, the same plant is identified and named as Rik who also use it for medicine.
4. *Aconites:* Aconites are some of the oldest well known items of trade between the hill men of frontier tracts and the Ahom rulers of Brahmaputra valley. Aconites provide deadly arrow poison for defense by the local people. Aconites are strong base of Ayurvedic medicine for preparing vital life saving drugs. Presently aconites are widely used under Ayurvedic preparations.

If herbal production in the State is known to the rest of the country, it can create an exhaustive job of collecting and collating in all researches and extension studies. It will create a new avenue in the job markets.

SECTION II

This section concentrates itself about the sustainability of the Herbs in the State. As much as the State is going to be developed day-by-day in different aspects of economies, there is a negative impact on forestation of the State. As we see after independence, there is a positive correlation between economic development and deforestation. The conservation of biodiversity is central to the idea of sustainable development. For human development to be sustainable, environmental issues and biodiversity conservation are critical. Can the rich biodiversity of the State continue to be protected, as development comes? The forest cover as well as the diversity in its highly rich flora and fauna has declined, but it is one of the key biodiversity hot spots in the world. Can a development path be forced that is not destructive, but is environmentally sustainable? A path recognizes the lessons that people here have learnt and practised for centuries in the indigenous management and harvesting of resources. In recent years, the State's rich biodiversity has increasingly come under threat. The hastening pace of development activities in the last three decades and the improvement in the communication network have meant increased access in the State. Now, we search the different impacts of economic development on sustainability of environment and biodiversity conservation in Arunachal Pradesh.

Impact of Shifting Cultivation

Agriculture occupies an important major occupation of the people of the State. According to 2001 census, about 79.66 per cent of the State's population is living in rural areas and 58.44 per cent of the total workers are cultivators. Due to scarcity of plain land in the State, the rural people have to practice shifting cultivation, *i.e.,* Jhum cultivation in order to fulfil their minimum requirement for food. The shifting cultivation is called slash and burn method of cultivation. It is labour-intensive process of farming with extensive use of land. The technology being primitive, the level of production and income is very low. It occupies a distinct place in the socio-economic fabric of tribal economy of this state. The man who practices jhum cultivation *i.e.*, shifting cultivation is called jhumia. The jhumia selects the field on the slope of the hill on rotation basis. Due to deterioration in fertility of soil the jhumia is compelled to shift his cultivation on another plot. He keeps the land fallow for a number of years for regeneration of forests. Again he uses the same land after a number of years. That is why, this process is also called shifting cultivation. This practice is not only done in Arunachal Pradesh but also in all north-eastern states due to lack of sufficient plain land.

The area under shifting cultivation and number of families are engaged are shown in Table 3.1: in context of North-Eastern States.

Table 3.1: Shifting Cultivation in the North East Region

State	*Annual Area under shifting cultivation (sq.kms)*	*Fallow period (in years)*	*Minimum area under shifting cultivation one time or other (sq.kms)*	*No. of families practicing shifting cultivation*
Arunachal Pradesh	700	3-10	2,100	54,000
Assam	696	2-10	1,392	58,000
Manipur	900	4-7	3,600	70,000
Meghalaya	530	5-7	2,650	52,290
Mizoram	630	3-4	1,890	50,000
Nagaland	190	5-8	1,913	1,16,046
Tripura	223	5-9	1,115	43,000
Total	3869		14,660	4,43,336

Source: The Task Force Report on Shifting Cultivation, Ministry of Agriculture, 1983.

Deforestation, due to practice of shifting cultivation, is considered world's most pressing land use problem. The effects of deforestation on ecology are too well known. The role of forest in maintaining ground water level, preventing soil erosion and land slide, controlling flood in plains, reducing air pollution have been discussed at length in several publications. The extent of deforestation of tropical forest has caused world wide alarm as tropical forests provide more than 50 per cent of modern medicine. Tropical forests are living museums and laboratories that have yielded only a tiny fraction of their treasures to scientific study. In course of shifting cultivation remarkable varieties of flora and fauna are disappearing, which need immediate attention for extensive and intensive studies.

The type of vegetations destroyed depends upon the length of jhum cycle. A dense forest of long cycle has more tree species than grasses, whereas a forest of short cycle has more number of grasses. All the forest resources are disappearing and become rare due to deforestation and illegal felling of trees. The ecological balance favouring the complete hydrological cycle has been seriously upset over vast areas due to ignorance or lack of appreciation of methods of conserving and managing natural vegetation (whether a forest, grass land or mixed type) and of clearing the vegetation for cultivation. This misuse and destruction of plants cover combined with great increase in human and livestock population has created intense competition for natural resources. In the continued absence of conservation and correctly integrated land use system, overall habitat deterioration has become very widespread.

Impact of Urbanization

Till 1961 census the State of Arunachal Pradesh was entirely rural. There was bi-urban centre in the State. Census-wise trend in urbanization is shown in Table 3.2.

Table 3.2: Census-wise Urban Centres

Census	*No. of Census Towns*	*Name of the Census Towns*
1961	NIL	–
1971	4	Bomdila, Along, Pasighat and Tezu
1981	6	Bomdila, Along, Pasighat and Tezu, Nharlagun and Itanaga
1991	10	Bomdila, Along, Pasighat and Tezu, Nharlagun and Itanagar, Ziro, Roing, Namsai and Khonsa
2001	17	Bomdila, Along, Pasighat and Tezu, Narlagun and Itanagar, Ziro, Roing, Namsai and Khonsa, Tawang, Seppa, Daporijo, Basar, Changlang, Jairampur and Deomali

Source: Various Census Reports,

All these towns are administrative centres in most cases. Before the establishment of administrative centres, these places were full of jungles.

According to 1991 census, a total of 12.80 per cent people live in ten urban areas while as per 2001 census, approximately 20.41 people live in seventeen urban areas. The decennial urban growth rate in the State has been recorded as 139.63 in 1971-81, 167.04 in 1981-91 and 101.24 in 1991-2001.

Impact of Population Growth

The human population census was conducted for the first time in Arunachal Pradesh in 1961. Population increases in 2001 by 326.23 per cent in comparison to the population of 1961. The growth of population and density of population census-wise are shown in Table 3.3.

Table 3.3 : Population Growth and Population Density Since 1961

Census	*Persons*	*Population Density*
1961	336558	4
1971	467511	6 (5.58)
1981	628050	8 (7.50)
1991	864558	10 (10.32)
2001	1097968	13 (13.03)

Notes: (i) Figures in the parentheses show actual values.
(ii) Population Density = Total Population ÷ Area in sq. km.
Source: Census Report, Arunachal Pradesh, 1971, 1981, 1991 and 2001.

More population means more shelter, more food, etc. which directly accelerate the deforestation. The decennial population growth rate since 1961 in the State has been recorded as 38.91 per cent in 1961-71, 35.15 per cent in 1971-81, 36.83 per cent in 1981-91 and 26.21 per cent in 1991-2001. It is more than all-India average.

Impact of Transportation

Till 1947, there were only three jeepable roads between Pasighat and Kobo by 35 kilometres, Sadiya-Tezu-Denzing by 77 kilometres and still well road 56 kilometres (NCAER – Techno-Economic Survey of NEFA, 1967, p.91). So, the total length of roads was only 168 km. till 1947. Before independence, the colonial government did not take any effort to initiate the development process and the British indifference towards the area was mainly due to the fact that the area did not possess any readily exploitable resources. After the independence of the country, the Government of India undertook the development of transport and communication with a view to open up this remote state of India and therefore, to facilitate the rapid development of the State.

In the development plans, the government has been attaching high priority to the construction of roads and as a result the total length of roads constructed in the State stood at about 15021.80 km. including 399.80 km. under National Highway giving the road density of 17.9 km. per 100 sq. km. of area at the end of March 2004. The development of roads and its density (Road length per 100 sq. km.) are shown in Table 3.4.

Table 3.4 : Category-wise Length of Roads and Its Density During 9th and 10th Plans (*in km*)

Year	*Total length of roads*	*Density of roads*
1	5	6
31.03.2000	13982.20	16.70
31.03.2001	13982.20	16.70
31.03.2002	13982.20	16.70
31.03.2003	14450.47	17.26
31.03.2004	15021.791	17.94

Note: Density of Road = Total length of roads ÷ total area.
Source: Directorate of Economics and Statistics, Govt. of Arunachal Pradesh, Itanagar.

The impact of road transport is wide ranging which includes agriculture, industry, trade and commerce which cumulatively affect overall development of a region. But at the same time the State has to face deforestation and thereby to destroy the herbs.

Impact of Industrialization

Arunachal Pradesh, though endowed with abundant natural resources is still lagging behind in industrial development as compared to other States of the country. Lack of transport and communication, dearth of skilled/technical personnel, poor literacy among local people, and low capital formation for setting up industries in this hilly region are some of the major factors for industrial backwardness. At present the main thrust of the Industry Department is to promote traditional village and small scale industries and thereby provide employment opportunities and improve the economic conditions of the people of the State. At present there are 14 district industries centres (DICs) in the State. Three DICs provide all possible help and guidance to the prospective entrepreneurs for taking up industrial ventures and provide services for identification of suitable schemes, preparation of project reports, supply and management of raw materials and marketing of finished product, etc. The DICs also organizes trainings at district level to create awareness amongst the entrepreneurs. They also assist entrepreneurs to avail incentive packages and facilities given by both Central and State Governments. In Arunachal Pradesh at the time of independence, there was almost absence of industry excepting cottage industries in the village. But at present there are 15 medium scale industries which are mostly saw mill, plywood and 11 veneer mills functioning in the State. In spite of many obstacles in the way of development of large and medium scale industries, significant number of small-scale industrial units have come up in the State over the years due to active support and positive policy of the government. There were 471 registered small scale industrial units functioning at the end of March 2003 mostly engaged in activities like blacksmithy, tin smithy, carpet making, carpentry, wool knitting, handloom and weaving, cane and bamboo works, printing press, etc.

Due to the shifting cultivation, growth of urbanization, growth of population, growth of transportation, growth of industrialization and overall development programmes, the hitherto virgin vegetation has become a victim of sudden large-scale changes upsetting the balance of nature. At conference in Guwahati, experts from the State Forest Research Institute, Itanagar, Botanical Survey of India and the G. B. Pant Institute of Himalayan Environment and Development, Itanagar made an assessment of 47 plant species lying under threat. Out of the 47, five are threatened at the global level and are red-listed by the International Union for Conservation of Nature (IUCN). This endemic species include *Amentotaxus asamica, Coptis teeta, Gymnocladus assamicus, Piper Pedicellatum, P. Peepuloides, Aquilaria malaecensis, Dienia muscifera, Rauvolifia serpentina* and *Smilax glabra* are reported to be critically endangered.

SECTION III

This section tries to focus on the economic viability of natural resources like herbs. In order to harness the vast and varied natural resource endowments of Arunachal Pradesh, the following steps may be suggested. They are:

1. A quick survey should be undertaken through a team of young and enthusiastic field experts borrowed from different organizations dealing with indigenous medicinal herbs and drugs to assess the nature and extent of availability of economic plants and above all to extract herbs of economic value from the forest should be encouraged.
2. This should be followed by detailed survey for identification, classification and codification of economic medicinal herbs.
3. Considering the market demand both inside the country

and the export market, projects should be drawn to cultivate herbs of medicinal value for their desired active ingredients.

4. Bankable projects should be drawn for cultivation and processing of known medicinal herbs.
5. Promotional programmes on the aspect of research and development should be undertaken of selected herbs of known use but unknown economic exploitation for their gainful utilization.
6. The authority should undertake the possibilities for establishment of pharmacological perfumery and other specialized industries.
7. The floral assemblage in the State can cause immediate concern to any investigator. The effects of growth of urbanization, population, transportation, industrialization and overall shifting cultivation on biological resources will have to be assessed on data base and do accordingly for the preservation of natural resources.
8. The only one university, Rajiv Gandhi University in the State should establish a Herbal Science Department with following major areas of research as part of teaching and extension programmes:

    - Development of natural products as drugs from living resources.
    - Standardization of herbal drugs that are already developed.
    - Validation of commercially available herbal drugs and formulation.
    - Development of Agro-technics for herbal plants.
    - Development of human resources by commencing job oriented short-term teaching and training programmes on herbal sciences.

9. The existing Research Institute (Ayurvedic), Itanagar should be well equipped with enthusiastic field experts

who have considerable expertise in dealing with herbal research so as to be awarded national and international patents on herbal products.

10. Government (Central/State) should sell cooking gas (LPG) at subsidized rate so that the people can use fire wood as least as possible.
11. The women especially village women should be given training how to preserve bio-diversity in the State. Because in most cases, the women in the State are collecting fire wood from the forest. Deforestation for domestic fuel supply adds to the environmental crises.

Conclusion

Roy Barman Committee's Report (1982) on Forests clearly stated that banning the practice is not likely to achieve the object in view and it might even provoke reaction. CSE (1985) reports that a number of features have led to the failure of schemes to settle shifting cultivators; low productivity, absence of tools and implements, failure to understand water management in settled cultivation, short-term government policies and above all change of socio-cultural ethos, have been listed as probable factors. Question arises if a change is brought looking at the entire terrain conditions of the region, will it be acceptable to the local people and fit into their pattern of life. In this regard it may be suggested that some scientific measures should be taken to put an end to the erosion of top soil and studies should be carried out to explore the possibility of introducing modern innovations on jhum land so as to obtain higher yield per unit area. Besides, replacements of crop cultivation by other types of alternative livelihood like plantations, economic and conservational forestry, horticulture, development of animal husbandry, *i.e.,* livestock rearing like poultry farming, sericulture, bee keeping and so on may also be encouraged. The problems arising out of jhuming in Arunachal Pradesh can be solved keeping in view the many facts of shifting cultivation, the socio-cultural life of the people, the feasibility of change over the expenditure involved and the maintenance of a changed pattern. Effects should be so made as to bring the change from within the society. The cultivators should be imparted proper training and education to adopt new innovations. They must also be educated about the danger of jhuming.

For conserving and managing natural vegetation the jhum cultivation and illegal felling of trees, which are the root cause of deforestation, must be stopped immediately but not without rehabilitation of the jhumias. If the government is successful to protect the natural vegetation, the State will be the richest in having the Herbs which can be sold in national and international markets. Hence, it is necessary first to develop the market for Herbs within the State where the local cultivators will be benefited economically. It will give an incentive to the local people to protect the valuable Herbs from extinction.

For the betterment of lives, urbanization, transportation, industrialization are necessary but we can try to minimize the deforestation due to shifting cultivation and illegal felling of trees which are the main cause of disappearance of flora and fauna in Arunachal Pradesh. The Central Government as well as the State Government should give top priority to protect the herbs of economic value in the State which are endowed more than 50 per cent of herbs of the country. Days are not far when the Governments can generate employment as well as earn foreign currency from the export of the State's herbs if they have keen interest to protect the existing herbs from disappearance due to impact of the factors mentioned under Section II.

The recent debates and developments with regard to the draft of National Environment Policy (NEP), 2004 and the Scheduled Tribes (Recognition of Forest Rights) Bill (STB), 2005 are illustrative in different ways of the manner in which social concerns are dealt with in environmental policy and legislation in India. Yet, while the pros and cons of specific policies and legislations have been central to the academic debates on the environment, very little attempt has been made to trace the changes in environmental policy-making and the way of social concerns have been still problematized.

References

Anderson, L.A. and J. D. Phillipson (1985): Herbal medicine, education and the pharmacist, *Pharm.J.* 236: 303-305.

Eisenberg, D. M., R. C. Kessler, C. Foster, F. E. Norlock, D. R. Calkins and T. L. Delbanco (1993): Unconventional medicine in the United States. Prevalence, costs and patterns of use. *N. Engl. J. Med.* 328: 246-252.

Fahishi, A. (1996): *Complementary Medicine*. Vol. 1. London: Financial Times and Health-care Publishing.

Ghosh, A.K. (1990): "Impact of Shifting Cultivation in Living Natural Resources", in Majumdar, D.N. (ed.), *Shifting Cultivation in North-East India,* Omsons Publications, Guwahati and New Delhi, pp.178-197.

Govt. of Arunachal Pradesh (2004): *Economic Review*, Directorate of Economic and Statistics, Itanagar.

Hegde, S.N. (1988): "Coptis Teeta Wall (Mishmi Teeta): A Rare Medicinal Plant from Arunachal Pradesh", *Arun for News* 6(I), pp.27-29.

Jain, S.K. (1987): *A Manual of Ethnobotany*, Scientific Publishers, Jodhpur.

Johnston, G. A. (1997): Market Report. *Herbalgram* 40: 52.

Josh, M.C. (1997): "Role of Herbs and Drugs in Economic Development" in Pandey B.B. (ed.), *Patterns of Change and Potential for Development in Arunachal Pradesh*, Himalayan Publishers, Itanagar, New Delhi, pp.174-184.

Kanjilal, U.N., Kanjilal, P.C. and Das, A. (1934): *Flora of Assam*, Vol.I, Govt. of Assam, Shillong.

Maclennan, A., D. H. Wilson and A. W. Taylor (1997): *Prevalence and Cost of Alternative Medicine in Australia*, London: Mintel International Group.

Mandal, R.K. (2005): *Arunachal Economy: Socio Economic Transformation*, Champion Publishing, Itanagar, pp.116-117.

Mandal, R.K. (2006): "Sustainability and Economic Viability of Medicinal Plants in Arunachal Pradesh, India " *Plant Archives: An International Journal of Plant Research*, Vol.6, No.2.

Mehta, D.K., (1998): *British National Formulary*. British Medical Association and the Royal Pharmaceutical Society of Great Britain. London : The Pharmaceutical Press.

Pantuck, E. J. (1996): Stimulatory effect of vegetables on intestinal drug metabolism in the rat. *J. Pharmacol Exp. Therapy*, 198 : 278-283.

Pandey, H.C. (1988): "Some Healing Herbs of the Monk's Amongst the Minor Forest Produce", *Arun for News* 6(I), pp.1-10.

Rao, V.M. (2003): *Tribal Women of Arunachal Pradesh*, Mittal Publications, New Delhi, p.21.

Rimo, Y., Tamuk, A. Ranjan, S. & Mishra R. (2004): "Some Prominent Medicinal Herbs of Arunachal Pradesh" in Mishra, R. (ed.), *Recent Advances in Environment Biology and Ethnobotany*. Sunview Centre, Itanagar, p.77.

Shrivastava, S., R., Barik, N. Mishra, S. Vengurlekar, G. Shrikarthi, S., Revathi, S., Jain (2006): "A Review of Herb-Drug Interactions", *Plant Archives: An International Journal of Plant Research*, Vol. 6, No. 2, October, pp. 423.

ANNEXURE I

TROPICAL AND SUBTROPICAL ZONE

Habit	*Botanical name*	*Trade name*	*Purpose*
Herb	*Amomum subulatum*	Sthul Ela	Digestion, tonic
	Andrographis paniculata	Kalmegha	Liver disorder
	Asparagus racemosus	Shatavari	Tonic
	Curcuma cassia	Kali Haldi	Joint pain/sprain
	Curcuma Longa	Haridra	Cough/pain
	Mimosa pudicaa	Lajjalu	
	Rauvolfia serpentine	Sarpagandha	Hypertension
	*Solanum Khasianum**	Kantakari	Swas cough
	Solanum nigrum	Kakamachi	Digestion
	Zingiber officinale	Adraka	Cough, arthritis
Climber	*Cissampelos pareira*	Ambastha/Patha	Liver tonic
	Tinospora cordifolia	Guduchi	Tonic

TEMPERATE AND ALPINE ZONE

Habit	*Botanical name*	*Trade name*	*Purpose*
Herb	*Aconitum heterophyllum**	Visha	Tonic
	*Coptis teeta**	Maira	Liver disorder
	*Picrorhiza kurroa**	Katuki	Liver tonic
	*Swertia chirayita**	Chiraita	Liver disorder
	*S.Ciliata**	Chiraita	Liver disorder
	*Valeriana hardwickii**	Tagar	Cardiac, hepatic and

(Contd...)

			nervine tonic
	Thalictrum foliolosum	Mamiri	Liver tonic
Climber	*Embelia ribes**	Vai bidang	Worm, liver
	*Rubia cordifolia**	Manjishtha	Blood purifier
	Tinospora cordifolia	Guduchi	Tonic

Note: * indicates that these Herbs are largely available in Arunachal Pradesh.
Source: *Regional Research Institute (Ayurveda)*, Itanagar, Arunachal Pradesh.

4 SHGs and Women Empowerment

A Preliminary Investigation

Ritu Hazarika

Introduction

Rural development has been an important agenda in development planning of third world countries. In India, poverty alleviation programmes have been launched and implemented with twin objectives of providing wage employment and additional money income. As a result, IRDP, PMRY, IAY, DWCRA, SGSY are important schemes implemented in rural areas to realize the above objectives. In these schemes, there are specific considerations for women and weaker sections. More importantly, there are also schemes exclusively for women, women empowerment has been recognized as an important strategy for rural development. Among the schemes, SHG is a comprehensive one with more scope for women in income earning and decision-making at family levels.

In order to understand the impact of SHG strategy in the role of women, two SHGs of Telahi Block of Lakhimpur district, Assam have been selected. The paper shall be a preliminary enquiry to understand the decision-making power of the women forming into SHGs.

Locating SHGs in Poverty Alleviation Programmes and Women Empowerment

Poverty alleviation programmes have to be viewed in the wider perspective of socio-economic transformation in the country. It is necessary to ensure that the pattern of overall economic growth itself is such as to generate adequate incomes for the poorer sections through its greater impact on employment generation and on the development of the less developed regions. The programmes for poverty alleviation should thus be regarded as supplementing the basic plan for overall economic growth in terms of generating productive assets and skills as well as incomes for the poor.

In almost all plans for poverty alleviation and social change, disadvantaged women became a 'target' in developmental activities rather than a group to be co-opted as active participants (Beijing Conference, 1996). Since 1970, policy makers and academicians started thinking as to how development programmes could be linked to poor women. Women issues are development issues and by-passing them in development programmes means leaving almost half of human resources outside development intervention (CIRDAP Development Digest, 1998). Female members of a poor household are often worse off than its male counterpart, because of gender discrimination in the distribution of food and other entitlements within the household. In the context of rural poverty, "increasingly poverty has a women's face" (Human Development Report 1995) and the Human Development Reports of UNDP from 1990 onwards attest to the fact of growing feminization of poverty. Therefore, the Government of India had implemented some important schemes in rural areas in order to provide wage employment and additional money income with specific considerations for women and weaker sections.

The important implemented schemes in the country are:

1. Integrated Rural Development Programme (IRDP)
2. Prime Minister's Rozgar Yojana (PMRY)
3. Indira Awaas Yojana (IAY)
4. Development of Women and Children in Rural Areas (DWCRA)
5. Training of Rural Youth for Self-Employment (TRYSEM)

6. Swarnajayanti Gram Swarozgar Yojana (SGSY)

The SHGs were formed under the Swarnajayanti Gram Swarozgar Yojana (SGSY) scheme of the government. SGSY is a new self-employment programme to assist the rural people to enhance income and quality of life. It was introduced on 1st April, 1999 in Assam with an aim to help the poor people to uplift than from the poverty line. The people who got the benefits under this programme are known as Swarozgaries instead of beneficiaries. Under this programme, the SHGs were formed in villages.

SGSY has been conceived as a holistic programme of Self-employment. It covers all aspects of self-employment of the rural people, namely, organization of the poor into Self-Help Groups (SHGs) and their capacity building, training, selection of key activities and planning of activity clusters, infrastructure build up, technology and marketing support.

Concept of SHG

Today the concept of Self-Help Groups is catching up as the most viable means of mobilizing credit support for the poor at the grassroots, particularly for the women folk; women have shown extraordinary dynamism to organize themselves for group activities, for income generation, better bargaining power and improvement in the quality of life.

The concept of SHGs is not new for our country. Our country has a long tradition of people coming together voluntarily for performing various socio-cultural and economic activities collectively. Most of the employment and income generation programmes of the government are routed through the SHGs. The major objective of SHG is socio-economic empowerment of women through group initiatives of training production and marketing.

Self-Help Group is a “small, economic, homogenous and affinity groups of rural/urban poor, voluntarily formed to save and contribute to a common fund known as Group Corpus to be lent to the members as per group decision and for working together for social and economic uplift of their families and community" (TNCDW, 1999). The SHG is a viable attentive to achieve the objectives of rural development and to get community participation in all rural development programmes.

It is a well-known fact that the goal of poverty alleviation can not be achieved without the full and active participation of women who constitute a large section of work force. Women's development is directly related to nation's development. It is a belief that "When women move forward, the family moves, the village moves and the nation moves". These words of Pandit Jawaharlal Nehru is the central theme in the socio-economic paradigm of the country as it is an accepted fact that only when women are in the main-stream of progress, the economic and social development be meaningful (Saha and Banerjee, 2001). The development of women is an integrated and unified concept stretching across economic, social and cultural field (Mehta and Sethi, 1997). The national and state governments have formulated some strategies for rural development particularly for women empowerment.

Women Empowerment

Empowerment is a term widely used in the context of development particularly Women's Development. While 'power' is the key to 'Empowerment', it implies control and say in decision-making and participation in social, economic or political development of the society. At family level, it implies participation of women in household decision-making, access and control over the productive resources. Empowerment is particularly complex because it is multidimensional and takes place in multiple domains of home, community, state and society. It is locally defined and is embedded in social, cultural and political contexts. It has personal, group and political components although discussions about the measurement of empowerment have primarily focused on the personal psychological aspects. The concept of empowerment is broken down to personal factors like attitudes, traits, skills which together enable one to exert control over aspects of one's own life and to participate effectively in group efforts for social change. Empowerment is also a state of mind and is sustained by certain supportive factors in the environment. As a state of mind, it reflects self-reliance and determination to fight for one's right and interest. Empowerment in a nutshell, is a way of defining, challenging and overcoming barriers in one's life through which the individual develops the ability to shape life and environment. It is an active process enabling the women to realize their full identity and power in all spheres of life.

In order to empower women and to bring them to the mainstream, an enabling environment with requisite policies, programmes, institutional mechanisms at various levels and adequate financial resources have been created. The Government of India declared the year 2001 as the women's empowerment year. With gradual spread of education and empowerment, the status of women has begun to change. A woman is empowered when she gains productive skills, access to capital and self-confidence. Education and training leads to economic, social, legal and collective empowerment. Women's role as educators in family, community and in formal school systems and in public life is highly recognized by UNESCO (2000).

Depending on the context concerned, empowerment is defined variously. In our present context, empowerment may be defined ideally as 'a continuous process where the powerless people become conscious of their situation and organize themselves to improve it and access opportunities, as an outcome of which women take control over their lives, set their own agenda, gain skills, solve problems and develop self-reliance.'

Different social scientists have defined women's empowerment differently:

1. Griffen (1989) defined women's empowerment as "adding to women's power".
2. Kabeer (1990) interprets it as a radical transformation

of power relations between women and men, so that women have greater power over their own lives and men have less power over women's lives.
3. Andre Betille (1999) said "The main point behind empowerment is that it seeks to change society through a rearrangement of power."
4. Gidden (1984) views it as transformative capacity.

The World Bank has suggested that empowerment of women should be a key aspect of social development programmes (World Bank, 2001). The 'National Policy for the Empowerment of Women' (2000) states that "The women's movement and a widespread network of NGOs which have strong grassroots presence and deep insight into women's concerns have contributed in inspiring initiatives for the empowerment of women."

The World Bank's 'Empowerment and Poverty Reduction: A Sourcebook' defines empowerment in its broadest sense as the "expansion of freedom of choice and action" (Narayan, 2002). United Nations (2001) defines empowerment as the processes by which women take control and ownership of their lives through expansion of their choices. Kabeer's (1998, 1999) view of empowerment refers to the processes by which those who have been denied the ability to make choices acquire such ability.

The concept of women's development has undergone a metamorphic evaluation. Initially, it was welfare oriented. In the Fifth Plan (1974-1978), this approach was shifted from 'welfare to development'. During the Sixth Plan (1980-1985), the concept of welfare with development services was integrated with multi-disciplinary needs of women, *viz.*, health, education etc. In the next plan (1985-1990), the government has given a major thrust on education and social enlistment of women. The 9th Five Year Plan is committed to women's empowerment. The National Policy for Women, 2001 is a step in building up strong women's movement and is declared as "the year of

Empowerment of women." The goal of this policy is to bring about the advancement, development and empowerment of women. In due course, many social and economic programmes were evolved exclusively for women or with a percentage set aside solely for them. Studies have shown that "practical gender gains" improved livelihood, education, nutrition and sanitation, are not sustained and easily reversed (Menon and Mehta, 1998).

SHGs and Women Empowerment

Women empowerment has been recognized as an important strategy for rural development. There are many schemes exclusively for women empowerment. Among the schemes, Self-Help Group (SHG) is a comprehensive one with more scope for women in income earning and decision-making at family levels.

The SHGs disburse microcredit to the rural women, for the purpose of making them enterprising and encouraging to enter into entrepreneurial activities. Credit needs of the rural women are fulfilled totally through SHGs. It enhances equality of status of women as participants, decision makers and beneficiaries in the democratic, economic, social and cultural spheres of life. SHGs encourage women to take active part in socio-economic progress of our nation.

Micro-financing: Shift from the Traditional Banking System

Micro-finance programmes for women are promoted not only as a strategy for poverty alleviation but for women's empowerment as well (Mayoux, 1996). Since early 1980s, empowerment has become a key objective of development. Empowerment has been considered both an end and as a mean of development.

Micro-financing has turned out to be an effective strategy for formal financing agencies. Group lending minimises transaction cost and at the same time the members of a group can avail small loans through that group. The chances of misutilisation are minimal and there are assured repayment because of peer monitoring by the group. The group concept has enabled the rural poor to develop the savings habit and minimise extravagance. Also the rate of interest of group lending is much less as compared to loans from bank.

For the SHG members, the system has been found beneficial because of minimal procedural formalities, access to institutional credit without collateral offering, full autonomy in the selection of activity, and the availability of thrift for meeting urgent needs. The absence of procedural formalities has made the programme customer-friendly. Besides, the flexibility repayment schedule enables them to repay as and when it is convenient. The group will see to it that prompt repayment is made, as they are likely to get repeat loans. The smaller unit size allows women to pursue the activities in their spare time and contribute to the family's income.

SHGs in Assam — A Brief Profile

In order to ameliorate the rural people, the Government of Assam has also taken many employment generation and poverty alleviation schemes. In rural development schemes the focus is shifted to programmes meant for only women.

The programme focuses on organization of the poor at grassroots level through a process of social mobilization for poverty eradication. Social mobilization enables the poor to build their own SHGs in which they fully and directly participate and take decisions on all issues that will help them in coming above the poverty line. A SHG may consist of 10-20 persons belonging to families below the poverty line and a person should not be a member more than one group. Each SHG selects a leader called "Animator" among its members. In some special cases, five members could also form a SHG.

The group takes up economic activities, of their choice for income generation. This phase would include Entrepreneurship

Development as well as Skill Development Training of the members of the Group to enable them to successfully implement the chosen activity. The weaving skill of the women of Assam is a potential opportunity. It is necessary to upscale weaving from household activity to market oriented enterprise for better income and employment generation. Training, design, inputs and market linkages are necessary so that women can make the most productive use of their skills and resources.

The main objectives of the study were to see the type of activities of the SHGs, the economic gain of the female members of the SHGs and the benefits that the female members get to improve their social status. Four hypotheses of the study are:

1. Female members of the SHGs are engaged in different productive activities with a common goal.
2. Female members of SHGs are getting economic gain.
3. Members of SHGs take independent decisions in spending their income.
4. To examine the impact of SHG and micro-credit on women empowerment.

Methodology

For this study, the survey method was applied using structured questionnaires to collect data from the sample groups collected randomly from different villages under Telahi Block. Two women SHGs were selected for the purpose of a primary investigation.

Frame of Analysis

The results were discussed on the following heads such as—

1. Socio-economic profile of women in SHGs.
2. Activities of SHGs.
3. Formation and operation of SHGs.
4. Income and expenditure by the members.

Sample and Sample size

Each of 27 districts of Assam is divided into a number of blocks. There are 219 Community Development Blocks in Assam. In each block there is a number of Gaon Panchayats (GP) and under each GP there are number of villages. In each village a number of SHGs were formed. Lakhimpur district of Assam has nine Community Development Blocks, of which Telahi Block has been selected for this study.

Table 4.1 : Profile of Lakhimpur

Population of Lakhimpur	889,325
Male Population	455,689
Female Population	433,636
No. of villages	1,185
No. of towns	3
Community Development Block	9

Source: Census Report, 2001.

Table 4.2 : Profile of Telahi Block

Population of Telahi block	51,037
Male Population	26,390
Female Population	24,647
No. of SHGs	1,337

Source: Census Report, 2001.

Many SHGs are formed only by the female members. As female lag behind, the investigator felt the need to study how far the SHGs could empower the women. So, the female SHGs in different villages under Telahi block of Lakhimpur district has been selected for the study.

Socio-economic Profile of Women in SHGs

From Table 4.3, it is found that, out of 21 members, 19 were formerly engaged only in household activities. Two members of different groups are graduates, whereas 16 have completed schooling at different levels and 3 are illiterate. Among the members, most of them are married, i.e., 15 members whereas only 6 of them are still unmarried.

Table 4.3 : Details of the SHGs Selected as Sample

Code of SHG	*Name of SHGs*	*Year of Formation*	*No. of Members*	*Educational Status*			*Marital Status*	
				Primary Level	*Graduate*	*Illiterate*	*Married*	*Unmarried*
01	Munmi SHG	2003	11	9	1	1	7	4
02	Sandhani SHG	2007	10	7	1	2	8	2

Source: Field survey, September 2008.

Analysis of Findings

From Tables 4.4 and 4.5, it is found that both the groups (Munmi and Sandhani), lending of money on interest was the prime activity. Production of rice, mushroom cultivation and poultry farming were other activities undertaken by group with code No. 01. The group with code No. 02 has undertaken weaving apart from money lending.

Table 4.4 : Money Lending Activity of the Groups

Name of SHG	Period	Type of Lending	Money Lent (Rs.)	Money Received (Rs.)	Amount Outstanding (Rs.)	Interest Received (Rs.)	Interest Due (Rs.)	Money at Hand (Rs.)
Munmi SHG	2003-2008	Internal	47,000.00	33,000.00	14,000.00	7,715.00	8,525.00	
		External	8.800.00	8,800.00	0.00	2,510.00	0.00	3,085.00
		Total	55,800.00	41,800.00	14,000.00	10,225.00	8,525.00	
Sandhani SHG	2007-2008	Internal	0.00	0.00	0.00	0.00	0.00	
		External	31,000.00	0.00	31,000.00	0.00	1,550.00	2,225.00
		Total	31,000.00	0.00	31,000.00	0.00	1,550.00	

Source: Field survey, September 2008.

From the analysis, it was found that the profit earned by the group with code 01 from money lending including both internal and external is Rs. 10,225 and Rs. 19,580 from other activities. As the group with code 02 is new, their activities are also less. They earned Rs. 3,500 from weaving.

Table 4.5 : Other Activities of the Groups

Name of SHG	*Activities*	*Year*	*Money Invested (Rs.)*	*Money Earned (Rs.)*	*Profit (Rs.)*	*Labour time spent (in Hours)*	
						Members	*Hired*
Munmi SHG	Mushroom Cultivation	2005	150.00	400.00	250.00	Average 1 hour daily	
	Production of rice (including amount for Land	2006	19,650.00	30,500.00	10,850.00	Average 2 hour daily	2 hours for 15 days (1 person)
	mortgage of Rs. 19,000.00 for 3 bighas land)	2007	20,780.00	29,000.00	8,220.00	Average 2 hour daily	2 hours for 25 days (2 persons)
			40,430.00	59,500.00	19,070.00		
	Broiler Farming	2007	5,000.00	5,260.00	260.00	Average 2 hour daily	
Sandhani SHG	Weaving	2008	3,000.00	6,500.00	3,500.00	Average 3 hour daily	

Source: Field data as on September, 2008.

From the analysis, it was also found that the scope of making more profit is external lending of money for longer period, rice cultivation and weaving. Lending of money is a much easier way of earning. In weaving also, one piece of cloth becomes free of cost in every two pieces, which they can either use for self or sell it.

Formation and Operation of SHGs

The stage of formation of SHGs may be said to be the 'foundation-stone-laying stage'. The formation of SHGs is "not ultimately a micro-credit project but an empowerment process" (Micro-Credit Summits, 2001). The concept aims at empowering women and thus uplifting their families above the poverty line. It is a gradual process resulting from interaction with group members through awareness and capacity building.

The voluntariness of the poor women in coming together is of crucial importance. The women are motivated by the agencies[1] through small informal gathering, at which the virtues of small savings and the importance of reducing wasteful expenditure and building up funds for meeting their contingency credit needs are explained to them. Though it is generally said that no promise of financial support is to be given at this time of group formation, this norm is rarely practised in any group. From the beginning, the members in the group have motivated to get financial support in terms of loan.

During the field survey, information on the factors that motivated the members to join the group was also collected. Table 4.6 shows the reasons given by the members for joining the SHGs.

Table 4.6 : Motivating Factors — Members Perception

Reasons	*Munmi N:11*	*Sandhani N:10*
For getting loan	7(63.6%)	5(50%)
For promoting savings habit	9(81.8%)	8(80%)
For availing loan and promoting savings habit	6(54.5%)	4(40%)
For family's welfare	2(18.1%)	2(20%)
Other reasons	7(63.6%)	5(50%)
Multiple reasons	11(100%)	10(100%)

Source: Field survey, September 2008.

Out of 21 members, 11 members were motivated by NGOs and the rest by bank personnels. All the members (100 per cent) joined the group for multiple reasons like getting loan, inculcating the savings habit and welfare of the family. 80 per cent opined that they joined the group for promoting savings and for getting loans. Only two members of each group reported that they have joined the group for the welfare of their families. Nine members thought that memberships in the group would raise their status in society as one of the reasons for joining the group.

Role of Promoting Agencies

Here, the government personals, NGOs and social welfare agencies have played a vital role to identify the interested persons, form SHGs and guide them in framing the rules and regulations for thrift and credit procedures and payment ethics.

Table 4.7 : Details of Training given to SHGs by Promoting Agencies

Name of the SHG	*Promoting Agencies*	*Training on*	*Duration*	*No. of participants*
Munmi SHG	NGO	Mushroom Cultivation	7 days	3
		Food processing	1 month	5
	Bank Personnel	Book keeping, transaction with bank, etc.	7 days	11
	Veterinary Personnel	Broiler Farming	i5 days	3
Sandhani SHG	NGO	Weaving	1 month	10

Source: Field survey, September 2008.

Both the groups have received training on different activities like mushroom cultivation, book keeping, transaction with bank, weaving etc. by various government personals, and NGO's as shown in Table 4.7.

Patterns of Income

The income of the groups included interest on money lending, profits from selling products, self deposits, and subsidy from bank etc. Self deposit amount of group 01 and 02 was Rs.30 and Rs.100 on monthly basis respectively. The rate of interest on internal lending for 01 was 5 per cent and for 02 was 3 per cent. For some special causes such as illness of any family members, meeting expenses of their children at the time of examination etc., the interest is exempted from the members for a limited period of time as decided in group meeting. The interest rate of lending money to other people was 10 per cent and 5 per cent per month for group 01 and 02 respectively.

The SHG utilize the group deposit and loan for purchasing raw material, lending of money, other expenses for group activities like meetings and miscellaneous expenses as shown in Table 4.8.

Table 4.8 : The Involvement of Accounts on Various Heads

Accounts Heads	*Munmi SHG (01)*	*Sandhani SHG (02)*
Starting Capital	Rs. 50 x 11 = Rs. 550	Rs. 120 x 10 = Rs. 1200
Initial Expenses	Rs. 220	Rs. 200
Monthly Contribution by the members	Rs. 30 each	Rs. 100 each
Loan from bank	Rs. 25,000	Rs. 30,000
Cash at bank	Rs. 3,085	Rs. 2,225
Cash on hand	Nil	Nil
Money on lent	Rs. 14,000	Rs. 31,000
Fixed assets	Office Room Rs. 10,000	Nil
Purchase of Raw materials	Rs. 7,580	Rs. 3,000
Expenditure for group activities, meetings and miscellaneous	Rs. 4,920	Rs. 2,275
Profit sharing among group members	Rs. 1,740/- each	Rs. 1,000 each

Source: Field survey, September 2008.

Utilization of Loan

Money lending is one of the prime activities of both the groups. The group with code 01 is involved in both internal and external lending whereas the group with code 02 is involved only in external lending. For group 01, 9 out of 11 members availed loan. It was found that the number of loanees is more than the number of members as some of the members took loan more than one time. All the nine members who took loan utilized it to meet their domestic needs, medical purpose and children's education. Five members availed loan for ceremonies and festivals, three members for repayment of old debts, two members took loan to purchase land, one member utilized it to release land mortgage and another one to start her own micro enterprise.

Analysing Impact on Empowerment

In this Section, it is important to examine the impact of SHGs and micro-credit on empowering poor women and their

Table 4.9 : Utilisation of Loan

Name of SHG	*Type of Lending*	*Loan Amount*	*No. of Loanees*	*Purpose of Use*
Munmi SHG (01)	Internal Lending	Rs. 200	3	Medical
		Rs. 300	3	Medical
		Rs. 500	7	Repayments of old debts, medical
		Rs. 1000	11	Domestic needs, medical, children's education
		Rs. 1500	3	Domestic needs, medical
		Rs. 2000	6	Domestic needs, medical, children's education
		Rs. 2500	1	Micro enterprise
		Rs. 3000	4	Ceremonies, medical, children's education
	External Lending	Rs. 1000	3	Medical, Children's education
		Rs. 1800	1	Release of land mortgage
		Rs. 2000	2	Ceremonies, Purchase of land
Sandhani SHG (02)	External Lending	Rs. 31000	1	Purchase of land

Source: Field survey, September 2008.

families. Here the empowerment framework developed at various workshops organised by various international agencies engaged in Micro Finance Programmes (MFPs) and other donors has been adopted and modified to suit the context, the area of study and the culture of the people.

Table 4.10 : Matrix for Analysing Impact on Empowerment

Type of Indicator	*Level at which impact on empowerment may be assessed*
Economic	Increase in savings
	Increase in income
	Increase in assets
	Repayment rates and repeat loans
	Skill development
Social	Increase in self-confident
	Change in attitude to women's role
	Improvement in communication skills and in social outlook
Political/Legal	Increase in participation in political process
	Removal of legal discrimination against women

Source: Adapted from the Action Aid, UK

But in our present investigation, economic indicator is taken into consideration for understanding impact of SHG strategy on women empowerment.

Dimensions of Empowerment

Independence in taking decision themselves for selection of loanees, fixation of interest rate and selection of activities shows the dimensions of empowerment of the group members. Selecting paddy cultivation as a source of income was also their decision which showed a handsome result by making profit. At the time of execution of the decision, in fact they take the help of technical person like NGO personnels. This is an indication of empowerment.

Conclusion

In conclusion, it can be said that the Self Employment Programme implemented by the Government under SGSY is really a promising programme to uplift the socio-economic status of the women in rural areas. Rural Development is possible only when women are involved in the development process to keep the society on the desired path. Women's empowerment through SHGs has gained wider recognition in the developing countries like India. It can be used as a tool to root out poverty and bring prosperity to the women. On the whole, SHGs could trigger the development impulses to blossom among the down trodden.

Note

1. As per Field Study.

References

Jha, P.K. (2005). *Education for Rural Development*: Vista International Publishing House, New Delhi.

Patil, A., Mathu, A. (2007). *Women and Entrepreneurship Issues and Challenges*: Kalpaz Publications, New Delhi.

Ray, B.D., Das, Gurudas (2004). *Dimensions of Rural Development in North-East India*, Akansha Publishing House, New Delhi.

Ray, Ashok Kumar (2008). *Female Emancipation Trends and Issues in North East India*, Om Publications, New Delhi.

Setty, E.D. (2008). *Effective Strategies for Rural Development:* Akansha Publishing House, New Delhi.

5 Communitisation in Nagaland
An Overview

Komol Singha

Introduction

The Nagaland government has introduced a unique concept of empowerment of community through the process of Communitisation. It was borne out of Nagaland Communitisation of Public Institutions and Services Act, 2002 on 15th April, 2002. This system has evolved from an effort to transfer certain management responsibilities to the village community, to take charge and to develop further and to own it. Community functions through a means of cooperation based on consent coordinate division of labour among people towards a socially desirable direction.

The programme of Communitisation in Nagaland is a very unique programme based on the intrinsic social capital in the State. The community bond or social norm in a tribal society, particularly in Naga society is very strong and firm, that is how the social capital is very strong in their society. The role and significance of community in economic development (particularly, the rural-based communities) has been recognized by the all and has been proved by different scholars in the past (e.g. Adam Smith, 1776; Robert Putnam, 1993; Hayami and Godo, 2006; and others).

By giving a change of responsibility to the community (investing social capital), the efficiency and governance of public institutions sought to be improved. The problem of common property and inefficiency of public institutions is one of the most important problems in the developing countries now. The same idea was also well-highlighted by G. Hardin (1968) in his study 'Tragedy of Commons' in regard to the environmental degradation. In order to improve the situation, the Nagaland Government proposes to share management responsibility for such institutions with the community for whom the 'institutions' have been set up; this is what we called '*Communitisation*'.

The preamble of Nagaland Communitisation Act states that 'Whereas the expedient to provide for empowerment of the community and delegation of powers and functions of the State government to the local authorities by way of participation of the community in matters connected with the management of local public utilities, public services and activities of the State government connected with education, water supply, roads, forest, power, sanitation, health and other welfare and development schemes and also to provide for promotion of community-based schemes incidental thereto.'

Objectives of the Study

Nagaland's programme of Communitisation of Public Institutions and Services has helped in moving the state towards fulfilling the Millennium Development Goals. The programme has won the coveted United Nations Award for Public Services from the Asia and Pacific Region. It has been recognized by the world and became a catch word now.

Keeping the achievement and recognition in mind, the *objectives o*f the present study are to understand the implications and reliability of the scheme in the present Naga society. How far has it helped in the rural development in Nagaland? Even after six years its implementation, the scheme has not been heading towards the speed of expected level. The present study will look into this direction.

Some of the *Specific Objectives* of the study are as follows:

- To study the need and importance of Communitisation in Nagaland

- To study the operational system of Communitisation
- To study the implication of Communitisation in Naga society
- To study the role of Communitisation in rural development
- To study the challenges and lacunae confronted in the process of Communitisation
- To recommend possible suggestions

Methodology of the Study

The programme of Communitisation is the first ever step towards the smooth functioning of the public institutions in Nagaland. Since, it is the first ever programme and there is no similar work done in the past, the present study is based purely on the primary field survey. In this study, exclusively three sectors, namely, Education, Health and Power sector have been included.

For the purpose of the study, a primary survey was conducted during the month of February 2009 in a village called 'Thizama' under Kohima district of Nagaland. During the survey, village council leaders, government officials, and villagers were interviewed as per the requirement of the paper. To substantiate the primary survey, personal observations, interviewed method are also included. Personal observations regarding the Communitisation in the village was also incorporated in the paper. Different institutions, including government, private and other related organizations (NGOs) were also surveyed for the purpose. Village councils (VDB) and other village organizations have been given more weightage in the survey.

Genesis of Communitisation in Nagaland

The concept of Communitisation, which was introduced by none other than the Former State Chief Secretary R. S. Pandey under the 'Nagaland Communitisation of Public Institutions and Services Act, 2002' on 15th April, 2002. In reality, the genesis of Communitisation in Nagaland can be traced back from the time of traditional village institutions and more precisely from the inception of Village Development Board (VDB).

Under the provision of the Nagaland Village and Area Council Act, 1978, every government recognized village is authorized to constitute a Village Development Board (VDB) under the Village Council. It came into force in 1980 as an experimental basis. To be very precise, a village level body called "Village Development Board" came into being for the first time in Nagaland at *Ketsapomi Village* in Phek district prior to the inception of the Act of 1978 (Ao 1993). Some time in the month of October 1976, a group of villagers from *Ketsapomi* came to the DC office of Phek to withdraw some money, which was due to them. The then DC suggested them to form a committee or body, which was readily accepted by the villagers. In this direction and in the presence of the DC, they passed a resolution to form 'Ketsapomi Village Development Board', consisting of different *Khels* (clans in the village), with the DC as its Chairman. Accordingly this was done on 11th December, 1976; this is how the VDB programmes began in Nagaland.

Keeping the success experiences of VDB and stringent traditional village law of Nagas in mind, Former State Chief Secretary, R. S. Pandey introduced the very unique scheme of "*Communitisation*" through a legislation called 'Nagaland Communitisation of Public Institutions and Services Act, 2002' on 15th April, 2002. Under this scheme, many social sectors, like Health, Education and Power (Electricity), which are the backbone of economic development, have been included.

Need and Significance of the Study

Since the introduction of the Communitisation of Public Institutions in Nagaland, various departments like Education, Health and Tourism have already started working with the Village Communities by setting up various Village Committees and Water Supply and Electricity are also coming under the purview of the programme. Every village has school and there are health facilities, water supply, electricity and rural roads are reaching almost all the villages in the State.

But the feeling is many of our institutions are not functioning properly, and to improve the situation, the Government proposes to share 'management responsibility' for such institutions with village community for whom the 'institutions' have been set up. One thing is understood from the study of Singha (2007), that the contribution of Public Sector Units and Public Institutions on development front in the tribal region is very negligible. Working hour in the government institutions is comparatively very less, and contribution to the society by these institutions becomes very minimal. Offices are being opened lately and closed early in the State. There is no body to supervise and oversee the institutions, because most of the officials or the authoritative powers are under the control of the leaders or the well-to-do people of the community. In this context, the role of Communitisation is very significant.

In the finding of Kumar *et al*. (2003), there are three critical sectors, education, health and electricity, Nagaland already has the basic infrastructure. The State has elementary schools readily available almost for the entire population. But the schools are not effectively functioning. The situation is not different in the case of healthcare sector in the State. In the case of electricity, Nagaland is one of the states in North East India which consumes power lavishly.

Now, this unique experiment of Communitisation began out of a need, to improve the functioning of grassroots level Public Institutions through the input of age-old social community participation, exists in the Naga society. The very concept is borne out with the idea of a unique partnership between the government and the community involving empowerment, decentralisation, delegation, building capacity, tapping resources latent in the community — to ameliorate the state of affairs of the government institutions in the villages delivering essential services like education, health and power. In this type of society, sensitisation of this unique scheme has become need of the hour. This system (Communitisation) can be replicated as a model of rural development at the national level. In the same line, internationally, many research works have been done by the scholars in the past (e.g. Richard K. Beardsley, 1959; G. C. Hickey, 1964; M. Nurul Haq, 1973; Robert Putnam, 1993, 1995, 2000; Ella Schmidt, 2006, etc.).

Success Experiences and Functional Mechanism

The reports of success story of Communitisation in Education sector are immense. The department had already introduced the Communitisation of elementary education in 90 villages and they are still collecting more data for expanding to more villages in the current. In the system, they had constituted Village Education Committee comprising teachers, parents of the children (Students), representatives of the NGOs, the churches, Village Council. Therefore, the system of education has become more effective and they are now responsible for managing the affairs of the school. The staffs and teachers of the school will be overseen by them and they are empowered under the Communitisation to even deduct salaries of those teachers who do not perform their duties or absent from the duties. These amounts will be deposited in their welfare fund. This checks the irregularities of the teachers. For instance, *Khuzama* ME School (under Kohima district) was done complete electrification and a school room extension in Peren district by the Village Council with the amounts deducted from the absent teachers. All these rapid developments in Education sector are because of the introduction of Communitisation of Education in the State. Communitisation of school education is not shifting responsibility, but involving Community in its functioning of the schools.

The water supply is also being brought in under the Communitisation. Under the new programe, the department will now hand over the operation and maintenance of the water supply to the Village Council. In order to effectively managing the affairs, Village Water and Sanitation Committee are being constituted with the women representations too. Earlier, the Department had never collected water tax from the rural and village consumers but under the new system, the Committee is now empowered to collect minimum tax and this will be deposited in a separate account. Only little portion of it will go to the Government, besides the Government will contribute some lump sum grant to welfare funds of the Committee.

It is now believed that the problems of water pilferage, damages of pipe lines and dereliction of duties by departmental field staffs will tremendously reduce and Village people themselves will now be the owners. Therefore, people will immensely be benefited out of the new system once it is fully implemented. Its functional mechanism is concerned; the procedures for communitisation of public sectors are very simple. The Department approaches the village council to communitise and with the consent of the village council the responsibility of the particular sector is handed over to the village authority. After that the community looks after or oversees the functioning of the sector with the existing manpower (without retrenching the existing employees). Village council takes the charge of smooth functioning of the system, does not have any legal authority to appoint or suspend any employee.

The Power Department has also handed over the management of electricity in villages to the Village Councils. But this will be managed through the dully constituted Village Electricity Management Board that consists of 5 to 9 members including women representations and the tenure of the Board will be for three years. The departmental staffs posted in a particular village shall not be eligible to be a member of the Board of that village. The field staffs shall otherwise be eligible to be member of any Board other than of the village of posting/ assignment. The Village Council and the Village Development Board shall, however, coordinate and assist in the work of clearing of trees or other objects touching the electrical lines within the vicinity of the village, for the prevention of accidents and interruption of power supply.

Under the Communitisation of Power Supply, the Board is empowered to check theft of energy within its respective villages, besides it is responsible in recovering of loss following theft of energy and should report the matter to the Village Council for taking punitive action in accordance with law. In this way, the sense of ownership will prevail to the community and ultimately effective working culture would inculcate to the minds of not only communities but also staffs. The Board shall also operate the balance amount of electricity charge realized from the individual consumers, after making payment to the department. They can also operate any money that may be realized from the defaulters by way of recovery for theft of energy. Besides grants or any other contributions made by the Village Council and Village Development Board, voluntary donations can be operated by them.

Communitisation in Thizama Village

The Thizama village belongs to the *Angami* community of Nagaland, having 172 households. It lies about 5 km away on the northern side of the State capital, Kohima. So, the community lives in this village is considered as *Northern Angami*. Since, the village lies within the Kohima district and close to the city, majority of the people are educated and well-to-do in totality.

Communitisation is concerned in *Thizama* village; four sectors, (i.e. Electricity, Education, Health and Water & Sanitation in 2004, 2005, 2006 and 2007 respectively) have been communitised till the survey was conducted. For clear understanding of the system and the functional mechanism, sector-wise study is given separately in the following manner:

- *Communitisation of Electricity in Thizama*: After

communitisation through the process mentioned above, the electricity committee formed in the village (not Governmant Deplartment) collects the bill payments at the rate of Rs. 2 per unit and deposits to the government electricity department. Unlike before, the electricity bills are being collected regularly every month and 20 per cent of the collected amount is retained by the Village Council as commission or remuneration. Any repairing or installation of the line is done by the line man appointed by the government. Benefits of the communitisation is concerned, it is fairly noticed that after the communitisation, the village council pays electricity bill to the government regularly (which was not happening before communitisation) and there is perfect regularity of electricity in the village. Line-man or electrician and other government employees cannot ignore in discharging their duties in the village, because they are being overseen by the village council, and the department also gives more importance to the communitised village.

- *Communitisation of Education in Thizama*: The communitisation process of education sector was initiated in the year 2003 and finally, communitised in 2005 in this village. In the village, only one school, i.e. 'Government Lower Primary School' is there and it has been communitised. Coming to the functional mechanism, a committee is to be formed to operate the sector in the communitisation process. The committee is headed by a Village Education Chairman with some other members, like head *Gaon Bhura* (GB), one member from the women society of the village, one member each from the different Churches of the village (if there is Church more than one), one from youth society, two parents from the students of the school, one or two students from the school, etc. This committee calls meeting every month and keeps strict vigil over the performance and the functioning of the school.

Table 5.1 : Enrolment after and before the Communitisation (Government Lower Primary School, Thizama)

Year	*Enrolment after Communitisation*	*Enrolment before Communitisation*
2001	—	24
2002	—	34
2003	—	37
2004	—	37
2005	29	—
2006	30	—
2007	42	—
2008	40	—

Source: Survey.

- *Communitisation of Health Sector in Thizama*: This sector was communitised in the village (Sub-health Centre, Thizama) quite lately compared to other two sectors, i.e. in 2006. Similar to Education sector, this sector also needs to form a committee. The committee is headed by a Chairman appointed from the village along with some other members including one Secretary, one member each from the village Churches, one teacher, one member from the village council. For smoothly functioning of the health centre, government sanctions Rs. 20,000 to the committee annually, apart from the monthly salary of the employees and necessary medicine provided by the government. The amount is given for two broad heads, like, Rs. 10,000 for maintenance and the other half, Rs. 10,000 for buying medicine.

Overview of the Study

Now, the question that arises is what the leaders (those who look after the system) get from the process. Will they be sincere enough without any profit? Definitely, all the villagers including the leaders are getting benefits (even if not monetarily) out of the system. They are paid at least some maintenance expenses regularly by the government. On the other hand, government is also getting benefit out of the system. Before communitisation, government did not have any specific account of the revenue and expenses due to one reason or the other. For instance, villagers did not pay regular electricity bills before communitisation. The regularity and transparency of services of the communitised sectors in the village are quite visible now.

On the other side of the picture, the system is not completely free from the complicacy. Very often, misunderstanding arises among the members of the committee. They face the problem of making rules and regulations on the ground of favouritism and nepotism. Since the members are not benefited monetarily directly, they lack interest sometimes, the attendance in committee meeting becomes very thin, and it creates further problems. From Table 5.1, we can visualize the trend of enrolment in the school after communitisation. Despite Nagaland being the highest growth rate of population in the country and commendable improvement of the Communitisation system, the enrolment rate in the school of this village rather declines. If the communitisation becomes a new salvation to the community, why the students of the village go to private schools, is the question that poses in front of us.

By and large, the communitisation brings a new change in the Naga society. After communitisation, the degree of transparency and regularity of the sectors has been dramatically increased in the State. This system suits very much to the society like Nagas, in which people are bounded by the village or community laws. Definitely, communitisation will uplift the Naga society sooner. Everything cannot be changed overnight. For speedy development of the village under the communitisation system, leaders and village council members are to be enthused with modernization and quality education.

Concluding Remarks

Although the programe is in its infancy, encouraging scenes are already visible. All this is possible because of the abundance of social capital available with the community which sought to be invested by way of Communitisation. Capacity building is critical for the success of the programe. The State Government is committed to further promote the programme. So, the kind of political support which is proclaimed by the present Government and given the richness of the Naga tradition in which community bonds are extraordinarily strong, Communitisation is indeed hope for future.

In practice, the community and the State often overlap. For example, a village is a community by the fact that villagers cooperate voluntarily. However, if villagers authorize a particular individual or individuals to exercise coercive power in the administration of village affairs, this village can be regarded as a small state. For the rural development, strong social system or well oriented community is the prerequisite condition. So, the Communitisation of Nagaland can be a model for rural development.

References

Books

Ao, A. L. (1993): *Rural Development in Nagaland,* Har-Anand Publications, New Delhi.

Haq, M. Nurul (1973): *Village Development in Bangladesh: A Study of Monagram*, Bangladesh Academy of Rural Development, Comilla, Bangladesh

Hayami, Yujiro and Godo, Yoshihisa (2006): *Development Economics: From the Poverty to the Wealth of Nations*, Oxford University Press, New Delhi.

Hickey, Gerald Cannon (1964): *Village in Vietnam,* Yale University Press, New Havena.

Putnam, Robert D. (2000): *Bowling Alone: The Collapse and Revival of American Community,* Simon and Schuster, New York.

Putnam, R. D. (1993): *Making Democracy Work: Civic Traditions in Modern Italy,* Princeton University Press, Princeton NJ.

Richard K. Beardsley *et al.* (1959): *Village Japan.* The University of Chicago Press, Chicago.

Smith, Adam (1776): *The Wealth of Nations*, W. Strahan and T. Cadell, London

Journals

Hardin, G. (1968): The Tragedy of the Commons, *Science*, 162(3859): 1243-48.

Putnam, Robert D. (1995): Bowling Alone: America's Declining Social Capital, *Journal of Democracy*, 6 (1): 65-78, Baltimore, USA.

Schmidt, Ella (2006): Sustainable Community for Sustainable Development: A Case Study of the Mujeres Reunidas Co-operative in Hindalgo, Mexico, *Journal of Developing Societies*, Vol. 22 (4): 379-400. Landon.

Singha, Komol (2007): Nagaland is the State with Highest Population Growth Rate: *Is It an Issue? Southern Economist*, Vol. 46 (6): 14-16, Bangalore.

Kumar, S. *et al.* (2003): Primary Education in Rural Areas: An Alternative Model, *Economic and Political Weekly*, XXXVIII (34): 3533-36.

SECTION II

PHYSICAL INFRASTRUCTURE AND FINANCE

6 Role of Infrastructure in Rural Development in North Eastern Region of India

P. C. Dutta

Introduction

Infrastructure is the prerequisite factor for development in any society. Socio-economic development can be facilitated and accelerated by the presence of social and economic infrastructures. If these facilities and services are not in place, further development will be in vein. The provision and development of infrastructures has been the subject of much theoretical analysis and empirical studies. We shall start by examining some of the theoretical analyses of socio-economic infrastructures.

'*Economic*' infrastructures, particularly power (energy) facilities, transport and communications, banking facilities are the main thrust of the privatisation debate so far. '*Social*' infrastructures, including education, health, etc. have traditionally been public goods. Apart from underpinning economic infrastructure, it is an indicator of the long-term prosperity of a region. Social infrastructure is the glue that holds a regional community together. As privatisation extends into new areas, it is important for the governments to better understand the interaction between economic and social infrastructure in the regions. However, there are some constraints occur in the process of development which should carefully be noted to overcome the constraints.

The rural population constitutes the country's major populace: around 70 per cent of the entire population (Rural-

Urban ratio is 72.2: 27.8 in the 2001 Census) with 62 per cent of the total unemployed in the country. The rural subsystem of the North Eastern Region (NER) economy consists of some 35 thousand villages inhabited by over 32 million people who constitute about 85 per cent of the total population in the region. Of approximately 10.6 million main workers in the NER economy, about eight million workers are directly engaged as cultivators or agricultural labourers. The land-base of the rural economy in NER is not much promising. Except in some parts of Assam, Manipur and Tripura, the landform is not very attractive for cultivation. The area under the reported land-use forms about 88 per cent of the total geographical stretch of the region.

Despite concerted efforts, the rural populace remains poor in the midst of abundant resources. The programmes of the Government of India to assist the rural poor could not do much to alleviate the sufferings of the poor. The projects fell short of providing accessibility to education, infrastructure, electricity, telecommunication, water supply, employment, etc. to the rural areas in spite of the schemes' commendable objectives.

Literature Survey

According to the theory of unbalanced growth (UG) by A.O. Hirschman, no Less Developed Countries (LDCs) has sufficient endowment of resources as to enable it invest simultaneously in all sectors of the economy in order to achieve balanced growth.

The removal of poverty and unemployment has been the major goal of India's development strategy. The prime focus of most of the anti-poverty programmes has been on the rural areas where most of the absolutely poor and chronically unemployed live (Chadha and Chadha, 2008). However, the increasing pressure of population growth has made it difficult to provide productive employment and income to this section of population (Chadha, 1993). Thus, it is being increasingly realised that rural industrialisation may offer great scope for labour absorption (Ho, 1986), though the evidence suggests that the industrialisation strategy pursued by many developing countries has favoured the alliance between the urban sector and large-scale farmers, at the expense of rural industries (Lipton, 1993).

Saith (1991) perceives rural industries as including those non-farm activities, which, besides being located in designated rural areas, also have strong linkages with rural economy as well as with urban economy. Again, Saith (1992) and Mukhopadhyay (1985) have made out a strong case for rural industrialisation in the developing world by corroborating evidence of tremendous potential of this sector for labour absorption in the South and East Asian countries. Only rural industries have the prospects to absorb unemployed rural labour, and at the same time affording them a wage and work of dignity (Papola, 1982 and Eapen, 1994).

Dutta (2003) also observed that in the era of globalization, rapid socio-economic transformation has been taking place in Indian economy without addressing the problems of regional disparity, for which they argued that the states of NER are suffering from paucity of funds to improve their socio-economic backwardness. The study reveals that the States of NER are far behind from other states of the Indian Union so far as the basic amenities of life such as health, education, safe drinking water, food security, banking facilities, communication, etc. are concerned.

Education can affect lives of people in several ways. It enables women to assume more autonomy or power in traditional gender stratified family settings and also in more egalitarian ones, giving them greater control over their own lives and a stronger voice in matters affecting themselves and their families. Female education is perceived as an important factor not only in imparting new knowledge and information, skills and values for improving their participation in the labour force or earnings, but also in enhancing their status within and outside their immediate family. Thus, schooling is envisaged to have a long-term effect on women's position in family and society (Jeffery and Basu, 1996).

Dutta and Pradhan (2004) have rightly pointed out that under the backward conditions of the North Eastern Region, special initiative will have to be taken up by the governments of the concerned states to improve infrastructure as well as to ensure food and nutritional security to the poor. Steps taken up through Public Distribution System by the governments are not sufficient.

Hooda (1997) remarked that the rural development involves all agents of change and policy makers to activise the passive majority of rural people, to assist them by providing schemes, funds, skill, training, technology and opportunities to participate in the process of development and to raise their share in production and wealth. It is wrong to suggest that more investment in social sector development is anti-growth and it is more wrong to say that economic growth is unnecessary for social and human development. Keeping in view of the above discussion, the present paper tries to investigate the role of infrastructures in the development process of rural areas of NER of India based on published and unpublished secondary sources of statistical data.

Discussion

By bracketing the eight northeastern Indian States, called as NER of India, with its diverse tribes, customs and cultures, into what is called the 'North-East,' we tend to ignore the distinct identity and sub-national aspirations of these ethnic groups. More so, such clubbing together of the region, in an attempt to look at it as a single entity, has led to stereotype of the problems that plague the area. The region has been neglected by the centre from the very day of Independence though the fact that each State has a different set of location-specific concerns and grievances often gets blurred in the scheme of things of policy framers and public representatives who are supposed to address these issues.

As per the UNDP's Global Human Development Report (GHDR) 2007, in spite of the absolute value of the Human Development Index (HDI) for India improving from 0.577 in 2000 to 0.611 in 2004 and further to 0.619 in 2005, the relative ranking of India has not changed much. India ranks at 128 among the countries with medium human development out of 177 countries of the world as against 126 in the previous year. In terms of Gender Development Index (GDI), India ranks 113 out of 157 countries ranked on the basis of their GDI value. In India, around 260 million people are living below the poverty line. In the NER, around 13 million people live below the poverty line according to NSSO 55th Round Survey.

Inter-state comparisons based upon important socio-economic indicators bring out disparities between States in development outcomes. The performance of States across various sub-sectors, be it poverty, health or education related, reinforce each other. To some extent, this disparity in performance between states may be accounted for by extraneous factors but largely can be attributed to governance and delivery of services. This calls for a greater emphasis on governance issues.

NER of India had long been virtually out of focus barring usual financial supports from the Federal Government of India for different reasons. While the GDP of the country as a whole is growing at 9.2 per cent per annum, the growth rate in the NER as a whole is under 4 per cent. Nearly 98 per cent of the frontiers of the region constitute the international frontier of India and the remaining 2 per cent is connected with the rest of the country. Still the region has virtually not much trade relationship with those bordering countries. Lack of skilled manpower is one of the most important factors for industrial backwardness of the region. The region's trade with other States is not worth mentioning either. The region has been caught in a vicious cycle of poverty and opportunities causing unrest and militancy, and thus militancy and the resultant violence retarding the economic growth. A sense of 'alienation and neglect' had brewed over decades. It is natural to find the people of the region harbouring a great sense of alienation from the Indian mainstream and feel they are being neglected by this distant mainstream. As a result, the regional stability has been threatened by occasional insurgencies in some of the states.

Problems and Prospects

In the contemporary phase of liberalisation and globalisation in which the survivability of any industry will depend on its competitive strength in terms of the quality and value in terms of cost of its products in the market, the prospects of NER's rural industry apparently seem to be bleak, given the above mentioned along with other constraints. But due to inherent positive features and strengths of this sector, consistent with the socio-economic parameters and requirements of the economy and society in the State, rural industrialisation is the most suitable alternative conducive for the substantial development of the state (Chadha and Chadha, 2008).

Poor governance has been a major problem in the region. The region did not figure high on Union Government's agenda during the preparation of budget and planning, after independence, except, perhaps, the realization that this was a strategic area that needed concentration of military strength. This led to an impression that the Indian leadership actually regarded the region as a buffer against possible foreign aggression and hardly anything else. Another important problem – Lack of capacity by the States in the region to absorb the huge quantity of funds in the absence of training and expertise to successfully come up with implementable location-specific projects and the infrastructure to get some of these projects off the drawing board stage.

Leakage of funds at various levels of the government machinery is an important problem stands as obstacle in the road of economic development of the region. Another familiar problem is that of not implementing of the economic package announced by the Union Government from time-to-time. This was because of poor monitoring, lack of accountability and non-adherence to the set time frame for project execution.

Human resource development is instrumental in increasing productivity which in turn gives rise to faster economic development. Adequate provision of basic minimum services such as education, health and nutrition is both necessary and sufficient condition for attaining higher economic growth with social justice and equitable distribution of income. Since human resources being the key to economic development, the Government has been scaling up the quantum of public expenditure on social services through time. The share of expenditure on education stood at 2.7 per cent against the norm of 6 per cent, as recommended by the Kothari Commission. With respect to health, the share stood at 1.12 per cent against 5.0 per cent, according to the norms set by World Health Organisation. It emphasises that the share of expenditure on education and health needs to be hiked considering the recommendations made by the above two organisations.

Another fact that needs to be taken into account is that the continuity of the programes gets snapped with the change in governments at the Centre and in the States concerned. The tragedy in so far as the region is concerned; New Delhi changes its policy to this area with the change of governments and political parties heading the government. The biggest policy gap in so far as the Union Government is concerned is lack of a set of response mechanism towards this backward region of India.

The media plays an important role in the development of a region by projecting in the right perspective. While developmental agencies and financial institutions are striving to make the region's enormous potential known to the outside world, very little of such efforts is reflected in the mainstream as well as regional media. The region's image as an area of breathtaking natural beauty and a vibrant arts and culture arouses interest and fascinates the rest of the country or the world do not reflect much in the national and international media. While the reports about insurgency, ethnic strife, and under-development that plagues the region abounds in the media. This holds back would be investors and visitors, as only the dark side of this vibrant area, wedged between Bhutan, Bangladesh, Myanmar and China's Tibet region, gets projected.

Without any trained journalist in 'developmental journalism,' it is difficult to imagine that the existing print media in the region would ever be able to play the role of an effective medium to spread the good words regarding the efforts to transform the economy of the area through outside investment.

The degree of electrification of villages in the region is almost at par with India (NER 82.8; India 84.4) but per capita consumption of electricity is much lesser (201 kWh/year against 631 kWh/year in India) compared to the national level in the region. The ratio of surfaced road to total road length in the region is only 0.27 against 0.51 in India. Per 100 sq. km of area road length in NER is only 46 km against 64 km in the nation. Except in Assam and Tripura, there is hardly any access to the railways.

Investing in the health and education of citizens is basic to any human capital development and economic growth. Stark disparities in access to health in urban and rural areas, poor service delivery, and inequities between and within the states remain challenges. At the same time, malnutrition, prevalence of HIV and a slowing down in the decline of infant and child mortality rates are jeopardising India's chances of achieving the MDG targets for health.

The education sector faced challenges of inequality, lack of access, and poor quality of education services, despite basic education being recognised as a fundamental right. People are largely dependent on the private sector for services, over 80 per cent of the population access private healthcare services and education is growing outside the government systems and poor are unable to access such facilities as the services are priced and most often are not affordable for the poor. But the government has done very little to regulate the private sector and enforce existing regulations.

The number of registered educated and semi-educated jobseekers in the region shows an upward trend, increasing approximately at the tune of 2.65 lakhs every year out of which only 3 to 4 per cent actually obtain placement during a year. Education policies are largely responsible for the malady. The present education system has failed to produce skilled person which is essential in the modern age of development. Change in the educational policy in the region is perhaps overdue. It is worth noting, however, that educational institutions are scarcely mindful of the need for such changes. Technical and vocational education must be made a priority to solve the problem. However, the malady has its roots in the faulty economic policies as well.

Economic Infrastructure in NER

Development of infrastructural facilities opens the path of economic development of a particular region. The State largely remains backward in respect of infrastructural system. Due to its peculiar geographical features, the entire region was neglected from the very early period. The states of the region were lagging behind the other states of the country in respect of *transportation, communication, electrification, credit facilities, etc.* Due to infrastructural backwardness, industrialisation was either absent in some part or started very belatedly in some other parts of the region.

The transportation system of the region was very backward from the very beginning. The surface transport facilities of the region which includes Road transport, Railways and Airways along with the links with the neighbouring States and the rest of the country are totally inadequate and subject to severe hardships during monsoons, especially the roadways.

Transport and Communication

Under the successive Five Year Plans, the plan outlay on transport and communication varied significantly. Although, 17 per cent of the total outlay was allocated on transport and communication during First Plan but the share was declined in subsequent three years and reached to 4.8 per cent during *adhoc Plan* and again after 4th Plan (13.1 per cent), the declining trend has been observed up to 8th plan (6.3 per cent). However, the share has been increased in subsequent two plans, i.e. in the 9th and 10th Plans from 10.24 per cent to 10.57 per cent, which are still far below of 1st Plan period (Fig. 6.1). Figure 6.1 reveals the fact that the transport and communication did not receive much priority under the successive Five Year Plans.

Particularly, considering the most populous State of Assam in NER, it is observed that it has total road length of approximately 69,000 km covering both metalled and non-metalled surfaces that accounts for approximately 60 per cent

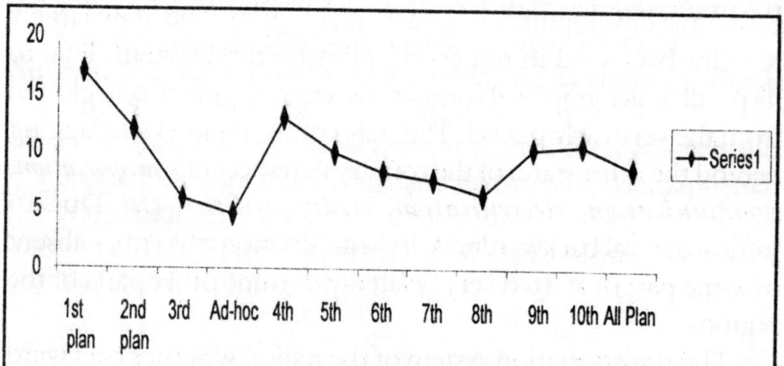

Fig. 6.1 : Percentage of Outlay on Transport and Communication with respect to Total Outlay (1951-2007)

Table 6.1 : 10th Plan Outlay, Energy Development : India, 2002-07 and Annual Plans (2002-03 to 2006-07), Amount (Rs. Crores)

	Tenth Plan 2002-07	*Annual Plan 2002-03*	*Annual Plan 2003-04*	*Annual Plan 2004-05*	*Annual Plan 2005-06*	*Annual Plan 2006-07*
Energy	403927.0 (26.5)	44710.0 (21.3)	50199.1 (22.3)	60729.5 (23.0)	71305.8 (20.3)	90498.9 (20.5)
Power	(N.A)	25280.8 (12.0)	30784.7 (13.7)	34315.5 (13.0)	39939.0 (11.4)	52090.3 (11.8)
Non - Conventional Sources of Energy	(N.A)	1712.2 (0.8)	1205.3 (0.5)	896.4 (0.3)	719.2 (0.2)	1093.9 (0.2)

of the total road length in the North-east. National Highways connect the major towns in the State. The length of National Highways is 2044 km while State highway occupies 2028 km and the other PWD roads occupy 29271 km. The East West Corridor spans over 713 km in Assam.

The present telecommunication network in the region is growing fast. Assam has 269 telephone exchanges with approximately 1,20,000 working connections. But it is not so in other States of the region. The region has the unique locational advantage of being situated close to South East Asian countries and hence it has the potential to emerge as a strategic base for domestic and foreign investors to tap the vast potential markets of countries like Bhutan, Bangladesh, China, Myanmar, Malaysia, Thailand, Philippines, Cambodia, Indonesia, etc.

Energy

Energy plays a crucial role in the socio-economic development of a country as growth in energy consumption is intrinsically linked to growth in the economy. The degree of economic growth is correlated with the generation and consumption of electricity. The household sector is the largest consumer of energy in India, accounting for 40-50 per cent of the total energy consumption in the country. In rural areas, the domestic sector 1 accounts for nearly 80 per cent of total energy consumption.

A close look at Table 6.1 points out that in 10th Plan (2002-07), 26.5 per cent of the Plan Outlay was allotted for energy which was amounting to Rs. 403927 crores for the country as a whole. It is also to be noted here that during 5 Annual Plans of 2002-2007, the percentage of allotted amounts were ranges from 11.4 per cent to 13.7 per cent. While in case of non-conventional energy sector, the percentages vary from 0.2 to 0.8 per cent during the same Plan Periods.[1]

Coming to the NER, Assam has a huge potential for development of infrastructure for generation, transmission and distribution of electricity. Assam is blessed with abundant reserves of natural gas and potential generation of cheap and eco-friendly power from small hydro-electric stations. Assam can be a boast of being one of the pioneers in utilisation of natural gas for power generation. The total installed capacity of electricity generation plants in the State is 574.4 MWs, while the total generation of electricity is 840.4 MU. The per capita consumption of electricity is 120 kWh.

Higher electricity use per capita correlates with a higher score on the Human Development Index (1997). Developing nations score much lower on these variables than developed nations. The present per capita consumption of electricity in India is little over 600 kWh, which is much lower than that of the developed countries. It is also observed that the Indian per capita consumption of electricity is more than three times of the consumption level in North East Region (NER). Although, NER is a vast storehouse of potential power generation, the per capita power consumption is very low in comparison to all India level. The demand for energy has been growing over time with the increase of development effort during last six decades.

NER is a vast storehouse of potential power. But the problems of exploration are many, particularly of hydel-electric development as major potential hydel power areas are located in intense seismic zones where construction of high dams may trigger earthquakes. There are also sociological problems of rehabilitation of affected people. The region is endowed with various sources of power. It has vast potential of hydel-power; its natural gas resources are substantial.

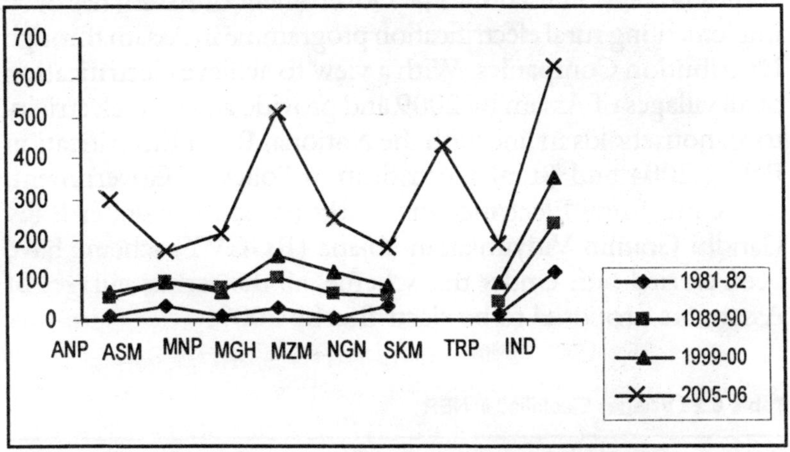

Fig. 6.2. Per Capita Consumption of Electricity in NER (in kWh)

From Fig. 6.2 it is clear that during the 25 years period (1981-2006), per capita consumption of electricity (in kWh) has increased very little in all the states of NER in comparison to next 6 years period (2000-06). However, during 2005-06, per capita consumption in all the States of NER including NER as a whole (201.44 kWh) are below the national level (631.41). It is to be noted here that, per capita consumption in the State of Assam is the lowest (170.65) and the highest in the State of Meghalaya (517.54) among the States of NER. The average per capita consumption of electricity in the State (Assam) was 120 kWh in 2002-03 and 116 kWh in 2003-04 as reported by the ASEB.

In modern day world, electrification is a key ingredient for facilitating rural economic development including alleviation of poverty, realization of socio-economic goals and overall human development. In Assam, as per census 2001, only 70 per cent villages are electrified and it includes only 16.5 per cent rural households. The total number of villages electrified in Assam was 19039 as on March 2003, out of the 24685 inhabited villages of the State as per 1991 Census. Thus, the percentage of villages electrified in the State was 77.13 per cent at the end of March 2003. The Government of Assam has been implementing rural electrification programme in Assam through Distribution Companies. With a view to achieve electrification of all villages of Assam by 2009 and provide access to electricity to all households in line with the National Rural Electrification Policy, 2004 and Rural Electrification Policy of Government. of Assam. Rural Electrification works particularly under Rajiv Gandhi Gramin Vidyutikaran Yojana (RGGVY) scheme have been carried out. Under this scheme, all the census villages of Assam are proposed to be electrified by 2009.

Table 6.2 : Villages Electrified in NER

States	*P.C. of Inhabited villages electrified*		*P.C of Rural households*
	1980	*2000*	—
ANP	9.9	60.5	44.53
ASM	20.4	77.1	16.54
MNP	16.5	91.7	52.53
MGH	13.5	47.1	30.26
MZM	11.8	99	44.14
NGN	36	98.4	56.88
TRP	17	94.7	31.75
NER	18.5	—	73.5
IND	44.6	86.3	43.52

Table 6.2 reveals the fact that during the period of 20 years (1980-2000), drastic change took place in the state of Mizoram where the percentage of electrification in inhabited villages increased from 11.8 per cent in 1980 to 99 per cent in 2000. The same is true for Tripura where it increased from 17 to 94.7 per cent, but it is unfortunate that same is not true in the States

of Assam and Meghalaya. There is a regular feature of the shortage of power in the State of Assam. As per 2000-02 figure, only 16.54 per cent of rural households in Assam have been electrified which is the lowest among the States in NER. While the highest is observed in the State of Nagaland (56.88 per cent) followed by Manipur (52.53 per cent). The respective percentage for the country is 43.52 which show the fact that three States, *viz*. Assam, Meghalaya and Tripura of NER are below the national percentage.

The task of rural electrification in NER is relatively difficult because of hilly terrains and wide valley, mighty Brahmaputra, Barak and their tributaries – low density of population spread over the hills separated by forests, especially the Arunachal Pradesh. Poverty of the people with their low purchasing power also retards the Rural Electrification programme. Rural electrification despite being a basic source of enlarging outlook of rural masses, it can also help them by enabling them to adopt modern technology in the process of production. In spite of having immense potential of power generation in the State, the performance of this sector is not encouraging.

About 87 per cent of the State population live in rural areas, that is 26,247 villages. Of these, as on March 31, 2006, only 21,586 villages have been electrified of which only 16.54 per cent of the total households in these electrified villages have electricity connection. The remaining 4661 villages are still to see light of electricity. Again, 2145 un-electrified villages have been identified as remote and thus to provide 'Electricity to All' by 2012 slogan of the government is a far cry. In order to provide power to all by 2012, additional capacity of 100,000 MW will have to be set up in the next decade. Capacity addition plans for 41,110 MW have been finalized, state-wise and project-wise for the Tenth Plan period (2002-07). In the central sector, state sector and private sector, the capacity addition would be 22,832 MW; 11,157 MW and 7,121 MW respectively[2].

As on 31st March, 2005, a total of 60.46 per cent villages were electrified in the State of Arunachal Pradesh while the percentage of rural households having electricity was 44.53 per cent only as on March 31, 2004. As per Power Ministry data, 2004, share of Arunachal Pradesh in Central sector stations was 117 MW and installed capacity in the State sector was 45.43 MW. The total installed capacity was 162.43 MW. The percentage of villages electrified was 60.46 per cent as on March 31, 2005. The percentage of rural households having electricity was 44.53 per cent as on March 31, 2004. Per capita consumption of electricity was 68.61 kwh in 2000-01 (Dutta, 2008).

It is important to note that, as on August 31, 2004, the percentage of villages electrified was 100 per cent. As compared to the national average of 355 kWh, the per capita consumption of electricity in Nagaland was 84.74 kWh and the percentage of rural households having electricity in the State was 47.16 per cent. According to the Annual Administrative Report of the Department of Power, the total power generation was 3.21(MU) and the total purchase was 230 (MU) in 2000-01. Thus the state could generate only 1.39 per cent of the total power requirements.

Despite commendable successes in the State of Tripura, the position in relation to needs remains highly unsatisfactory. It is observed that a large expansion of this source of energy is required. As such about 79.80 per cent of the villages and 100 per cent towns are electrified which raises both the income and expenditure of the department .But it is found that expenditures far exceeds the income. The percentage of rural households having electricity was 28.50 per cent. Out of the two major sources of power generation in the State of Tripura, thermal power accounts for more than 77 per cent. The percentage of rural households having electricity was 28.50 per cent. But due to the increase in the demand for electricity, the state is also experiencing persistent power shortage.

However, it is to be noted here that in all the States of NER, except in the States of Manipur and Tripura, installed capacity either decreased or remain unchanged during the period 1997-

2002 which can be considered as a un-healthy situation for the economic development of the region. A minute look at Fig. 6.3, observes that during the period 1996-2002, installed capacity has not been changed so much in all the states of NER. In the year 1996-97, the total installed capacity in state sector was 938.8 MW which further increased to 994.26MW in the next year (1997-98) and 1048.35MW in the year 2001-02.

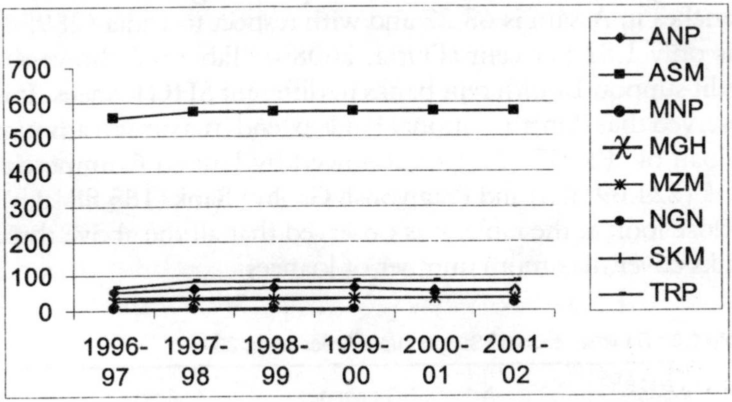

Fig 6.3 : Installed Capacity State Sector Unit (MW)

However, the Government of India has approved a package of fiscal incentives and other concessions for the NER, namely the *'North East Industrial and Investment Promotion Policy (NEIIPP), 2007'*, effective from 1st April, 2007. NER, of India has been identified as India's *"future powerhouse"* and 168 large hydroelectric projects, having a capacity of 63,328 MW (megawatt) , have been proposed in the region. A target of capacity addition of 78577 MW has been proposed for the 11th Plan by the Government of India.

Banking

Financial infrastructure is essential for economic development. The number of branches of scheduled commercial banks (SCBs) in NER was 1935 in 1996 which gradually increased to 1952 as on March 31, 2005. However with respect to India (66970 nos.), there are only 2.87 per cent branches in NER as on March 2004 which increased by 1.67 per cent as on March 2005. The credit-deposit ratios (CDR) of banks in NER have fallen from 47 per cent as on the end of March 1991 to 26 per cent as on the end of March 2003. But after that it has increased to 35 (as against the national average of 66) as on the end of March 2005. With respect to NER (1952), the percentage of number of branches in Assam is 63.27 and with respect to India (28958) it is only 1.81 per cent (Dutta, 2008b). Table 6.3 shows the credit support by different banks to different SHG loanees. It is observed that Punjab National Bank extends maximum amount of loan of Rs. 573.22 lakh followed by United Commercial Bank (224.09 lakh) and Pragjyotish Gaoliya Bank (185.88 lakh). A close look at the table, it is observed that all the above three banks cover maximum number of loanees.

Table 6.3 : Bank-wise Credit Support up to December, 2003

Name of Bank	*No. of SHG Loanees*	*Amount of Loan (Rs. in lakh)*
Punjab National Bank	456	573.22
UCO Bank	317	224.09
State Bank of India	162	181.10
United Bank of India	127	131.4
Union Bank of India	91	92.59
Lokhimi Gaoliya Bank	121	122.42
Pragjyotish Gaoliya Bank	166	185.88
Bank of Baroda	40	64.53
Central Bank of India	59	46.71
Others	272	268.74
Total	1811	1890.68

Source: State Institute of Rural Development, Assam.

During the financial year 2004-05, there were 228 bank branches of all type of commercial banks. Out of these 138 branches in rural areas, 44 branches in semi-urban areas and rest 46 branches in urban areas are functioning in the State of Arunachal Pradesh.

Commercial Banks located in Meghalaya have an important role to play in its development particularly in the rural areas.

Social Infrastructures

There are several aspects of social infrastructure that are fundamental to the competitiveness of the Region. Human resources development is instrumental in increasing productivity which in turn gives rise to faster economic development. Adequate provision of basic minimum services such as education, health and nutrition is both necessary and sufficient condition for attaining higher economic growth with social justice and equitable distribution of income.

Increasing trend of expenditure on social services by the government in recent years reflects the high priority attached to these sectors. Health and nutritional status of the population contributes to improvement in overall labour productivity. The Health policy desires that the under-served and underprivileged sections of the population have to have easy access to utilisation of health services. A sound health infrastructure and manpower at primary, secondary and tertiary care in Government, voluntary and private sectors should be built up immediately. Improvement in penetration of technology and health status of the population can be gauged with reference to birth rate, death rate, infant mortality rate and life expectancy at birth.

Since human resources being the key to economic development, the Government has been scaling up the quantum of public expenditure on social services through time. Expenditure on social sectors as a proportion of total expenditure, after decreasing from 20.4 per cent in 2002-03 to 19.5 per cent in 2003-04, increased steadily to 22.3 per cent in 2006-07 and 22.5 per cent in 2007-08.

With respect to health, the share stood at 1.12 per cent against 5.0 per cent, according to the norms set by World Health Organisation. It emphasises that the share of expenditure on education and health needs to be hiked considering the recommendations made by the above two organisations.

Health

Health is a key determinant of human capital and thereby economic growth of a region. Health and sustainable development are mutually dependent: neither is possible without the other. Good health is essential to keep the labour force productive and efficient. Frequent illnesses and inadequate nutrition will have adverse impact on the incomes of households making them vulnerable. Good health not only increases productivity and earnings of an individual but also improves the overall quality of life and the socio-economic development of the general population.

Public Health Centre (PHC) is the first contact point between village community and the Medical Officer. The PHCs were envisaged to provide an integrated curative and preventive health care to the rural population with emphasis on preventive, promotive aspects of health care and Family Welfare Services. There are 22,370 PHCs functioning as on March 2007 in the country. The PHCs are established and maintained by the State Governments under the Minimum Needs Programme (MNP)/ Basic Minimum Services Programme (BMSP). Based on mortality estimates from the IACMEG for 2005, 72 per cent of all under-five deaths in India occur during the first year of life: 45 per cent in the neonatal period and another 27 per cent between the first and the eleventh months. The remaining 28 per cent occur between the second and the fifth years of age. According to DHS 2005-06, the highest under-five mortality rates of the 29 states in India were seen in Uttar Pradesh and the lowest in Kerala.[3] Among the States of NER, Arunachal Pradesh occupies the first position followed by Assam, Meghalaya and Nagaland. The lowest mortality rate is observed in the state of Sikkim followed by the states of Manipur, Mizoram and Tripura. Share of health in total expenditure has been increased from 4.4 per cent in 2004-05 to 4.9 per cent in 2006-07.

Table 6.4 gives a picture of health facilities available in different States of NER. A minute look at the Table 6.4 confirms the fact that the health service facilities is the poorest in the State of Assam (11980 persons served per doctor) followed by Mizoram (10360 persons served per doctor) and Nagaland (5422 persons served per doctor).

Table 6.4 : Population Served per Doctor in North-eastern States

State	*Number of Doctor*	*Population served per doctor*	*Reference Year*
ANP	464	2352	2002-03
ASM	2160	11980	1.1.19.99
MNP	945	2427	2002-03
MGH	389	5411	1998
MZM	89	10360	1.1. 1999
NGN	367	5422	2002
SKM	174	3108	2001-02
TRP	860	3720	2003-04

Source: Basic Statistics of NER 2006.

Education

Education, like health, has a very significant role in accelerating the pace of socio-economic development of any region. But the condition of rural education in the region is not at all satisfactory, in spite of spending huge amount in that field. The purpose of education is to inculcate skill, modernization ideals, will to economize and develop as well as the need for achievement. The present education system in the region has failed the target and it continues to turn out to be only potential clerks and big *babus*. Change in the educational policy in the region is perhaps overdue. It is worth noting, however, that educational institutions are scarcely mindful of the need for such changes.

More than 838 million adults in the developing world are illiterate, according to surveys by UNESCO. Around the world, one of every seven children is not enrolled in primary school, and more than one-third of adolescents are not in high school. Again, Education is the most basic necessity after those that are vital to life itself – food, clothing, and shelter. The truth is that all people have a right to have these basic needs fulfilled, and they also have a right to education. In this regard, the world is not doing very well.

From a dismal statistic of 16.67 per cent literacy, and despite the burgeoning population, India has achieved an impressive growth of literacy, which stands at 65.38 per cent (male – 75.85 per cent and female – 54.16 per cent), according to the 2001 Census. Literacy rates have shown an impressive growth of 11.72 per cent for males and 14.87 per cent for females, over the last census decade (1991-2001). The Female Literacy Rate in the region ranges from 44.24 per cent to 65.41 per cent. Except Arunachal Pradesh (44.24 per cent), the region's rate is higher than the national average of 54.16 per cent. The decadal growth rate of female literacy in the States of NER has shown an increase of 7.17 (Nagaland) to 15.76 (Tripura) points during the period 1991 to 2001.

The National Policy on Education (1986) which provides the broad policy framework for the development of education in the country had set a goal of expenditure of 6 per cent of the GDP on education. A high priority was accorded to this sector in the Tenth Five Year Plan (2002-2007), with an allocation of Rs. 43,825 crore as against Rs. 24,908 crore made available in the Ninth Plan, representing an increase of 76 per cent. The per capita budgeted expenditure had been Rs. 819.65 in the country in 2001-02. Expenditure on education as a proportion of total expenditure has increased from 9.8 per cent in 2004-05 to 10.4 per cent in 2006-07. The share of expenditure on education stood at 2.7 per cent against the norm of 6 per cent, as recommended by the Kothari Commission.[4]

In comparison to Indian women (41.42 per cent), NER women occupied only 1.74 per cent in case of general education. The school completion rates are found to be very poor in the region comparison to all-India level. A large percentage of the villages are still without an upper primary school. This especially accounts for a large chunk of girls dropping out after primary level. Surveys indicate that the majority of school dropouts belong to the poorest and the least developed areas. Gender discrimination against girl child is a major cultural issue. The absence of women teachers in the village schools and the lack of separate toilet facilities for girls are other factors, which keep girls away from school. It is very important to tackle the problem of dropouts in order to achieve universal elementary education.[5]

Access to educational institutions promoting skill development is a prerequisite for providing trained manpower. As per 1991 census literacy rate of NER was 58.09 per cent [all India 52.2 per cent] while in 2001 it was 68.5 per cent [all India 64.8 per cent]. Mizoram has the second highest literacy rate in India. Table 6.5 gives the number of registered educational institutions in the NER.

Table 6.5 : Number of Educational Institutions in NER

Prim + UP	*Sec + HS*	*Arts/Sc. Colleges*	*Engg.*	*Medical*	*Universities*	*Polytechnics*	*ITIs*	*IIT*
56677	7716	497	6	6	13	18	49	1

Source: Draft Report of the Task Force on Development Initiatives for the NER, September, 2005.

Assam Human Development Report (AHDR) 2003 pointed fault lines in the State's education system. The report noted, "At the primary level, the enrollment rate for girls is 48 per cent. At the higher secondary (HS) level, the enrollment rate is little over 35 per cent. Overall, in higher secondary education, the enrollment rate for women is less than 33 per cent". This is made worse by the dropout rate for girls – 42 per cent at the primary stage, 72 per cent at the middle school and 75 per cent by high school. Tribal girls are particularly affected; the overall illiteracy among tribal women in the State is as high as 75 per cent. "As women journey along the path to higher education, many fall by the wayside and dropout".

Figure 6.4 shows that the pass percentage of students in HS Examination over the period of 12 years (1997-2008). As per results declared in 2008, in Assam, the pass percentage for 2,39,606 students taking the High School Living Certificate (HSLC) examinations touched a new height, as did the results

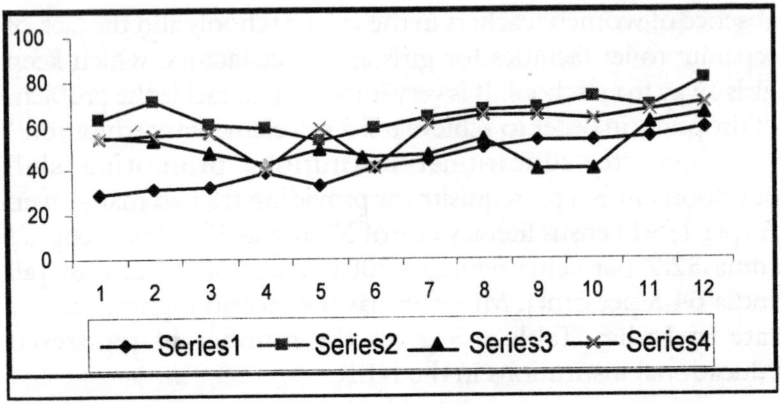

Fig. 6.4 : Pass Percentage of Students in H.S. (1997-2008)

for those in the Arts and Commerce streams of Higher Secondary (HS) examinations. The pass rate was 58.68 per cent (series -1) in the HSLC examinations which doubled the figure in 12 years. More granular analysis of the HSLC 2007 results, however, reveals there are still significant challenges to be overcome. Performance varied between government-run schools and private schools; between schools located in urban and in rural areas; and between vernacular medium schools and English medium schools.

A comparison of the pass percentage of the last twelve years showed the 2008 as the best, with the highest climb in performance recorded in the Science stream (series-2). Considering the Arts (series-3) and Commerce stream (series-4), the respective percentages are 65.33 and 69.96, a noticeable improvement over last year. Rising pass percentages at the high school level have led to challenges in college and university education. Currently, to accommodate the pass outs in HSLC and HS examinations, the State has a total of 317 colleges for general education, 114 junior colleges, three medical colleges and one for aquaculture, two Homeopathic colleges, one Ayurvedic college, one dental college, one nursing college, three engineering colleges, two veterinary colleges, two agricultural colleges and 27 Industrial Training Institutes and Polytechnics for vocational education. It also has two State run universities, two Central universities and one Indian Institute of Technology. But while there are sufficient institutions to accommodate these students, out-dated curricula as well as limited options for choices in courses, however, have made many pass outs opt for pursuing study outside the state. Another worry is of declining interest in science education. While the pass percentage in HSLC exams has nearly doubled over the last 10 years, enrollment in the Science stream at Higher Secondary level has remained static between 12,000 to 15,000. The increasing "success rates" in HSLC did not reflect in more science education at the higher secondary level. It is also observed that our current education system selectively discards talented students with inquisitiveness, ability to ask questions and dream to do something challenging, something better for the society. Now we only produce private tuition and coaching enabled, mugging-up grade technicians who are great to do routine jobs or imitating others, but not capable of doing original research, despite of having many world class physical infrastructure, huge budget and some so-called "elite" institutes.

"Colleges and universities are no more an attraction for most of the brilliant students now. This is mainly because of an approach of gradual downgrading the universities. We need brilliant engineers, but only engineers cannot build the complete human resource of the country. We need more researchers, as so many issues of human development are yet to be addressed at academic level. It is observed that there is acute funds crunch in the State run universities and colleges. It is a matter of great concern that the centre of gravity of scientific research appears to have moved away from universities. Only the Ministry of Human Resources Development is to be blamed for such a situation in General Science education at higher education stage.

Initiatives taken up by the Government

The economy of Assam is predominantly an agrarian economy.

There is ample scope for development particularly in the rural areas for processing of cereals, fruits, vegetables, milk, meat and other agricultural products like jute, ramie etc. The Government will encourage development of Agro and Food processing industries by providing possible basic infrastructure to the industries. Apart from that, Government will take necessary action to motivate the investors for commercial exploitation and processing and setting up of projects on medicinal herbs, aromatic plants, rubber plantation and processing, small tea garden etc. The Government of Assam is very much aware about the viability of setting up of Industries like diversified Jute products and Ramie based Industries in Assam by prospective entrepreneurs.

The State of Assam is traditionally known for its rich Handloom and Handicraft products and the Government will ensure promotion of this sector through various development schemes. The Government will take all possible steps for getting Financial and Technical assistance from the Government of India for implementation of various schemes. The Government will strengthen the Handicraft Research and Design Centre, Cottage Industries Training Institute in the State. All possible measures will be taken to assist the craftsmen, artisans of various crafts for the development of Handicraft Industries in the State. The Government will take necessary measures to export the Handicraft products to outside the country.

The Rural Non-Farm Sector (RNFS) has a tremendous scope for development in the State. In a recently conducted survey, NABARD has identified 10 sectors for development which includes sectoral schemes like agriculture, fish rearing and processing, rural retail trade, sericulture and silk textile, fibre products, construction, small plantation products, handloom and handicraft mainly cane, bamboo and wood products. These activities are to be developed for creation of additional employment in the rural areas.

In consonance with the commitment to faster social sector development under the National Common Minimum

Programme (NCMP), the Central Government has launched new initiatives for social sector development during 2007-08. Central Government expenditure on social services and rural development has gone up consistently over the years. The share of Central Government expenditure on social services, including rural development in total expenditure (plan and non-plan), has increased from 11 per cent in 2001-02 to 16.4 per cent in 2007-08 (BE) in Assam.

Under the new scheme called "Aam Admi Bima Yojana" (AABY) launched on October 2, 2007, insurance to the head of the family of rural landless households. The Rashtriya Swasthya Bima Yojana was formally launched on October 1, 2007. All workers in the unorganized sector who come in the category of Below Poverty Line (BPL) and their families will be covered under the Scheme. National Rural Employment Guarantee Scheme (NREGS), which was launched on February 2, 2006, in 200 most backward districts in the first phase, has been expanded to 330 districts in the second phase. The remaining 266 districts have been notified on September 28, 2007 where the scheme will come into effect from April 1, 2008. As against the employment demanded by 2.61 crore rural households, 2.57 crore households have been provided wage employment during 2007-08. The programme of 'Bharat Nirman' was launched in 2005-06 for building infrastructure and basic amenities in rural areas, has six components, *viz*. rural housing, irrigation potential, drinking water, rural roads, electrification and rural telephony. Bharat Nirman has received a budgetary outlay of Rs. 24,603 crore in 2007-08 as against Rs. 18,696 crore (including NER component) in 2006-07.

Suggestions

A much better understanding is needed of the development capacity of regional economies and how to build competitive advantage. Governments must find better ways of making their programmes 'hit the ground'. They must convert their political rhetoric – about empowering local leaders, facilitating and business-government partnerships – into consistent and coordinated actions. Emphasis should be given for the development of managerial capability to the local youths through intensive Entrepreneurship Development Programme (EDP).

Women entrepreneur should get due priority for their economic development as well as to meet the ends of social justice. To encourage the woman entrepreneurs as well as for generation of employment among the women, the Government should give preference to them for the actual development of the society.

The 'mindset' of the people in the region needs to be changed and made forward-looking; a sustained campaign needs to be carried out through the media, dedicated to the cause of development and progress. This campaign must reach the common man as well as policy makers or policy influencers who play a key role in matters concerning this region. Work-culture should be brought in the minds of the people of the region for the true progress of the society and hence the region.

Effective steps should be taken to promote handloom and handicraft sectors by providing, *inter-alia* marketing access to handloom and handicraft producers through any means. The provisions of adequate infrastructure are the prerequisite for any industrial development. Thus, existing infrastructure shall be strengthened and should be upgraded to suit the ever increasing demands of the industrial sector.

The Governments should actively promote direct investment in the projects that involve and improve infrastructures like power, roads, social and health care facilities. Credit facility should be facilitated in a simple way for the availability of credits from the banks and other financial institutions for promoting industrial activity. The process of Foreign Direct Investment (FDI) should be enhanced and welcome by the government, especially in the infrastructure sectors. The willingness was also shown by many giant foreign investors during the last NE

Business Summits. Now, the ball is in the court of government.

In the backdrop of the ongoing process of liberalization and privatization, the public sector enterprises, especially in the non-core sectors, are losing their relevance. Therefore, in keeping with the present trend, the governments should make a distinction between the promotional and purely commercial Public Sector Undertakings (PSUs). The general policy should be made to progressively reduce financial and budgetary support to all the PSUs so as to make them stand on their own feet.

The situation of the region reinforces the need for greater focus on health and proper education in our development planning. It is this concern that it should be reflected in Planning of the governments of the region which seeks to reduce not only poverty but also the various kinds of disparities across regions and communities by ensuring better access to not only basic physical infrastructure but also health and education services to one and all.

Peace is another prerequisite condition for creating congenial atmosphere for any developmental process. Therefore, the Governments of the region should strive to create a congenial atmosphere for sustained growth by maintenance of law and order.

Notes

1. Planning Commission, 10th Plan Outlay by Heads of Development: Centre, States and Union Territories, 2002-07 and Annual Plans 2002-03 to 2006-07, from the website: http://indiabudget. nic.in
2. UNDP Human Development Reports 2002 and 2007.
3. World Population Prospects – the 2006 revision, UN Population Division. New York, 2007; 2 UNICEF. *The State of the World's Children 2007*; 3, WHO, *World Health Statistics 2007*.
4. PIB FEATURE, 19 August, 2002.
5. Dutta, P.C. and B.C. Pradhan (2007) : 'Gender Issues and Development in North Eastern Region of India,' in *Women Emancipation Focus North East India* (ed.) Asok Kumar Ray and Basudeb Datta Ray, Om Publications, New Delhi.

References

Chadha, G.K. (1993): "Non-Farm Employment of Rural Households in India: Evidence and Prognosis", *Indian Journal of Labour Economics*, Vol. 36, No.3, pp. 296-327.

Chadha, V. and N. Chadha (2008): "A Regional Perspective on Rural Industrialisation in India: The Case of Punjab Economy", *Journal of Rural Development,* Vol. 27, No. 2, pp. 213-230.

Dutta, P.C. and B.C. Pradhan (2004): "Agricultural Development and Security of Life" in *Food Security and Public Distribution System Today – Failures and Success,* (ed.) Amalesh Banerjee, Kanishka Publishers, New Delhi.

Dutta, P.C. (2003): "Regional Disparity and its Consequences in North Eastern Region of India" in *Economic Liberalization and Regional Disparities inIndia – Special Focus on the North Eastern Region* (ed.) A.C. Mohapatra and C.R. Pathak, Star Publishing House, Shillong.

Dutta. P. C. (2008): "Some Aspects of Sustainable Socio-Economic Development in the North Eastern Region (NER) of India" in *Society, Culture and Development in NE India : Essays in Memory of Dr. Basudev Datta Ray* (ed.), A. Ray and Chakrabarty, Concept Publishing Company, New Delhi.

Dutta. P. C. (2008 b): "Constraints of Industrial Development in North East India", Paper presented in the National Seminar on *Problems and Prospects of Industrial Development in North East India,* organised by Dera Natung Govt. College, Itanagar, Arunachal Pradesh, 14th - 16th February, 2008

Eapen, M. (1994): "Rural Non-Agricultural Employment in Kerala – Some Emerging Tendencies", *Economic and Political Weekly*, May 21, p.1285.

Ho, S.P.S. (1986): "Off-farm Employment and Farm Households in Taiwan", in R.T. Shand (ed.), *Off-farm Employment in the Development of Rural Asia*, Canberra: Australian National University.

Hooda, I.S. (1997): "Rural Development – Some Conceptual Issues" in *Rural Development – Theory and Practice* (ed.), Spellbound Publications, Rohtak.

Jeffery, Roger and Basu Alaka M. (ed.) (1996): *Girls' Schooling — Women's Autonomy and Fertility Change in South Asia*, Sage Publications, New Delhi.

Lipton, M. (1993): "Restructuring South Asian Agriculture", in M. Lipton and C. Simkons (eds.), *State and Market in Post Apartheid South Africa*, Johannesburg: Witwatersrand University Press.

Mukhopadhyay, S. (1985) : "Rural Non-Farm Sector in Asia : A Characterisation", *Economic and Political Weekly*, Vol. 20, No. 22, pp. 966-68

Papola, T.S. (1982): *Rural Industrialisation: Approaches and Potential*, Bombay: Himalaya Publishing House.

Saith, A. (1991) : "Asian Rural Industrialisation: Context, Features, Strategies", in J. Breman and S. Mundle (eds.), *Rural Transformation in Asia*, New Delhi, Oxford University Press.

Saith, A. (1992): *The Rural Non-Farm Economy : Processes and Policies*, Geneva : ILO

Basic Statistics of North Eastern Region, NEC, (1982 and 2002).

7 Role of Infrastructural Facilities in Rural Development

Problems and Prospects

K. H. Nakhro

Introduction

The economy of Nagaland is passing through the initial phase of development where majority of workforce of the State are engaged in the primary sector, while secondary and tertiary sectors are weak and developing in and around the urban centres. A wide gap of rural-urban inequality is seen in the State. Majority of the people of the State lives in the rural areas and it covers around 80 per cent of the total geographical area of the State. To develop the State at par with national level, a common infrastructure for the well-balanced development of all sectors of economy and sustainable growth is required. As far as infrastructural facilities in the course of development are concerned, it is an absolute prerequisite to growth. Hagen (1975) states that power-communication-transport-labour coefficients in production are fixed, in the secular course of development and without these facilities advance is throttled. It is true that economic growth is stagnant without proper infrastructures. In dealing with local community for growth promotion, it emphasizes the presence of good infrastructure facilities for development that the smooth delivery service always keeps things ready for the next move.

The inadequate infrastructure and even the lack of basic facilities and services in rural areas such as roads, safe drinking water, electricity, schools, hospitals, police protection, transport and communication provide the basis of rural development.

These public facilities and amenities are not only inadequate, but are very poorly organized and under-dependable in India. As a result, poor villagers are dammed generation after generation to poor education, poor health, unemployment, and in poverty. Improvement of such distressing situation also requires intensive government intervention. Of course, government has already intervened in development initiatives of the rural development by launching various development programmes to create and provide infrastructural facilities; still it is not reaching to the needy persons. Campbell (1990) views that villagers in developing societies are the last persons, they are socially, economically poor and ignored. They should be put unto the first priority, if any government tries to make policies for development.

According to the World Development Report (1994), the infrastructure for overall development has been classified into four main groups and again subdivided into various sub-groups. Second important aspect of balanced development of an area is the vocational characteristics and the distributional pattern of the elements of such infrastructure (Singh, 1999). Movement of man, material and ideas from one place to another is the function of communication activities. In fact, socio-economic movement of ideas, goods, and of people by means, ranging from walking to telecommunication makes possible the specialization of location. Communication is the means of progress in modern development economies. Whether, it is physical or human communication, it plays a very important role in rural development. Physical communications consist of roads, railways, shipping, aviation, and posts and telegraph, whereas human communication comprises mass communication, institutional communication and face-to-face communication.

With the growing economics, the political and social integration of rural localities into mass society and the improved infrastructure facilities and telecommunication have enhanced the homogenizing tendencies of popular culture, creating 'a planet reduced to village size' (Hoggart and Henry, 1987). At the same time, the impact of television has also induced a reorientation in social linkages from horizontal to the vertical (Warren, 1978), as the intra-local social ties (horizontal linkages) have been replaced with ties to the inter-local persons and institutions (vertical linkages). Many social analysts commented that social change in rural areas had largely comprised replacement of the horizontal with the vertical.

Another aspect of infrastructure is its accessibility, which is location specific. Location of a facility/amenity will determine its utilization. An optimal location of a facility/amenity minimizes the distance between user and the facility and reduces the user's transport costs. There are a lot of literatures available on these locational aspects in which the accessibility criteria is used for spatial planning, Campbell (1990) and various models for space partition was developed by many scholars (like, Cooper, 1963; Haggett, 1977; Scott, 1975; and O'Kelly, 1986, etc.). On the basis of the locational aspects and accessibility of infrastructural elements, the available infrastructure for the development has been studied at district-level break up of collected data. The detailed analysis of available infrastructure for human resource development and overall development of the state is persuaded in the preceding sections.

Transport Network and Road Accessibility

Optimal spatial organization of transport facilities play an important role in the process of regional development over space. Transportation has become one of the most significant factors of development progress. Economic vitality of a region flows through the efficiency and facilities of a good transport network. Rural transport may be regarded as one of the main spatial interactions between the central places and numerous villages scattered within their perspective hinterlands (Singh, 1964). It naturally links a centre point, markets and usually located at a junction and numerous villages scattered around them. But lack of surface roads and bridges is the main problem facing rural transportation in general. In our country, where one out of every three village, is more than five miles away from an improved road (Singh, 1964).

The aerial perspective of road distribution can be stated by preparing road intensity index which would reflect a realistic picture of utility and accessibility of road for use of the local people; this refers to the road length in relation to its aerial extent. Hence, the higher the road intensity index, the greater is the degree of its accessibility and more is its utility for local people and *viceversa* (Singh, 1999). Development of roads has been recognized all over the world as a basic and important infrastructure for the development. Roads not only provide important link between rural and sub-urban areas of the country, but also connect the country with other international centres of trade and commerce (NEC, 1985). While discussing about road and transport network planning for development, the work of Singh (1988) on transport planning in Rohilkhand is worth mentioning.

In the State of Nagaland, road is the main means of transportation, which controls directly and indirectly the supply of materials, services and people mobility. The State is fully depended on the roads network. Railway line is connected only to Dimapur, the last border town of Nagaland. While the National Highways serve as the main arteries, other types of roads are to be linked up, but due to the absence of improved roads, market and industrial units are still lagging.

According to administrative status of roads, they have been categorized as National Highways, State Highways, District roads and Village roads. The National Highway (NH) 39 passes through Dimapur to Imphal *via* Kohima, stretching a total length of 110 km within the State, and the NH 61 from Kohima to Amguri *via* Tseminyu, Wokha and Mokokchung covers a total length of about 250 km. Total road length in the State under the Public Works Department is about 9,859 km (1999-2000) of which 4,116 km is surfaced and 5,743 km is still unsurfaced. Thus, the road density of the State is 59.47 km per 100 sq. km.

Table 7.1 : District-wise Road

Districts	*Total Area (in sq. kms.)*	*Total Road length (in km.)*	*Road Density (km per 100 sq. km)*
Kohima	4041	1551	38.38
Mokokchung	1615	494	92.50
Tuensang	4228	2474	58.51
Phek	2026	1126	55.57
Mon	1786	1311	73.40
Wokha	1628	977	60.01
Zunheboto	1255	927	73.86
Total	**16,579**	**9,859**	**59.47**

Source: Department of Economics & Statistics, Government of Nagaland, Kohima (1999-2000).

Road accessibility refers to the distance of villages from *pucca road.*[1] Classifying villages according to road accessibility classes, namely, connected villages (0 km), highly accessible (0-4 km), moderately accessible (4-8 km) and inaccessible (above 8 km distance from the surfaced/*pucca* road), the district-wise figures of accessibility categories are calculated. The following results of the distributional pattern of transport network are emerged.

(a) About one-third villages (28.87 per cent) of the State are well connected with the surfaced/*pucca* roads. Wokha District has the lowest percentage of villages (12.38 per cent) under this category as against the highest (42.85 per cent) scored by Mokokchung and then followed by Mon (41.66 per cent). The very low connectivity in Wokha district may be because it lies on the border with Assam, where border area disputes are frequent in this part of the State and the people are not much interested to improve the road connectivity, and also the NH 61 passes through the district from the two major urban centres of the state (Kohima to Mokokchung), where Wokha is located in its middle (Table 7.2).

(b) Highly accessible (0-4 km) areas have been recorded only nearly 15 per cent villages of the State in which this percentage prevails in almost all the districts except

Table 7.2 : Road Accessibility

Accessibility Class Distance in km	Kohima		Phek		Zunheboto		Wokha		Mokokchung		Tuensang		Mon		State average (%)
	No. of villages	*%*	*No. of villages*	*%*	*No. of villages*	*%*	*No. of villages*	*%*	*No. of villages*	*%*	*No. of villages*	*%*	*No. of villages*	*%*	
Well connected (0)	125	33.33	33	33.00	31	17.12	14	12.38	45	42.85	50	21.73	45	41.66	28.87
Highly accessible (0-2)	47	12.53	5	5.00	9	4.97	9	7.96	9	8.57	17	7.39	1	0.92	6.76
Moderately accessible (2-4)	36	9.60	8	8.00	11	6.07	11	9.73	9	8.57	17	7.39	0	0.0	7.05
Accessible (4-6)	45	12.00	3	3.00	14	7.73	5	4.42	10	9.52	14	6.08	1	0.92	6.23
Moderately in accessible (6- 8)	35	9.33	2	2.00	12	6.62	7	6.19	8	7.61	8	3.47	4	3.70	5.56
Highly in acce-ssible (8-10)	18	4.80	7	7.00	8	4.41	6	5.30	6	5.71	5	2.17	3	2.77	4.59
Remote (10-12)	11	2.93	3	3.00	5	2.76	3	2.65	1	0.95	9	3.91	4	3.70	2.84
Highly remote (12-14)	4	1.06	0	0.0	2	1.10	3	2.65	3	2.85	8	3.47	6	5.55	2.38
Extremely-remote (14 & above)	57	15.20	39	39.0	89	49.17	55	48.67	14	13.33	112	48.69	41	37.96	36.00
Total	375	100	100	100	181	100	113	100	105	100	230	100	108	100	100

Source: Directorate of Economics and Statistics, Government of Nagaland, Kohima, 1997.

Mon where a few villages have been classified in this category (Table 7.2). Mon villages are generally big in size. It is considered to be one of the least developed districts in the State. Road facilities (surfaced road) were connected to the bigger villages and thus, 41.66 per cent of the villages are well connected in the district but highly accessible villages or villages within 4 km distance are insignificance.

(c) One-third area of the State falls under the category of highly remote (inaccessible), where *pucca* road is available only after a walk of 14 km. In such extremely low conditions of road connectivity, the pace of development is very slow. These areas are found in Eastern part of the State in Tuensang and Mon districts bordering with Myanmar, southwestern part of Peren subdivision in Kohima district, in the central part of the State in Zunheboto and western part of Wokha district. Topography is the main constraint to road-accessibility in these areas.

Though all the villages in the State have been connected with either *pucca* or village approach road (unsurfaced or *kutccha* road); the State being pre-dominantly hilly, there are various constraints to the development of railways. Using of bullock carts as is used in plain areas, is also not advisable in the hilly terrain, deep gorges and streams region. Foot-track and head loads are the only solution but for how long these people can go on like that situation with a dream of modernization. Road is the only possible alternative mode of transport, which may be intensified to connect the villages. Unlike in plain areas, villages in the state are scattered on hilltop and ranges, this makes it more difficult to connect the road facilities and it is very difficult to achieve the goal of hundred per cent road connectivity to the villages in the State.

Postal Services

The network of postal service facilities is an organization

controlled by the public sector, and the foremost aim of the postal services is to convey the private or public messages of various types from one location or individual to the other. Also, Post and Telegraph have been taken into consideration as their normal postal service; the Department also discharges certain agency functions like the work of postal saving bank, national saving certificate, postal life insurance, etc. special scheme for women and children. Besides, telephone for public utility is also installed in some of the offices.

According to the State Directorate of Postal Services, there were 322 Post Offices and 864 nos. of letter boxes in the State in 1999 (Government of Nagaland, 2000). In this regard, an average area served by a Post Office in the State is 51.48 sq. km. Similarly, the population served by a Post Office is 6,175 persons.

The distributional pattern and the service approach of Post Office are important aspects for the development of the rural areas. Accessibility of postal services based on distance between the location of Post Office and user's village would provide the basis of its effectiveness. Classifying villages into 9 categories based on accessible distance of the villages, the following distributional characteristics of postal services in the State are highlighted.

- The perfectly accessible villages, where post office is located in the village itself are noticed only in the 21 per cent villages of the State. The percentage share varies from 7.73 per cent in Zunheboto to 42.85 per cent in Mokokchung. It means growing townships influence the distribution of Post and Telegraph facilities (Table 7.3).
- The 60 per cent villages of the State falls under highly to extremely high inaccessible categories in which the villagers will have to walk more than 8 km to avail postal facilities. The condition of extremely inaccessible areas is noticed especially in Mon, Tuensang and Zunheboto districts, which are far from the main township, where more number of Post and Telegraph facilities are available.

Table 7.3 : Accessibility to Postal Service

Accessibility Class Distance in km	*Kohima*		*Phek*		*Zunheboto*		*Wokha*		*Mokokchung*		*Tuensang*		*Mon*		*State Average (%)*
	No. of villages	*%*	*No. of villages*	*%*	*No. of villages*	*%*	*No. of villages*	*%*	*No. of villages*	*%*	*No. of villages*	*%*	*No. of villages*	*%*	
Perfectly accessible (0)	50	13.33	28	28.0	14	7.73	14	12.38	45	42.85	49	21.3	29	26.85	21.78
Highly accessible (0-2)	30	8.00	6	6.0	7	3.86	9	7.96	9	8.57	14	6.08	1	0.92	5.91
Moderately accessible (2-4)	28	7.46	6	6.0	8	4.41	11	9.73	9	8.57	9	3.91	2	1.85	5.99
Accessible (4-6)	34	9.06	7	7.0	19	10.49	5	4.42	10	9.52	14	6.08	3	2.77	7.04
Moderately in-accessible (6-8)	42	11.2	5	5.0	16	8.83	7	6.19	8	7.61	9	3.91	6	5.55	6.89
Highly in-accessible (8-10)	26	6.93	5	5.0	9	4.97	6	5.30	6	5.71	8	3.47	5	4.62	5.14
Extremely in-accessible (10–12)	18	4.80	4	4.0	6	3.31	3	2.65	1	0.95	15	6.52	1	0.92	3.30
Extremely in-accessible (12-14)	16	4.26	0	0.0	3	1.65	3	2.65	3	2.85	12	5.21	5	4.62	3.03
Extremely in-accessible (14 & above)	131	34.93	40	40.0	99	54.69	55	48.67	14	13.33	100	43.47	56	51.85	40.99
Total	375	100	100	100	181	100	113	100	105	100	230	100	108	100	100

Source: Directorate of Economics and Statistics, Government of Nagaland, Kohima, 1997.

It is found that postal services are concentrated towards the villages well connected with *pucca* roads and is yet to extend its services to a large number of villages in all the districts. In this regard, Mokokchung district shows better facilities than the other districts. When the world is going ahead with the latest information technology, somewhere, in some part of the world is still depending on the age-old system, and some are even yet to avail it. The State is mostly hilly and mountainous, villages are scattered and the problem of transportation has also added to the poor facility of postal infrastructure.

Government has installed a Satellite Telephone and a Television set in each and every Village Council in the State during the early nineties. Recently, the Central Government has taken up a bold step on information technology (IT) to every doorstep for the North Eastern States. The Community Information Centre (CIC) Project is one of them and, it comprises setting up of computer rooms in each and every Rural Development Blocks in all 487 Rural Development blocks of the North Eastern Region.[2]

Financial Institutions (Banks)

In developing rural economy, finance plays an important role like the lifeblood of trade, industry and commerce (Singh, 1981). Smooth economic functioning of business, rapid economic development, and agricultural and small-scale industrial development are not possible without the availability of adequate finance. Credit facilities for agriculture development are the most essential one as far as modern agriculture is concerned. Capital is required not only for on-farm investment to improve the production apparatus and to provide various farm inputs and services, but also for the arrangement of infrastructure facilities such as power, roads, transportation, communication, markets, storage, education, training, extension and so on. The State largely depends on agriculture; eventhough the area does not have much scope for mechanical farming, because of its hilly terrain. Horticulture farming and cash crops farming have good potential in the state, so also does animal husbandry and poultry farming.

The financial institutions are also a major source of investment under various rural development programmes. The lending of institutional credit is being supplemented by the government subsidies to the beneficiaries at the grassroots level. These financial institutions are delivering good services to the villages in the State. As per the Village Development Board (VDB) record, each and every VDB has kept a fixed deposit of rupees one lakh to rupees two lakh fifty thousand in the banks of their respective districts. There are 45 per cent Commercial Banks in the State located in Kohima and Dimapur areas (RBI, 1999). Bank facility is far too low compared to the requirement of the population because one bank branch covers 28 thousand people in the State.

Some of the salient features of the distribution of bank facilities are presented below:

(a) In all the districts, bank facilities are poor and inaccessible to the villagers. In Kohima district, only 14.66 per cent of the villages have accessible to banking facilities within 4 km distance. More than 50 per cent are on a distance of 14 or more km away from the nearest bank. It means that the bank facilities are concentrated only in a few centres, which are located in and around the urban centres.

(b) The State has an average of 17.12 per cent of the villages within 4 km distance from bank, whereas 57.78 per cent are still at a distance of 14 or more km away from the nearest bank. The highest accessible areas (within 4 km) are recorded 25 per cent in Phek district, 20.33 per cent in Wokha and 19.98 per cent in Mokokchung, which are enumerated as higher percentage than the State average. Though, all the villages are maintaining their bank accounts through Village Development Boards, individual persons may not be aware of the financial facilities, loan system, etc. for economic development.

(c) The bank accessibility is in fact very poor in all the districts of the State. More than two-third number of villages fall under the categories of extremely inaccessible and remote location, which is more than 10 km from the bank (Table 7.4). Thus, bank facilities are concentrated only at a few points, which may be because of insecurity due to the insurgency problems and the topographical hindrances.

Role of financial institutions in providing increased financial support to the farmers, small-scale industries, cottage industries, craftsmen, etc. in the State is of prime importance for setting up new units/upgradation/modernization of the existing activities. The limited facilities of this institution are also a fact, which is due to insecure situations in the whole of the Northeastern region, as it is infested with insurgent activities. However, government can provide adequate security to these institutions, and bank facilities must be provided to the interior areas of the region for a balance development of the nation.

Educational Institutions

Education is one of the important factors that enriches human resources in achieving a desired quality of life and helps also in determining the human occupation and income levels, and measuring the socio-economic development of the society (Parik, 1967). This fact has also been revealed from various studies on the problem of education and economic development undertaken for the developing regions of the South and South-East Asia, by Haq (1965) and Latin America by Robertson (1974). An optimal spatial distribution of education and its facilities is a very significant factor in a balanced development of a region; it has a key role as they provide a distinctive social environment (Srivastava and Siddique, 1981). Lener, D. in his

Table 7.4 : Accessibility to Bank Service

Accessibility Class Distance in km	Kohima		Phek		Zunheboto		Wokha		Mokokchung		Tuensang		Mon		State average Total
	No. of villages	%	No. of villages	%	No. of villages	%	No. of villages	%	No. of villages	%	No. of villages	%	No. of villages	%	
Village Having Bank Branch (0)	14	3.73	8	8.0	6	3.31	10	8.84	3	2.85	18	7.82	6	5.55	6.73
Highly accessible (0-2)	11	2.93	9	9.0	8	4.41	6	5.30	10	9.52	9	3.91	0	0.0	5.01
Moderately accessible (2-4)	30	8.00	8	8.0	8	4.41	7	6.19	8	7.61	8	3.47	0	0.0	5.38
Accessible (4-6)	25	6.66	8	8.0	17	9.39	5	4.42	10	9.52	5	2.17	8	7.40	6.79
Moderately inaccessible (6-8)	29	7.73	4	4.0	15	8.28	7	6.19	8	7.61	6	2.60	4	3.70	5.73
Highly in-accessible (8-10)	31	8.26	9	9.0	9	4.97	6	5.30	8	7.61	8	3.47	2	1.85	5.78
Extremely in-accessible (10-12)	31	8.26	6	6.0	7	3.86	7	6.19	3	2.85	8	3.47	0	0.0	4.37
Remote village (12-14)	15	4.00	4	4.0	3	1.65	4	3.53	5	4.76	11	4.78	1	0.92	3.38
Highly Remote (14 & above)	189	50.4	44	44.0	108	59.66	61	53.98	50	47.61	157	68.26	87	80.55	57.78
Total	375	100	100	100	181	100	113	100	105	100	230	100	108	100	100

Source: Directorate of Economics and Statistics, Government of Nagaland, Kohima, 1997.

studies of a Literacy and initiative in a Turkish village, finds that the literates are more mobile than their illiterate co-villagers, who are firmly home rooted in their villages. This has shown a clear picture among the literates and illiterates that the illiterates do not want to change the old habits of their life, and also they are not keen on adopting the new technologies and practices.

Education is the single most important input in supply of manpower both in terms of quantity and quality. It creates awareness and adaptability towards new changes and the process of modernization. Education plays a crucial role in economic development and social modernization (Yogi, 1991). Education determines human occupation and income which together reflect the general economic status of a community where the educational, occupational and income levels are generally low with the low economic status. Inequality in income and wealth is positively correlated with educational development in the country (Hagen, 1975).

Education is helpful in reducing poverty for rural people who can use it to get better work/higher income, natural or physical assets or work yielding more, if one is educated (IFAD, 2001). As stated above, education is important in overall development of the society. Spatial distribution of educational facilities would provide a sound base of space-efficiencies and accessibility parameters of educational facilities of the state. It would help in understanding economic planning and manpower planning of the area.

As per the records of the School Education Department, there are 1,675 Government Primary Schools, 1,301 Middle Schools, 249 Government High Schools and 4 Higher Secondary Schools and also a large number of private schools as 1,468 Primary Schools, 374 Middle Schools, 309 High Schools and 12 Higher Secondary Schools in the State in the year 1999-2000. It means governmental and non-governmental agencies both are engaged in extending the educational facilities at lower and middle levels.

Since primary schools are located in almost all the villages of the State and this facility is accessible to all the children at home, the accessibility classification of the villages is persuaded here by considering high school facilities which are available only in 35.48 per cent villages and the children of about two-third villages of the State have to go everyday to the nearby high school. The percentage share of villages of the districts of Mon, Tuensang and Mokokchung has been recorded higher under the category of 'villages having high school' than the State average (Table 7.5). It shows that the villages having high school facility are concentrated in the northwestern part of the State, which is in the proximity of the Assam plains.

The Tenth Five Year Plan (2002-2007) lay down one of its objectives that all children to be enrolled in schools by 2003; and all children to complete 5 years of schooling by 2007. Literacy rate is to be increased to 75 per cent within the Plan period. Another target is to forward the reduction in gender gaps in literacy and wage rates by at least 50 per cent by the end of this 10th Five Year Plan. A careful locational plan for the intensification of educational facilities is needed for the same. But the target was not fulfilled as per requirement.

Medical Facilities and their Locational Characteristics

Health Service[3] is an important input for human beings. It fulfills the basic welfare need and also indirectly contributes to the efficiency of labour force. It is a fact that the individual's health contributes to higher productivity and economic development, which, in turn, provides them with higher wages and better prospects for good health (Singh, 1995). Thus, societal development largely depends on the health facilities. Census of India (1971) stated that the expenditure on improving the health of a nation is regarded as a good investment yielding indirect return in increasing efficiency and productivity. According to the International Fund for Agricultural Development (IFAD, 2001), human health assets comprise bodily and mental characteristics promoting longevity with full functioning and resistance to (or

Table 7.5 : Accessibility to High School Education

Accessibility Class Distance in km	*Kohima*		*Phek*		*Zunheboto*		*Wokha*		*Mokokchung*		*Tuensang*		*Mon*		*State Average*
	No. of villages	*%*	*No. of villages*	*%*	*No. of villages*	*%*	*No. of villages*	*%*	*No. of villages*	*%*	*No. of villages*	*%*	*No. of villages*	*%*	
Village having high School facility (0)	87	23.2	40	40.0	53	29.28	21	18.58	55	52.38	108	46.95	41	37.96	35.48
Highly accessible (0-2)	51	13.6	23	23.0	8	4.41	14	12.38	17	16.19	8	3.47	1	0.92	10.56
Accessible (2-4)	59	15.73	4	4.0	5	2.76	15	13.27	14	13.33	8	3.47	5	4.62	8.17
Moderately accessible (4-6)	46	12.26	0	0.0	11	6.07	9	7.96	9	8.57	8	3.47	4	3.70	6.00
Highly accessible (6-8)	34	9.06	0	0.0	17	9.39	10	8.84	3	2.85	8	3.47	5	4.62	5.46
Highly in-accessible (8-10)	21	5.60	4	4.0	3	1.65	5	4.42	3	2.85	9	3.91	6	5.55	3.99
Extremely in-accessible (10-12)	16	4.26	1	1.0	3	1.65	5	4.42	0	0.0	12	5.21	6	5.55	3.15
Remote (12-14)	12	3.20	1	1.0	1	0.55	2	1.76	0	0.0	6	2.60	11	10.18	2.75
Highly Remote (14 & above)	49	13.06	27	27.0	64	35.35	32	28.3	4	3.80	53	23.04	29	26.85	22.48
*					16	8.83					10	4.34			
Total	375	100	100	100	181	100	113	100	105	100	230	100	108	100	100

* Distance not available

Source: Directorate of Economics and Statistics, Government of Nagaland, Kohima 1997.

rapid recovery from) illness and injury. Thus, health is the primary essential input for a person to be productive and prosperous.

Today, most of medical facilities are concentrated in urban centres. Out of many medical officers and staffs, hardly 25 per cent of hospital beds and 34 per cent of the doctors are available in rural areas, where more than 80 per cent of our population lives in the rural area. Major portion of the expenditure on health services marked for curative services is predominantly incurred in the urban areas. They are accessible to the more privileged sections of the society (Banerjee, 1974).

In this study, Hospitals, Community Health Centres, Primary Health Centres, Sub-Centres having bed facilities are considered as basic infrastructure facility for health care. Dispensaries in villages are not counted here, as these are available in almost all the villages.

The locational characteristics of health services reveal that nearly one-fourth, *i.e.,* almost 25 per cent of the villages of the State have these services while nearly one-third villages of the State fall under the category in which a patient has to walk from 2 to 14 km to avail medical facilities. A large number of villages (36.63 per cent) have to suffice with health facility, that is located beyond 14 km from the nearest health centre. As a result, such areas are extremely inaccessible due to their remoteness (Table 7.6).

Mokokchung district of the State shows the best distribution of health facilities. In more than two-third of the total villages of the district (*i.e.,* 72 villages out of a total of 105), the health facility is available in them. The district is well developed and dominated by the Ao tribe, who are also educationally advanced as compared to the rest of the different tribes in the State. On the other hand, Zunheboto and Mon districts are included in the category, where nearly one-half of the total number of villages are extremely inaccessible to health facilities. There are 36.63 per cent of the total villages still in the category of extremely inaccessible medical facilities (14 km distance and above); only

Table 7.6 : Medical Facilities and their Locational Characters

Accessibility Class Distance in km	Kohima		Phek		Zunheboto		Wokha		Mokokchung		Tuensang		Mon		State Average
	No. of villages	%	No. of villages	%	No. of villages	%	No. of villages	%	No. of villages	%	No. of villages	%	No. of villages	%	
Available at village (0)	63	16.8	15	15.0	19	10.49	18	15.92	72	68.57	58	25.21	21	19.44	24.49
Highly Accessible (0- 2)	13	3.46	2	2.0	8	4.41	10	8.84	3	2.85	11	4.78	1	0.92	5.95
Accessible (2-4)	29	7.73	0	0.0	9	4.97	11	9.73	8	7.61	11	4.78	1	0.92	5.10
Less accessible (4-6)	25	6.66	1	1.0	14	7.73	4	3.53	8	7.61	8	3.47	5	4.62	4.94
Moderately inaccessible (6-8)	23	6.13	1	1.0	16	8.83	6	5.30	3	3.85	10	4.34	7	6.48	5.13
Highly inaccessible (8-10)	25	6.66	2	2.0	7	3.86	5	4.42	3	3.85	13	5.65	7	6.48	4.70
Remote (10-12)	22	5.86	0	0.0	7	3.86	6	5.30	1	0.95	9	3.91	5	4.62	3.50
Highly Remote (12-14)	8	2.13	1	1.0	4	2.20	3	2.65	1	0.95	7	3.04	8	7.40	2.76
Extremely remote (14 & above)	87	23.20	43	43.0	88	48.61	50	44.24	6	5.71	98	42.60	53	49.07	36.63
*	80	21.33	35	35.0	9	4.97					4	1.73			9.00
Total	375	100	100	100	181	100	113	100	105	100	230	100	108	100	100

* Distance not available.

Source: Directorate of Economics and Statistics, Government of Nagaland, Kohima, 1997.

Mokokchung and Kohima districts are below the State average, easy accessible.

It may be said here that they are unevenly distributed and are not accessible to the people living in remote areas. The distribution of these services is highly influenced by the road network and road connectivity. The villages located along the roadside have the advantage of these services.

Concluding Remarks

Distributional pattern and locational characteristics of infrastructural facilities/services for the development created in the State of Nagaland reveal the following features:

(i) According to a criterion given by the Government of India for optimizing the service pattern, the State of Nagaland needs more number of health, postal and bank service centres (Table 7.2 to Table 7.6). It is obvious to say that there is need of intensification of these services for their efficient use and welfare of society.

(ii) Districts of Mokokchung and Kohima are more exposed to urban taste and are served by these facilities and are able to provide better services to the remote areas. The conditions in Zunheboto and Tuensang districts are deplorable, where a large number of villages are located at a distance of more than 14 km from the nearest Postal, Bank, Health, Education and Road facilities and, therefore, the populations of these villages are ill-served.

(iii) The locational decisions of services/facilities are in the hands of politicians who do not know the efficient use of these services. Accessibility or the distance between user and facility location is the major consideration for the efficient use and locational decision regarding these facilities, rather than political biasness of locational choices.

Notes

1. The *Pucca* road refers to surfaced or all weathered road and the *Kutcha* road refers to the un-surfaced or unmetalled road or un-weathered road or approach road in the present chapter.
2. The decision of CIC project has been taken few years back, which has come to reality. It has been conceived in response to the Prime Minister's call for "freedom from distance." The CIC projects have been set-up taking into consideration the convenience of the rural masses of the region at a cost of Rs. 242 crores. These computer rooms will be provided with VSAT connectivity; the centre will also bear the satellite charges and remunerations, 'Centre unleashes Information Revolution in NE with CICs, *The_Guardian*. Vol. XII (No. 216), Shillong.
3. Health Service, which includes hospital, primary health centre or sub-centres (centres with Hospital bed facilities). Dispensaries are not included in this study.

References

Banerjee, I. (1974): Social and Cultural Foundation of Health Service System, *Economic and Political Weekly,* (Vol. 9), p. 1339.

Campbell, J. F. (1990): Locating Transport Terminals to Serve an Expanding Demand, *Transportation Research B*, Vol. 24, pp 173-192.

Cooper, L. (1963): Location-Allocation Problems. *Operations Research*, Vol. 11, pp. 331-343.

Government of Nagaland (2000): Millennium Issue, *Statistical Handbook of Nagaland,* Directorate of Economics & Statistics, Kohima.

Hagen, Everett E. (1975): *The Economics of Development,* Richard D. Irwin, Inc. Illinois.

Haggett, P. (1977): *Locational Analysis in Human Geography*, Edward Arnold, London, Chapter 13.

Hoggart, Keith & Henry, Buller (1987): *Rural Development A Geographical Perspective,* Croom Helm Ltd., Kent, p.183.

IFAD (2001): *Rural Poverty Report: The Challenge of Ending Rural Poverty.* International Fund for Agricultural Development 2001, Oxford University Press, London, pp. 107-108.

O'Kelly, M.E. (1986): Activity Levels at Hub Facilities in Interacting Network, *Geographical Ananlysis*, Vol. 18, pp. 243-356.

Parik, G.D. (1967): Education and Economic Development, *Education Quarterly*, Vol. III. (3), p. 9.

RBI (1999): Quarterly Handbook of March, June, September, December, Reserve Bank of India, New Delhi.

Ramanujan, K. N. (1987): Rural Roads for Rural Prosperity, *Kurukshetra*, Vol. 35. (4), p. 25

Sharma, R.C. (1989): *Regional Planning for Social Development*, Criteriory Publications, New Delhi, p. 126.

Scott, A. J. (1975): Discrete Dynamic Locational Systems: Notes on a structural Framework, in Karlquist, A. (ed.): *Dynamic Allocation in Urban Space,* Saxon House, Lexington, Massa-chussets.

Singh, Hoshiar (1995): *Administration of Rural Development in India*, Sterling Publishers Pvt. Ltd., New Delhi, p. 93.

Singh, J. (1964): *Transport Geography of South Bihar*, BHU Press, Varanasi, p. 189.

Singh, M.L. (1981): Changing Pattern of Business Finance Company Deposits, *Yojana,* Vol. XXV. (3), p. 25.

Singh, Katar (1986): *Rural Development: Principles, Policies and Management*, Sage Publications India Pvt. Ltd., New Delhi.

Singh, S. (1999): *A Resource Atlas of Arunachal Pradesh*, Government of Arunachal Pradesh, Department of Planning, Itanagar, p. 113.

Singh, S. (1988): *Rural Development and Planning*, Shree Publishing House, New Delhi, p. 135.

Singh, S. (1990): *Integrated Area Development Planning*, Shree Publishing House, New Delhi, pp. 81-105.

Sinha, P.R.R. (1972): Infrastructure in Communication, in L.K. Sen (ed.) *Readings on Micro Level Planning and Rural Growth Centres,* NICD, Hyderabad, p. 82.

Srivastava, R.K. (1992): *Integrated Area Development — A case study of Rath Tahsil, Hamirpur, U.P.,* Rawat Publications, Jaipur, p. 161.

Srivastava, R.C. & Siddiqui, J.A. (1981): Spatial Organization of Education Facility (A Case Study of Banda District–U.P.), *Indian Council of Geographers,* Vol. 9, p. 36.

Thomas, Isabelle (2002): *Transportation Networks and Optimal Location of Human Activities: A Numerical Geography Approach*, Edward Elgar Publishing Ltd. Cheltenham, U.K.

The Telegraph (2002): Extract from the International Conference on

Financing and Development, Monlerrey, March 2002. *The Telegraph,* Vol. XX (356), Guwahati Edition, p. 9.

Warren, L.R. (1978): *The Community in America,* Chicago, Rand McNally, Third Edition (in Hoggart), p. 183.

Yogi, A.K. (1991): *Development of the North-East Region: Problems and Prospects*, Spectrum Publications, Guwahati, p. 269.

8 Infrastructure Development in Nagaland

An Overview

Pradip Brahmachary

Introduction

The term infrastructure has been used since 1927 to refer collectively to the roads, bridges, rail lines, and similar public works that are required for an industrial economy, or a portion of it, to function.[1] The World Development Report, 1994, refers to infrastructure as an '*umbrella*' which includes activities that share technical features such as economies of scale and spill over effects from user to non-user (World Bank, 1994, p. 2).

In general, infrastructure signifies the basic and key foundation of development. It can, therefore, be taken as basic to all activities in the economy. It refers to some kind of permanent installations, which are used over a long period of time for supply of basic inputs, like, railway, roads, power, education, health, etc. Infrastructure can broadly be divided into two groups, *Economic* and *Social* infrastructure. *Economic* infrastructure consists of transport, power, communication and irrigation, etc. *Economic* infrastructure directly helps in the production process and *Social* infrastructure is generally composed of health, education and housing, etc. which is a direct representation of the standard of living of the population.

Many studies have concluded the role of infrastructure in growth as substantial, significant and frequently greater than that of the investment in other forms of capital. A strong linkage between improved infrastructure and economic growth has been found with "a one per cent increase in the stock of infrastructure being associated with a one per cent increase in GDP" (World

Bank, 1994, pp. 2). Thus a well-aided infrastructure is an essential and prerequisite condition of economic development and the nature and degree of development of infrastructure in an economy determines to a large extent the pattern and the rate of growth of employment and income of the economy.

Nagaland, a State in North East India, is suffering from slow rate of economic development primarily of being inadequate infrastructure. As per a survey conducted by Planning Commission, Nagaland stands seventh from below in terms of social and economic infrastructure. It is an agrarian economy. Out of total population of 19,90,036 (Census of India 2001: Nagaland), 16,47,249 persons live in rural areas and 3,42,787 persons live in urban areas. Thus, 82.77 per cent of the total population lives in rural Nagaland. The working population of the State is concentrated in the category of cultivators signifying the fact that the economy is land based.

The statistical data on development of infrastructure in Nagaland reveals the following facts:

Transportation

When we talk about the transportation system in the State, road transport comes first in the scene. The length of National Highway roads is 365.38 km and State roads are 1094 km. Surface transport is the main method of communication in this land-locked hilly State. One of the significant achievements of Nagaland has been the consistent expansion of roads. This has resulted in the development of an impressive network of public and private sector road transport system. Over the years, there has been a steady progress of the road connectivity. Beginning with 1955-56, when Nagaland had only a road of about 322 km, the roads were principally meant to connect the main administrative centres with points on the arterial links in the Assam Valley. Thus, the National Highway No. 39, which is the most important road and connects the rail-head at Dimapur with Imphal in Manipur *via* Kohima passed through Nagaland

Table 8.1: Length of Roads in Nagaland

(in kms)

Year	*National Highway*		*Surfaced Highway*		*Major Dist. Road*		*Other Dist. Road*		*Village Dist Road*		*Road Under Border*		*Feeder Road*		*Total*	
Category	*Sur*	*Unsur*	*Sur*	*Unsur*	*Sur*	*Unsur*	*Sur*	*Unsur*	*Sur*	*Unsur*	*Sur*	*Unsur*	*Sur*	*Unsur*	*Sur*	*Unsur*
2002	248	–	675	357.5	1018.4	1319.5	1053. 37	1899.13	2129	3021	1020.85	408.2	81	140.5	6225.62	7142.83

Source: Chief Engineer Office, P.W.D. (R & B).

for a distance of 102 km. The Amguri (in Assam) to Mokokchung road of 103 km was connecting central Nagaland with Amguri rail head in Assam. The road connecting Kohima and Amguri *via* Wokha and Mokokchung district is now converted to National Highway 61. The other two important roads were, Mokokchung – Tuensang of 84 km. and Namtila–Mon of 37 km. There were a few bridle tracks and mule paths connecting the villages to the arterial roads, but there were no feeder roads[2].

However, village road transport has been handicapped by inadequate development and poor maintenance of roads. All weather roads linking the scattered villages are a prerequisite for development of potential areas. This holds true for agriculture, social, industrial, entrepreneurial and mineral development. As many villages are not still covered by all weather roads, the villages have been deprived of proper socio-economic development in education, primary health care, and ready access of farmers' products to the market.

The railway network in the State is minimal. The only rail station of the State is at Dimapur and the length of broad gauge lines is 12.85 km. (N. F. Railway, CME Office, Guwahati). It is expected to reach State capital Kohima in the 11th Plan programme.

Communication

Nagaland had 219 post offices and 2223 telephone connections during 1980-81. This has increased to 323 post offices and 25,193 telephone connections during 1999-2000. Telephone exchanges have been established in 46 towns and 3 villages in the State. The 3 towns of Kohima, Dimapur and Mokokchung have more than 50 per cent of these facilities. The telephone density is very low and the quality of services is still very poor, especially in the other towns and in the rural areas. The rural coverage in the districts other than Kohima and Dimapur is minimal or non-existence.

Power

Nagaland is not self-sufficient in power, generating only 29 MW (2001). Despite the vast potential, the power generated within the State is quite insignificant. In fact, the State produces only 10 per cent of its power need. The bulk of its requirement of power comes through the national grid from Central Sector Projects like NHPC, North Eastern Electric Power Corporation (NEEPCO), etc. and Meghalaya State Electricity Board (MESEB).

After the commissioning of Doyang Hydro Electric Power Plant, having an installed capacity of 75 MW, the State receives a share of 12 per cent of the generated power. The 24 MW Likimro Hydro Electric Project has already been commissioned and a few mini-hydro projects are under construction, which will add about 3 MW to the existing generation.

Out of 1317 villages, the number of villages electrified as on 31.03.2000 was 1196 (as per Statistical Handbook of Nagaland 2004), *i.e.,* almost 91 per cent of the villages had been electrified. The annual energy consumption of 225 MW (2001) provides a very low per capita consumption of about 130 units per year only compared to an Indian average of 370 units. The current peak demand is estimated at about 75 MW but it is restricted to only 50 MW. The quality too is low, with frequent curtailment and interruption, transformer failures and low voltage.

Table 8.2 : Generation, Consumption and per Capita Consumption of Electricity

Period	*Installed Capacity kWh*	*Generation mkW/h*	*Consumption mkW/h*	*Per Capita Consumption kWh*
1999-2000	5160	2.80	145.75	120.49
2000-01	4500	3.05	220	118
2001-02	4500	0.5	238	120

Source: Chief Engineer (Power).

As per Ministry of Power data, Nagaland's share in Central sector stations as on September 30, 2004 was 71.10 MW, while the installed capacity was 101.46 MW. As compared to the national average of 355 kWh, the per capita consumption of electricity was 84.74 kWh. The percentage of rural households having electricity was 47.16 per cent.

Banking

On March 31, 2004, the number of scheduled commercial bank branches in Nagaland was 69 down from 70 as on March 31, 2000. The bank deposits were Rs. 1223 crore and bank credit was Rs. 206 crore. On March 31, 2004, as compared to the national average of 58.72 per cent the credit deposit ratio in Nagaland was as low as 16.84 per cent. The Financial institutions operating in Nagaland are NEDFi, IDBI, SIDBI and NABARD. Till March 31, 2005, NEDFi sanctioned a total of Rs. 1237 lakh to various projects located in Nagaland.

Table 8.3 : Bank Branches and Credit Facility *(Rs in crores)*

Scheduled Commercial Banks	*2000*	*2001*	*2002*	*2003*	*2004*
Bank Branches	70	69	70	69	69
Bank Credit	118	124	132	161	206
Bank Deposit	770	890	1052	1231	1223
Credit Deposit Ratio	15.34	13.92	12.55	13.08	16.84

Source: NEDFi Databank Quarterly., July 2005.

Table 8.3 reveals that the credit deposit ratio of Nagaland in 2004 stood at Rs. 16.84 crore compared to the credit deposit ratio of the entire North East as a whole stood at Rs. 29.35 crore

Drinking Water

Most of the Naga villages are located on hilltops, which make supply of drinking water a challenging task. The number of villages having portable water supply sources in 1995-96 was only 950. Now, 1304 (fully covered – 261, partially covered – 1043) of the 1376 villages/habitations (approx 95 per cent) have been provided with drinking water supply. Efforts are also being made to augment the water supply/distribution in the State, both in the rural and urban areas, to keep pace with the increasing requirement of water as the population grows. The objective is to achieve the recommended norm of 40 litres per capita per day. Attempts are being made to involve the community in implementation and maintenance of the water supply schemes.

Education

Between 1961 and 2001, Nagaland's literacy rate increased from 17.91 per cent to 66.6 per cent. While Nagaland's literacy rate was higher than the national average in the period 1981 to 2001, the extent of improvement has not been as high as in some of the other NE states like Mizoram (literacy rate 88 per cent).

Table 8.4 : Growth in Percentage of Literacy in Nagaland

Particulars	*1961*	*1971*	*1981*	*1991*	*2001*
Total	17.91	27.40	42.57	61.65	66.6
Male	20.04	35.02	50.06	67.72	71.2
Female	11.34	18.65	38.89	54.75	61.5

Source: Census of India.

The educational infrastructure, particularly at the primary level, has expanded considerably, with nearly 1500 schools serving the children of Nagaland. The proportionate increase in trained teachers, however, has not been realized, leading to poor quality of teaching. This, with poor infrastructure in some parts of Nagaland, has contributed to the poor pass percentage of school students.

The growth in the number of educational institutions after the creation of Nagaland State has been significant. At the beginning of the 21st century, Nagaland has nearly 1500 primary schools, 500 middle schools, 300 high schools and 16 higher secondary schools. Table 8.5 reflects the growth trends between 2000-01 to 2003-04.

Table 8.5: Growth of Educational Institutions

Particulars	*2000-01*	*2001-02*	*2002-03*	*2003-04*
University	1	1	1	1
Colleges	53	54	54	54
H.S. Schools	16	23	32	35
High Schools	315	321	321	331
Middle Schools	469	479	482	489
Primary Schools	1491	1499	1501	1508

Source: Directorate of Economics & Statistics, 2004.

In Nagaland, the primary stage of education is from class 1-4 and upper primary stage is from class 5 to 8. The high school stage of education is from class 9 to 10 and the higher secondary education stage is from class 11 to 12.

From Table 8.6, it can be seen that the number of government sponsored primary schools has increased from 1309 during 2001-02 to 1318 during 2003-04 but the number of private primary schools remained same during that period. In case of government sponsored middle schools the number has gone up from 261 in 2001-02 to 271 in 2003-04, whereas the number of privately sponsored middle schools has remained unaltered in that period. In case of high schools the number of government sponsored schools has gone up from 123 to 125, as well as privately sponsored high schools also increased from 198 to 206 from 2001-02 to 2003-04. The number of government sponsored higher secondary schools has increased from 5 to 10 and that of privately sponsored higher secondary schools has also increased from 18 to 25 during the same year.

The total number of higher and technical educational institutions has increased nominally. These educational institutions include 1 university, 36 colleges of general education,

Table 8.6: Number of Growth of Educational Institutions (Schools)

Year	*2001-2002*			*2002-2003*			*2003-2004*			*2004-2005*			*2005-2006*		
Types of Institutions	*Govt.*	*Pvt.*	*Total*	*Govt.*	*Pvt.*	*Total*	*Govt.*	*Pvt.*	*Total*	*Govt.*	*Pvt.*	*Total*	*Govt.*	*Pvt.*	*Total*
Primary	1309	190	1499	1305	215	1520	1303	215	1518	1305	215	1520	1303	215	1518
Middle	261	218	479	270	210	480	273	215	488	270	210	480	273	215	488
High	123	198	321	116	220	344	125	215	350	116	220	344	125	215	350
Higher Secondary	5	18	23	9	34	46	16	45	64	9	34	46	16	45	64
Total	1698	624	2322	1700	679	2390	1717	690	2420	1700	679	2390	1717	690	2420

Source: Statistical Handbook of Nagaland, 2006.

2 colleges of professional education, 2 polytechnic schools, 3 law colleges and others.

Health

Nagaland is a State in the north east where the health care facilities are far from satisfactory. For the people of the State, most of their healthcare requirements are met from outside the State either in Guwahati or outside the northeast region. This is due to the poor public health infrastructure, lack of adequate infrastructure, lack of adequate qualified doctors, nurses and paramedics and shortage of medicine.

Table 8.7 : Growth of Health Institutions, Staff, Patients and Beds

Particulars	*1999*	*2000*	*2001*	*2002*	*2003*
Urban Hospitals	8	8	8	8	10
Rural Hospitals	9	2	–	–	–
Community Health Centres	10	12	14	14	21
Primary Health Centres	49	55	65	65	93
Subsidiary Health Centres	35	36	35	35	30
Dispensaries	-	18	16	16	16
T.B. Hospitals	2	2	2	2	2
Mental Hospital	1	1	1	1	1
Doctors	352	366	366	367	367
Compounders	492	497	497	497	505
Nurses	1209	1116	1116	1278	1232
Total number of beds in various hospitals	1951	2095	2043	2183	2197
Number of indoor patients	53181	67318	88150	109738	110203
Number of outdoor patients	361755	412455	626209	623618	640075

Source: Statistical Handbook of Nagaland, 2004.

Nagaland had 204 health centres – including urban hospitals, rural hospitals, primary health centres, and sub-centres – with 1367 beds and 156 doctors in 1980. This health care infrastructure and personnel helped achieve a doctor: population ratio of 20 doctors per 1 lakh population and 30 hospitals for every 1 lakh people. As on 31st March, 2000, 36.95 per cent of the villages in the State were served by dispensaries, while 26.28

per cent had primary health centres, and 33.33 per cent had sub-centres. However, even as per national pattern, the achievements are still far short of the actual requirements. Based of population – related norms, as per 2001 census, the State requires 25 CHCs, 100 PHCs, 666 sub-centres.

Specialised health services are limited and concentrated mainly in the State capital and two other districts headquarters – Mokokchung and Dimapur. In 2003, the number of hospitals, dispensaries, primary health centre, subsidiary health centre, community health centre, sub-centre etc. stood at 603. The numbers of subdivisional hospitals were 1, community health centre, sub-centre were 21 and primary health centre stood at 93 in 2003. In the same year, the number of doctors stood at 367 and that of nurses stood at 1232, the number of indoor patients treated was 109738 and that of outdoor patients were 623618.

Conclusion

The above mentioned statistical data on infrastructure in Nagaland reflects that the State made significant expansion of the development of road connectivity. Still, the condition of the village road transport has remained unaltered. The number of post offices is inadequate. The telephone density is low and the coverage in rural areas is minimal. 95 per cent of the villages have been provided with drinking water facility, but not still sufficient and very uncertain. The number of educational institutions has shown remarkable increase, but the increasing number of dropouts, and the lack of trained teachers have been the area of concern. The health care facilities are far from being satisfactory due to inadequate number of medical institutions, trained doctors, nurses and shortage of medicines. Thus the pace of development of infrastructure in the state is tardy, sluggish and far below the acceptable standards of development. It is clear that Nagaland has to go a long way to attain its status of a developed state. In order to achieve this end, adequate amount of public investment is crucial. Government must frame out suitable polices and measures, which are best fit for this hilly landlocked area, to bring up the State at par with other developed states of India.

Notes

1. Excerpted from Gautam Patikar (2008): *Rural Transport Development in Nagaland,* paper presented in the National Seminar on 21-22 November at St. Joseph's College, Jakhama, Nagaland.
2. *Ibid.*

References

Related Link

http:// www.eref-trade.hmco.com

http://www.nagaland.nic.in/

http://www.goidirectory.nic.in/naga.htm

Gowda, M.V. *et al.* (1997) (ed.) : *Infrastructural Development for Economic Growth*, Deep and Deep Publication, New Delhi.

Hokishe, Sema (1986): *Emergence of Nagaland – Socio-economic and Political Transformation and the Future*, Vikas Publishing House, New Delhi.

Joshi, Hargovind (2001): *Nagaland Past and Present*, Akansha Publishing House, New Delhi.

Roy Burman, B.K. *et al.* (1984): *Towards Poverty Alleviation Programmes in Nagaland and Manipur*, Mittal Publications, New Delhi.

Saleh, Swabera Islam (1989): *Nagaland's Economy in Transition since 1964,* Omsons Publications, New Delhi.

Journals/Articles

Bhatia, M.S. (1999): Rural Infrastructure and Growth in Agriculture, *Economic and Political Weekly*, March 27 to April 2, pp. A-43-A 48, Mumbai.

Ghosh, Jayanti, *et al.* (1997): All Dressed up and Nowhere to Go-India Infrastructure Report, *Economic and Political Weekly*, XXXII (16): 803, Mumbai.

Ghosh, Nilabja (2002): Infrastructure, Cost and Labour Income in

Agriculture, *Indian Journal of Agricultural Economics,* Vol. 57, No. 2 , April to June, pp. 153 to 168.

Kurane, Supriya (2005): The Long and Winding Road Controversy – The Infrastructure Survey, *Business World*, 31st January 2005.

Loganathan, P. and Asokan, R. P. (2005): Rural Infrastructure Development Fund, *Kurukshetra*, Vol. 55, No. 2, December 2005, p. 14, New Delhi.

Sharma, Sheetal (2006): Education: Foundation for Rural Development, *Kurukshetra* Vol. 55, No.1, November 2006, p. 8.

Shekhar, Chandra (2004) *:* Infrastructure Financing*, Yojana*, Vol. – 48, January 2001, No.1, p. 55.

Singh, Richa (2004): Rural Infrastructure, Agricultural Development and Poverty in India : An Inter-State Study, *Journal of Rural Development*, Vol. 23, January to March 2004, No.1, p. 32.

Wanmali, Sudhir (1992): *Rural Infrastructure, the Settlement System and Development of the Regional Economy in Southern India*, Research Report, 1991, International Food Policy Research Institute, Washington D.C.

Government Publications

Department of Planning and Co-ordination, Government of Nagaland *: State Human Development Report, 2004.*

Directorate of Economics and Statistics, Nagaland: *Statistical Hand Book of Nagaland, different years.*

Directorate of Economics and Statistics, Nagaland: *Economic Survey, different years.*

Directorate of Information and Public Relations, Nagaland, *Annual 1999.*

North Eastern Council, Ministry of Home Affairs, Government of India, Shillong: *Basic Statistics of North Eastern Region, different years.*

Registrar General and Census Commissioner, India: *Census of India 2001—Final Publication Totals and other reports relating to different census years.*

Village and Town Directory of Nagaland, 2001.

Census of India-1961,1971,1981,1991 & 2001.

9 Microfinance and Poverty Alleviation
A Case Study on RGVN-CSP

Jagadish Nath and Basabi Deb

Introduction

Not very long ago, poor people of the country did not have any option of borrowings or savings. Ironically, borrowing and saving options for this lot were most essential. As such, village money lenders and petty lenders would always have field days as these people were easy to exploit and they were the neediest. Not many experts from the field of finance and economics, or for that matter, policy makers had any panacea for it. In 1961, a US based NGO, ACCION[1] International, as a sort of Pre-peace Corps programe working on community development with the poor in Latin America, developed a concept called '*Microfinance*' which later on became the most effective panacea, so far, to the poverty stricken majority of the third world nations.

Microfinance is a special kind of financial service involving credit and savings to the needy and the poor or to them who primarily depend on their tiny business for income. These sections of people are generally not considered bankable because of their lack of collateral security, thereby making them high risk clients for any self-respecting bank. Marguerite S. Robinson in 1998 defined microfinance as the small-scale financial services for both credits and deposits which are provided to lower income people (farmer or fisherman or a micro-entrepreneur) either individually or collectively in groups, in both rural and urban areas, especially in developing countries. In the 1970s, ACCION International experimented with the concept and developed a lending model. In the 1980s it made two important observations: (1) The poor can pay for what they need, and (2) Scale is not a challenge but a friend.

However, in course of time, ACCION did not remain as the sole flag bearer of microfinance rather many other NGOs and institutions got involved in the movement. In fact, in early 1990s, commercial banks in some parts of the world also tried to put in some effort in the field of microfinance. Bolivia's Bancosol is credited as the first commercial bank to be dedicated to microfinance in the year 1992. Just in Latin America, there are now many others, in Colombia, Peru, Mexico, Honduras, Ecuador, and Venezuela. In our subcontinent, it was none other than, Nobel laureate Dr. Mohammad Yunus[2] of Bangladesh took the microfinancing movement to a spectacular level. Bangladesh Grameen Bank became a pinnacle of success with the microfinance initiatives of Dr. Yunus. And from then it spread to different parts of subcontinent.

In India too, microfinance schemes are fast becoming important tool of development for both government and NGOs[3]. Till now, variety of schemes have been floated and various approaches have been practiced by both government and NGOs. Credit has always been viewed as one of the missing inputs in the development sector and thus, emphasis on re-formulating and re-strengthening micro credit programmes is ever increasing. Some examples of microfinance has been spectacular successes and some not-so-successful. Some experienced high default rates and were unable to provide financial services in the long run but most have been getting very good yields.

Microfinance is now evolved as a need-based policy and programme to cater to the target groups which were so far was somehow neglected whether intentionally or inadvertently (women, poor, rural, deprived, etc.). This is mainly based on the concern of all developing countries for empowerment of these sections and thereby alleviation of poverty. It has been proved beyond doubt that access to credit is a major input in upgrading downtrodden. Thus, development organizations and policy makers now have started including access to credit for poor people as a major aspect of almost all poverty alleviation programmes. Capital is a limited resource. Developmental capitals are even scarce. Microfinance programmes, in recent periods, have become a promising way of effective and efficient utilization of these funds. Moreover, quite a few microfinance programmes have really made wonderful impact in the development field and beyond. The sole objective of microfinance is simple and very clear that if these population, which are in real need and are in substantial number, are facilitated with access to financial services, including credit, it may not be very hard for them to start or expand a micro-enterprise. It is not the lack of skill or enterprising attitude which most of these people have rather the lack of proper support to build on their skill and entrepreneurial capabilities holds them to poverty. Microfinance is a bridge which tries to reduce this gap.

That the microfinance programmes actually have succeeded can be gauged from the fact that, more often than not, in enabling the target segments of the society to increase their income levels. And because of this, the access to credit and the opportunity of this population started to expand which in turn helped micro-enterprises of these neglected or ignored lots, especially in comparison to other policy development initiatives, recognizable. This also enhanced the credibility of the individual group members.

As far as development practitioners are concerned, the success of microfinance programmes is inspiring. In majority of the cases in the past, costly large-scale development initiatives have failed to achieve any sustainable benefits, especially after funds have dried up. Rather, these costly large scale initiatives encouraged corruption and unwanted dirty results. In recent times, one of the most effective interventions for economic empowerment of the poor thus seems to be microfinance initiatives.

In an article in *The Economic Times* by Vinod Khosla and Vikram Gandhi on 15 June, 2006, has sited different researchers' to highlight the achievement of Bangladesh in this field. In

Bangladesh, almost 15 million families now benefit from micro-loans and other microfinance programmes such as micro-savings and micro-insurance. A total of around 40 per cent of the overall reduction of rural poverty in recent years is now attributed to microfinance. Some of the other studies also suggest that the microfinance has been more effective on the poorest than on the poor. (It is really heartening for the countries like India, Bangladesh etc.) Strong spillover effects of microfinance operations in the areas where it has bought significant economic gains are also evident on that of non-participating members of communities. Furthermore, the authors argue that well-managed microfinance institutions (MFIs) have shown a capacity to wean themselves off of subsidies and become sustainable within a few years (Vinod Khosla and Vikram Gandhi, 2006).

From the above discussions on the literatures, it is evident that the microfinance is playing a significant role in poverty alleviation and rural development, thus making it necessary to share experiences and materials which will help not only in analyzing successes and failures but also provide knowledge and guidelines to implement future microfinance programmes.

The final goal of microfinance is to attain social and economic empowerment. Effectiveness of any microfinance model is dependent on how each of the stages of the intervention has been carefully analyzed, dealt and customized with actual situation. The capacity and the efficiency of the executing agencies in achieving the final goal should also needs to be properly accounted for, *e.g.*, if credit is delivered without sound consolidation of SHGs[4], it might trouble the self-sustainability and credit recovery of the agencies. However, banks, central and state governments also do have few schemes where direct credits to potential individuals are offered even if they are not members of SHGs. In general, the documentation of the developmental process of the individual becomes the base for the communication materials in the directory.

A typical micro-finance infused development process can be depicted with the help of following Chart.

Chart

Development Process through Microfinance

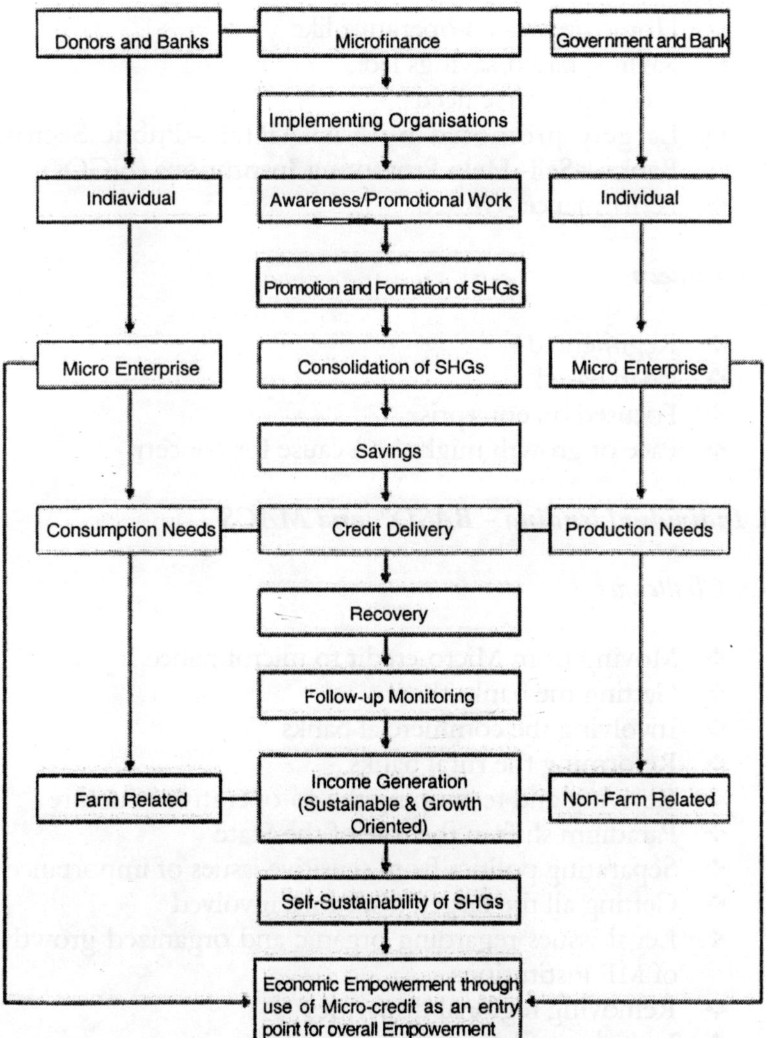

Source: http://www.un.org.in/iawg/icecd.section1.htm.

Microfinance: Delivery Models

1. Self-Help Groups

- Home grown–co-operative like
- Savings based/savings led
- Meeting diverse needs
- Largely promoted by NABARD[5]—Public Sector Banks—Self- Help Promoting Institutions (NGOs)
- Performance – mixed

2. Grameen

- Regimented
- Loan based
- Focused on enterprise
- Pace of growth might be a cause for concern

3. Individual lending – BASIX[6] and MACS[7]

Key Challenges

- Moving from Micro-credit to microfinance
- Getting the banks there
- Involving the commercial banks
- Reforming the rural banks
- Reviving and revamping the co-operative structure
- Paradigm shift in the role of the State
- Separating politics from sensitive issues of importance
- Getting all the targeted sections involved
- Legal issues regarding organic and organized growth of MF institutions
- Removing regional disparities
- Inclusion of left out urban poor
- Development of qualitative aspects of SHGs
- Expanding the diversity of products within the

microfinance category like Savings, micro-insurance, micro-pensions, remittances, micro-housing loans etc.

The Asian Age, a National Newspaper, in a news report in 2008 says that the Indian Microfinance sector is expected to grow 10 times to reach Rs.25,000 crore in the next 4 years. Today this sector is estimated to be at Rs. 2,700 crore. A study conducted by Sadhan[8] also confirms that, going by the current trends the microfinance sector will have a Compound Annual Growth Rate (CAGR) of 76 per cent. In India, both bigger and smaller organizations are engaged into microfinance and that too, both in the government sector as well as non-governmental sector. National financial institutions like the Small Industries Development Bank of India (SIDBI), the National Bank for Agriculture and Rural Development (NABARD), as far as government agencies are concerned, are playing quite significant roles of big players in the field of micro credit. Some of the big names from the non-governmental sector in this field are PRADAN, ICECD, MYRADA, SEWA etc. who have been successful in implementing microfinance schemes to the benefit of the poor. One such organization which has been doing a lot in this area is Rastriya Grameen Vikash Nidhi (RGVN) headquartered in Guwahati. This was founded as autonomous, non-profit organization in April, 1990, to improve the quality of life of poor and underprivileged. RGVN has a separate scheme called Credit Policy Scheme (CPS) which is currently being implemented in many districts of Assam. This study would like to analyse the different schemes, their *modus operandi* of the implementation and their impact in the poverty alleviation.

Credit and Savings Programme of RGVN-CSP

RGVN is an indigenous development support organization to reach the poorest, especially in the remote and less developed regions like north-eastern and eastern India. Its prime operations in those areas where the mainstream approaches and institutions often fail to reach. It has started basically in Assam and Meghalaya in May 1995. The Small Industries Development Bank of India (SIDBI) enabled RGVN to launch the programe with a loan of Rs.100 lakh. To enhance its operations, RGVN-CSP was sanctioned further loan support from NABARD and National Minorities Development Finance Corporation (NMDFC).

The credit and savings programe of RGVN was initiated to provide credit and other financial services to the people who cannot access the formal sector. The main focus of CSP was to enhance the livelihood of poor women and empower them in the process. To improve the quality of life of the poor and otherwise underprivileged rural and urban people through social action is the so called mission of this group. This is done basically through the Joint Liability Groups (JLGs) and the Self-Help Groups (SHGs). One more model for implementation is there which is known as Entrepreneurship Development Programme (EDP) which is now modified as Entrepreneurship Development Loans (ENL).

Vision

- To enhance the livelihood of the underprivileged of the society who have little or no access to formal banking system.
- To inculcate the habit of thrift amongst the poor.
- Woman empowerment through income generating activities.

The operation of RGVN-CSP though started in 1995, but it took a long time for them to prove their credibility among the masses. So, the initial period of more than 10 years is usually said as the set up period by them. It was only after 2005, the RGVN-CSP geared up their services. This is basically operating in twelve districts of Assam. There are almost forty-three branches as on September 2008.There are eight area offices and they publish a magazine called *Sarathi* quarterly every year.

RGVN-CSP's Process of Intervention

The operation of this organization is done in the following manner:

1. Area Survey
2. Ensuring Potentiality
3. Communication Programme
4. Group Formation
5. Individual Clients
6. Training of Groups or Clients
7. Group Recognition Test
8. Financial Transaction
9. Credit Plus Services

Objective and Methodology

In order to study the market system, the first and foremost thing is to know the population pattern. An interaction with the Gaon Panchayat is made and also a study on the Non-Performing assets of the Banks is being performed. After that by using residue method the target client survey is done and also the competitors are analyzed.

- *Ensure Potentiality:* Thorough analyses of the competitors are done and the credit needs of the customers are also justified.
- *Communication Programes:* Public meeting in relation to Credit and Saving programes are done and also its modalities are discussed. This also discloses the clarifications related to the rate of interests.
- *Group Formation:* Any area has a unit manager who promotes the group allocated in that area. In an SHG initially group meetings are held in 3 months and then each member is asked to contribute minimum of Rs.10. The money accumulated is then distributed inside the

group at a rate of interest decided by them. This reveals the credibility of the group. Loaning starts only after the group attains maturity. This is not so in case of JLG. Here the loaning starts only after the group is formed.

- *Individual Clients*: In case of individual entrepreneurs loaning starts after the completion of one to three cycles of loan in either SHG or JLG mode. Such kind of product is a market driven one. May group borrowers also ask for such loans? It has less transaction cost.
- *Training of Group or Clients*: Training is given on group functions and management, book-keeping and leadership, credit discipline. The entrepreneurs are motivated for the development and also training is provided for financial and risk management.
- *Group Recognition Test (GRT):* A GRT is given to test the effectiveness and strength of the group. There are some specified parameters to measure the group strength.
- *Financial Transaction*: After all these the loan disbursement process starts. The rate of interest charged changes over time-to-time depending on the economic situation prevailing.
- *Credit plus Services*: The basic credit plus services deals with training and micro insurance services.

With the objective of Providing "Food", "Cloth" and "Shelter", the RGVN-CSP tries to minimize the exploitation of money lenders through proper canalization of the loans to them. These loans create opportunities for self-employment. The main sources of fund for the organization are NABARD, IDBI, SIDBI, SBI, FWWB, ICICI, DCDL, NEDFi, etc. Among all these SIDBI gives grant. The rest provide loans. NABARD gives grant for SHGs. The monitoring of the loans disbursed is mainly done by the Branch Head or the so called unit Head. There are two to five credit officers in a Unit and one general purpose staff. The credit officers make the proposal and submit it to the Branch Head. After doing the verification the branch head makes the model.

Various Delivery Modes

1. *Joint Liability Groups (JLG):* This is formed by five to six members comprising both men and women who have experience of handling funds previously. This is a credit group and savings is compulsory only after loaning. Since the group has no treasurer so each member is individually liable to each other. Loan size varies from Rs.3000 to Rs. 30000. The rate of interest charged is 10 per cent flat. Repayment is done on a weekly or monthly basis.
2. *Self-Help Groups (SHGs):* In this mode the, 10 to 20 members are there and all the members are women who have no knowledge of funds handling previously. Under this mode, savings is compulsory prior to lending. It is formed with the broader vision of sustaining even without outside credit and support. This group is headed by a leader and a treasurer. The loan size varies from Rs.4000 to Rs.15000 each member. Here also the interest is flat 10 per cent and administrative charge is 5 per cent maximum and the repayment is on weekly or monthly basis.
3. *Entrepreneurship Development Programe (EDP):* An SHG or JLG loanee member who has good credit record from last three months are those who have attained at certain level to absorb more credit. They must also show entrepreneurial ability by virtue of their work. This kind of loan varies from Rs.15000 to Rs.40000. The same amount of interest is charged here also.
4. *JLG Cluster Loan/ SHG Preliminary:* In this kind of mode the individuals who are earning a very low income in urban, rural and semi-urban groups are targeted. For example small vegetable sellers, fast food vendors, bangle

sellers, rickshaw pullers etc. The maximum loan amount approved is Rs.2000. Here the rate of interest the CSP charges is as low as 7 per cent per annum. Repayment time is same as above.

5. *Micro Enterprise Loan:* Here the target customer is different. They are the educated men and women who are unemployed showing entrepreneurial ability. The loan amount is higher that is from Rs.25000 to Rs.50000. Interest rate is same as JLG Cluster loan but administrative cost is 5 per cent in this case.

Table 9.1 : Operational Highlights

Particulars	*March'08*	*August'08*	*Percentage Growth*
No. of Districts Covered	10	13	30
No. of Active Groups	3227	11152	245.6
No. of Members	44279	74922	69.2
No. of Active Borrowers (individual)	24147	55309	129.1
Outstanding Portfolio (Rs. in Lakh)	1322.34	3031.23	129.2
Average Loan size on outstanding portfolio (in Rs.)	5476.20	5533.58	1.048
Total Number of Loans	85935	134245	56.22
Cumulative amount of Loan Disbursed (Rs. in lakh)	5721.07	11444.91	100
Average loan Size Disbursement Amount (in Rs.)	6657.43	8525.39	28.06
On Time Repayment percentage	96.73	95.47	-1.3
Portfolio at Risk (Defaulter for more than 60) percentage	4.00	2.98	-25.5
Operating Costs in percentage	9	7	-22.2

Source: Monthly Operations Report-RGVN-CSP, September, 2008.

Conclusion

Table 9.1 almost has a picture perfect illustrations that any Microfinance organizations would like to achieve. Except for a tiny negative growth in the "On-time Repayment Percentage," all other figures are positive. Especially, the reduction in Operating Cost and reduction in Risked Portfolio, the achievements are remarkable. The table also highlights the fact that the model adopted by RGVN-CSP has been a success in the achievement of the objectives that they have set for themselves, albeit at a smaller scale.

The total number of families to be benefiting from the RGVN-CSP's micro-savings and credit programme is around 75000 throughout 13 districts of Assam with a significant 69 per cent growth in the penetration on previous quarter. The more notable fact that the along with the penetration level the average loan disbursement amount is also increasing which is from Rs. 6657.43 in March 2008 to Rs. 8525.39 in August 2008, a growth of around 28 per cent.

However, to have a noticeable impact on overall poverty situations, the need of the hour is to expand and scale-up this process. RGVN-CSP model has been a fairly successful in this venture and as such others, both NGOs and government organizations working in this field do have a known path to walk down now!

Notes

1. ACCION International was founded in 1961 to address the desperate poverty in Latin America's cities. Begun as a student-run volunteer effort in the shantytowns of Caracas, Venezuela, ACCION today is one of the premier microfinance organizations in the world, with a network of lending partners that spans Latin America, Africa, Asia and the United States. Over the last four decades, ACCION has built a tradition of developing innovative solutions to poverty.
2. Muhammad Yunus (born 28 June, 1940) is a Bangladeshi banker and economist. He previously was a professor of economics and is famous for his successful application of micro credit — the extension of small loans. In 2006, Yunus and the bank were jointly awarded the Nobel Peace Prize, "for their efforts to create economic and social development from below."
3. A non-governmental organization (NGO) is a legally constituted organization created by private organizations or people with no participation or representation of any government. In the cases

in which NGOs are funded totally or partially by governments, the NGO maintains its non-governmental status in so far as it excludes government representatives from membership in the organization.

4. SHG is group of rural poor who have volunteered to organize themselves into a group for eradication of poverty of the members. They agree to save regularly and convert their savings into a Common Fund known as the Group corpus. The members of the group agree to use this common fund and such other funds that they may receive as a group through a common management.
5. NABARD is set up as an Apex Development Bank with a mandate for facilitating credit flow for promotion and development of agriculture, small-scale industries, cottage and village industries, handicrafts and other rural crafts. It also has the mandate to support all other allied economic activities in rural areas, promote integrated and sustainable rural development and secure prosperity of rural areas.
6. BASIX is a livelihood promotion institution established in 1996, working with over a million and a half customers, over 90 per cent being rural poor households and about 10 per cent urban slum dwellers. BASIX works in 15 states of India. BASIX mission is to promote a large number of sustainable livelihoods, including for the rural poor and women, through the provision of financial services and technical assistance in an integrated manner.
7. MACS — Mutually Aided Cooperative Societies: [Act No. 30 of 1995], An Act to provide for the voluntary formation of cooperative societies as accountable, competitive, self-reliant business enterprises, based on thrift, self-help and mutual aid and owned, managed and controlled by members for their economic and social betterment and for the matters connected therewith or incidental thereto.
8. It was founded as an Association of Community Development Finance Institutions by SEWA Bank, BASIX, Sadhan Foundation, FWWB, MYRADA, RGVN, SHARE and PRADAN in 1999.

References

http://en.wikipedia.org/wiki/Muhammad_Yunus,31/10/2008.

http://en.wikipedia.org/wiki/Non-governmental_organization, 31/10/2008.

http://www.basixindia.com,31/10/2008.
http://www.iimahd.ernet.in/~mssriram/jmf.pdf,31/10/2008.
http://www.nabard.org/introduction.asp,31/10/2008.
http://www.sa-dhan.net,31/10/2008.
http://www.tn.gov.in/dtp/shg.htm,31/10/2008.
http://www.un.org.in/iawg/icecd/section1.htm.

Robinson, Marguerite S. (1998): *'Microfinance: The Paradigm Shift from Credit Delivery to Sustainable Financial Intermediation'*, in Mwangi S Kimenyi, Robert C Wieland and J. D. Von Pischke (eds), Strategic Issues in Microfinance, Ashgate Publishing: Aldershot.

Sriram, M. S. (2001). 'Case study of SHARE Group', in S. Datta & M. S. Sriram, *Flow of Credit to Small and Marginal Farmers in India* (report submitted to the Ministry of Agriculture, Government of India). Ahmedabad: Indian Institute of Management.

Sriram, M.S & Rajesh S. Upadhyayula (2002): "The Transformation of the microfinance sector in India—Experiences, Options and Future", *Journal of Microfinance,* Vol. 6, no. 2.

Sriram M. S. (2007): IIM-Ahmedabad, Presentation in the NAC on Microfinance.

The Asian Age, Kolkata, Tuesday 20th May 2008.

Vinod Khosla and Vikram Gandhi (2006): "Scaling up Microfinance in India", *The Economic Times*, 15 June, 2006, TNN.

10 Indebtedness in Nagaland

A Cursory Look

Subhendu Dutta

Introduction

Indebtedness has crippled the rural economy today. Almost every state has been suffering from this evil and rural households have been trapped in the vicious circle of poverty due to mounting debt. In some States like Maharastra, Andhra Pradesh and Punjab, the intensity of rural indebtedness is quite high. It has constituted a serious threat to economic, social and political life of rural India. Generally, the cultivator is poor and debt burden makes him poorer; extreme poverty does not allow him to improve his economic condition. More so, this burden generally passes on from generation to generation in multiple processes. It is aptly said that 'A farmer is born in debt, lives in debt and dies in debt'.

Rural indebtedness refers to the debts or loans taken by the rural people in order to meet their consumption and non-consumption needs. Due to small and marginal holdings and due to the lack of subsidiary occupation, farmers in India are reeling under heavy debt burden. In fact, the main cause of rural indebtedness is poverty, which is quite high in the country. Fig. 10.1 shows how debt is generated for an average person or family.

The burden of debt is indeed a big one because the number groaning under debt is very large. The amount involved is large too. And the repayment capacity of the debtors does not correspond to the amount of debt as most of the debt goes into unproductive uses. However, borrowing for the purpose of

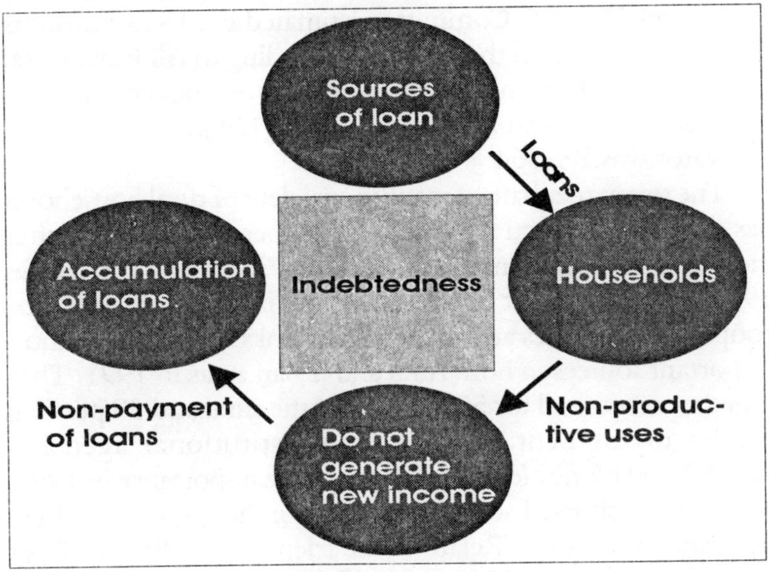

Fig. 10.1 : Cycle of Debt

agriculture is not to be discouraged. After the advent of technological breakthrough in agriculture, the need for capital has greatly increased to purchase various inputs. In fact, a loan for productive purposes is beneficial as it adds to the productivity of the land and income of the farmer. But, when this fund is diverted to unproductive channels, it becomes not only burdensome but a great cause of hardships and misery for rural households who are already fighting poverty.

Economically, increasing rural indebtedness has resulted in growing pauperization of the small and marginal farmers. The small farmers mortgage their landed property to the moneylenders and ultimately lose it to the latter. Then, they join the ranks of the landless labourers. In fact, rural indebtedness is the cause as well as the effect of the growing poverty of the Indian farmers.

The problem of rural indebtedness has been examined from time-to-time by various authorities, experts and committees, particularly with regard to the amount of indebtedness. In 1951, the National Income Committee estimated Rs. 1913.8 crore as the total rural debt in the country. According to All India Rural Credit Survey Committee, the quantum of outstanding debt per indebted cultivator was Rs. 526 and the average debt per cultivator was Rs. 364.

The rise in the share of institutional debt of rural households has slowed down and the share was 64 per cent in 1991, after increasing rapidly from 17 per cent in 1961 to 29 per cent in 1971 and 61 per cent in 1981. Among institutional agencies, cooperative societies and commercial banks were the two most important sources in both rural and urban areas in 1991. They together accounted for 55 per cent of the rural and 39 per cent of the urban debt. Among non-institutional agencies, professional money lenders were of prime importance in 1991, when they disbursed about 10 per cent of the aggregate debt in rural and urban areas. Relatives and friends had advanced 5 per cent of the rural and 10 per cent of the urban debt.

According to 'Indebtedness of Rural Households Debt and Investment Survey' (January-December 1992) NSS 48th round, out of the overall aggregate outstanding debt of Rs. 37,343 crore reported by the household sector, rural households accounted for roughly 60 per cent, *i.e.,* Rs. 22,211 crore. Cultivator households owed Rs.17,668 crores, which were about four-fifths of the outstanding debt of rural households. In 1991, over 23 per cent of rural households were found to be indebted. One out of every six rural households was indebted to institutional agencies. Only one out of 10 households was indebted to non-institutional agencies. A sharp rich-poor divide prevailed in rural areas with respect to the burden of debt. This burden was as high as 14 per cent for the poorest households *viz.* those owning assets less than Rs.5,000, but only 1 per cent for the richest, namely, those owning assets at least of Rs.2.5 lakh. Debt incurred just for household expenditure, other than those for expenditure on fixed capital, accounted for about third of the outstanding debt of households in both rural and urban areas in 1991. This share was even higher than – as high as 60 per cent — for the rural poor, who owned assets valued at less than Rs.10,000. Only about 11 per cent of the debt of such poor households was for productive purposes.

According to Rural Labour Enquiry Report on Indebtedness among rural labour households (55th round of NSS, 1999-2000), about 25 per cent of all classes of Rural Labour Households were reported to be under debt in the country. State-wise analysis of the report revealed that the incidence of indebtedness among all classes of Rural Labour Households was the highest in Dadar & Nagar Haveli (80.30 per cent) and the lowest in Nagaland (3.10 per cent). Andhra Pradesh, Assam, Gujarat, Haryana, Kerala, Punjab, Rajasthan, West Bengal, Jammu & Kashmir, Uttarakhand, Chandigarh, D & N Haveli, Daman & Diu and Lakshadweep reported the incidence of indebtedness higher than the national average of 25 per cent. The overall trend among the Agricultural Labour Households was almost similar to that of the Rural Labour Households. However, the incidence of indebtedness was marginally higher among the Agricultural Labour Households (25.10 per cent) than that among the Rural Labour Households (25.00 per cent) during 1999-2000.

At all-India level, the average debt per household and average debt per indebted household stood at Rs.1515 and Rs.6049 during 1999-2000 as against Rs.1113 and Rs.3169 respectively during 1993-94. While most of the states reported increase in average debt per household during 1999-2000 as compared to 1993-94, Assam, Orissa, Rajasthan, U.P. West Bengal, Nagaland, Tripura, and A & N Islands reported decline in average debt per household over the period. Andhra Pradesh, Gujarat, Haryana, Kerala, Maharashtra, Punjab, Rajasthan, Tamil Nadu, Mizoram, Uttarkhand, Chandigarh, Daman & Diu, and Lakshadweep reported average debt per household higher than the national average of Rs. 1515.

The main findings of the report on Indebtedness of farmer households of NSS 59th round (December, 2003) highlights that at all-India level, estimated number of rural households was 147.90 million, of whom 60.4 per cent were farmer households. Out of 89.35 million farmer households, 43.42 million (48.6 per cent) were reported to be indebted, *i.e.* having a liability in cash or kind with value Rs. 300 or more at the time of transaction. Estimated prevalence of indebtedness among farmer households was highest in Andhra Pradesh (82.0 per cent), followed by Tamil Nadu (74.5 per cent) and Punjab (65.4 per cent). Estimated number of indebted farmer households was highest in Uttar Pradesh (6.9 million), followed by Andhra Pradesh (4.9 million) and Maharashtra (3.6 million). Households with one hectare or less land accounted for 66 per cent of all farmer households. About 45 per cent of them were indebted. More than 50 per cent of indebted farmer households had taken loan for the purpose of capital or current expenditure in farm business. Such loans accounted for 584 rupees out of every 1000 rupees of outstanding loan. Marriages and ceremonies accounted for 111 rupees per 1000 rupees of outstanding loans of farmer households. Among the states the proportion was highest in Bihar (229 rupees per 1000 rupees), followed by Rajasthan (176 rupees per 1000 rupees). The most important source of loan in terms of percentage of outstanding loan amount was banks (36 per cent), followed by moneylenders (26 per cent). Average outstanding loan per farmer household was highest in the State of Punjab, followed by Kerala, Haryana, Andhra Pradesh and Tamil Nadu.

The important findings of various reports and committees bring out some important facts about rural indebtedness. It is evident that about 70 per cent of rural families in the country are indebted and incidence of debt among small farmers is heavier. Moreover, cultivators are more indebted than non-cultivators. Further, most of the debts are taken for short period and are of unproductive nature. It is also revealed that there is grip of private creditors and more particularly of the money-lender-*cum*-trader on the life of the rural people. The seriousness of the problem still exists and the rise in agricultural prices and planned development and its benefits have still not affected the majority of the peasants of the country, who continue to be in the grip of severe indebtedness.

Against this background, there arises a need to study and analyze the magnitude of rural indebtedness in the country. Analytical study of the subject will help in suggesting various measures to this end and assist in formulating relevant policies by the government, in an attempt at mitigating such debt.

Nagaland – A Breif Profile

Nagaland like other North-Eastern states is also suffering from slow rate of economic development. It is an agricultural state where about 16,35,815 persons live in rural areas out of total population of 19,88,636 (Census of India, 2001, Nagaland). Thus, 82.25 per cent of the population lives in rural Nagaland. The working population of the State is concentrated in the category of cultivators indicating that the economy is land based.

Rural people here mainly follow the primitive system of agriculture known as shifting cultivation. About 40 per cent of the total geographical area falls under shifting cultivation. Apart from shifting cultivation, the State also has irrigated terraces where rice is grown. Other important crops grown are maize, pulses, oilseeds, vegetables and sugarcane. Potato is gaining popularity in the State and it is grown in terraces. Horticulture is rapidly gaining the ground and is considered as one of the means of extending settled cultivation in the hill areas.

Poverty figures indicate that people are poor here. In 1999-2000, population living below poverty line was about 32.67 per cent, higher than the All-India average of 26.20 per cent. In rural areas, it was more pronounced at 40.04 per cent of total population. Rural households in the state are engaged in agriculture (including fishery, foresry and livestock) either as agricultural wage labourers or marginal farmers and self-employed. These are the most economically disadvantaged groups (weaker sections) in the state. It is assumed that households have also been burdened with indebtedness.

Like other north-eastern states, the rural credit scenario in Nagaland also shows a depressing picture. The credit-deposit ratio lags far behind the national ratio, which is an alarming situation. It was 43.4 in 1991-92, which sharply fell to 12.8 during 2001-02 and this was the lowest among the north-eastern states. The reasons for such low CD ratio in the NE states is due to lower level of utilization and misutilization of advances, improper identification of borrowers and lack of monitoring, poor recovery and writing off the bad debts by banks, etc. (Gogoi, 2004). The Commercial banks perhaps find it difficult to provide micro credit in the rural areas due to high cost of operation of banks and very high transaction cost for borrowers and the banks. One of the most crucial problems in the north east is the problem of recovery of agricultural credit that has become a constant source of anxiety for the financing institutions. As a result large chunk of banks' funds remain unloaded. The basic causes include weather conditions, drought and floods as well as the socio-political involvement in which the rural credit institutions function.

Methodology

The present paper is mainly based on the primary data collected during 2006-07 from four villages falling under Kohima district. Altogether, a random sample of 120 rural households belonging to various categories of cultivators was selected. Besides, rural households who are not agriculturists but engaged in non-farm occupations were also selected. Data were collected through scheduled questionnaire. Tabular analyses were carried out to derive meaningful conclusions. One of the major limitations of the study is that rural households provided data mainly by recollections and out of their memories. Most of the respondents were hesitant to provide information in regard to their income, loans, and utilization of the loans etc. However, most of the information have been obtained from the rural families by explaining them the usefulness of the study. Indebtedness was calculated on the basis of borrowed amount plus interest on the date of survey.

Review of Literature

Rural indebtedness is no longer a new area of research. A large number of studies have been carried out in India and abroad to look into problem of rural indebtedness. A brief review of a few selected studies is stated as under.

Darling (1930) examined the extent of indebtedness in Punjab. His study showed that if prosperity has increased in the State, so also the debt. It was seen that in 1873, 5 out of the 7 most heavily mortgaged districts of the province were amongst the most prosperous and wealthy. The main factor in the increase in debt in Punjab peasantry was the expansion of credit which followed the rise in the value of land. Lavish expenditure upon marriages was also found to be one of the important factors which increased debt. Further, falling prices, poor harvests, and a rapidly increasing population have all contributed to the cause of rising debt. The main reasons, therefore, for a Punjab peasant to borrow were – small size of holdings, constantly recurring losses of cattle from drought and disease, ingrained improvidence, extravagant expenditure upon marriage and other domestic ceremonies.

Singh and Mehrotra (1973) have made a comparative analysis of credit and indebtedness in rural Ballia district of Uttar Pradesh. It has been found that most of the highly indebted households belong to the landless labourers and the marginal farmers. He observed that the percentage of households in debt decreased with the size of holdings while the size of debt per household increased with it. Further, the village moneylenders were the main source of finance. The marginal and small farmers obtained about 80 per cent of their total borrowing from the institutional sources like the government and the cooperatives.

Mandal (1977) conducted a study of Kalipur village of Nadia district in West Bengal to analyze the nature of rural indebtedness and found that about 66 per cent families have taken loans from informal personal agency, about 11 per cent families from formal personal agency (businessmen) and remaining about 23 per cent families from government agency (BDO). The study revealed that the villagers are still under the clutches of the village moneylenders and 84.74 per cent of the total amount of loan is utilized for unproductive purposes.

Pratapaditya Datta (1989) conducted a study in one of the district in West Tripura to find out the nature and extent of the indebtedness of the farmers. It was revealed from the study that marginal farmers were more indebted than other categories of farmers. Farmers, in general, were more indebted to the non-institutional source (24.28 per cent of their total debt). It was found that farm size and indebtedness to non-institutional sources was negatively related. One of the purposes of loans for all types of farmers was found to be livestock purchase. Marginal farmers spent 25.02 per cent and 22.56 per cent of the loan in the home consumption and social obligation respectively. The study showed that about 61.29 per cent of marginal and 80 per cent of large farmers were defaulter on institutional sources.

Sukhpal Singh (1990-91) examined the extent and determinants of poverty and indebtedness among different weaker sections of rural Punjab. The study showed that 67.56 per cent of the weaker sections in rural Punjab were under debt and the amount of per indebted household came to Rs. 6019. The main reason for indebtedness, in general, was on account of borrowings from non-institutional sources, particularly moneylenders. The extent of outstanding loans was observed to be high in case of those weaker section households, which diverted the loans for use in marriage and social ceremonies and for construction of dwelling houses.

A. Lanunungsang Ao (1993) has made a study to project the problems and prospects of rural development relating to land, man and resources in Nagaland. He found that out of 150 households surveyed from 5 villages only 43.33 per cent were having saving accounts in banks. The main motive of opening bank accounts by the households was to avail loans. About 33.33 per cent of sample households had taken loans from the banks amounting to Rs. 185740. The purpose of loan taken was for development of their farms, purchase of animals, and paddy etc. However, loans had not been used for productive purpose. Most of the borrowers had used the money in contract work and also in log business. It was also found that 77.33 per cent were defaulters in case of loans. Most of the farmers used loans for purchasing items like electronic goods, furniture etc., merry making, rural politics, hiring of lawyers for cases of land disputes, children's education and festivals etc. Thus, it was found that loans had been used mostly for unproductive purposes.

Ramachandran and Swaminathan (2001) studied rural banking and credit policy in contemporary India and with the effect of the current policy of financial liberalization on the credit portfolios of rural workers. They examined, first, the major directions of rural banking and credit policy and indicators of performance of this activity in India since 1969. Secondly, they analyzed features of indebtedness of rural households, particularly rural worker households, in a south Indian village (Gokilapuram Village, Tamil Nadu). Thirdly, they attempted to evaluate the potential of a new policy alternative micro credit projects controlled by non-government organizations – as a solution for problems of rural indebtedness.

Main Findings

The survey of rural households in Kohima district revealed that out of 120 sample households investigated, 38 were found to be indebted. Thus, about 32 per cent of the rural households belonging to all categories were found to be indebted. About 50 per cent of large farmers were found to be indebted followed by agricultural labourers (40 per cent). About 42 per cent who are not cultivators were under debt. Average amount of debt per sample household was Rs. 12,450 whereas per indebted household, it was Rs. 39,318. Per capita debt of a sample household was Rs. 2,327 which for indebted household came to be Rs. 6,524. Percentage of indebted households by different categories in Kohima is shown in Fig. 10.2

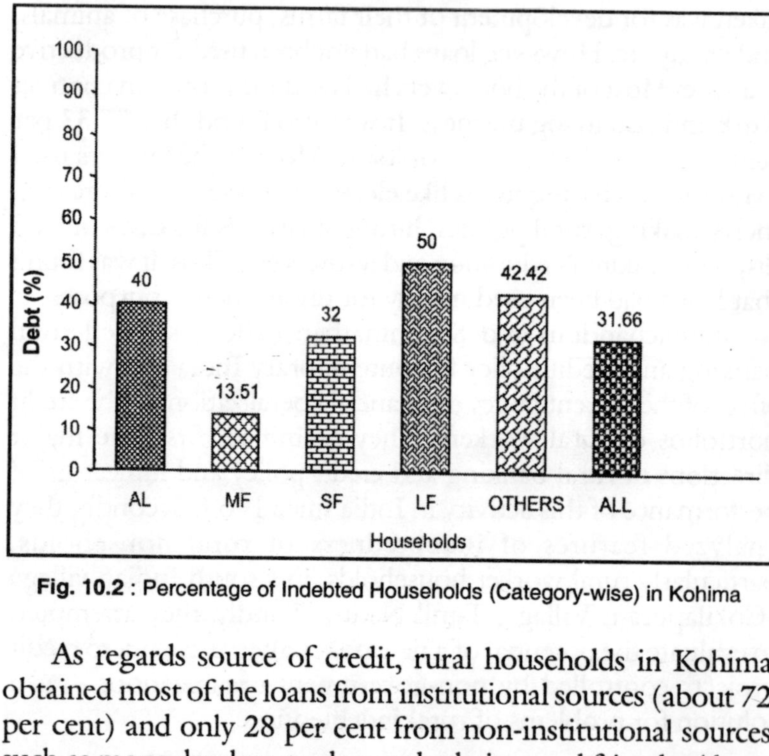

Fig. 10.2 : Percentage of Indebted Households (Category-wise) in Kohima

As regards source of credit, rural households in Kohima obtained most of the loans from institutional sources (about 72 per cent) and only 28 per cent from non-institutional sources such as moneylenders, traders and relatives and friends. About 17 per cent of non-institutional loans have been obtained from relatives and friends and only 1.3 per cent from moneylenders. This shows that the situation of Nagaland as compared to other states is better because in other states moneylenders rule the roost. It was found people in the state help each other in crises and financial need is met by taking loans for a short period from relatives and friends. The study revealed that agricultural labourers obtained 100 per cent of loans from non-institutional sources. In most cases, it was found that agricultural labourers are non-locals who take loans either from their landlord or relatives and friends. Banks generally do not provide loans to this class owing to their inability of pledging any security. Moreover, they are the most illiterate section of the rural society and as such have little knowledge about credit facilities available from banks and other institutional sources. About 70 per cent of total credit obtained by non-farm category households was from commercial banks. This section of the rural society is relatively educated and has better financial standing that helps them to get loans from commercial banks easily and quickly. Figure10.3 below depicts indebtedness according to source of credit in Kohima.

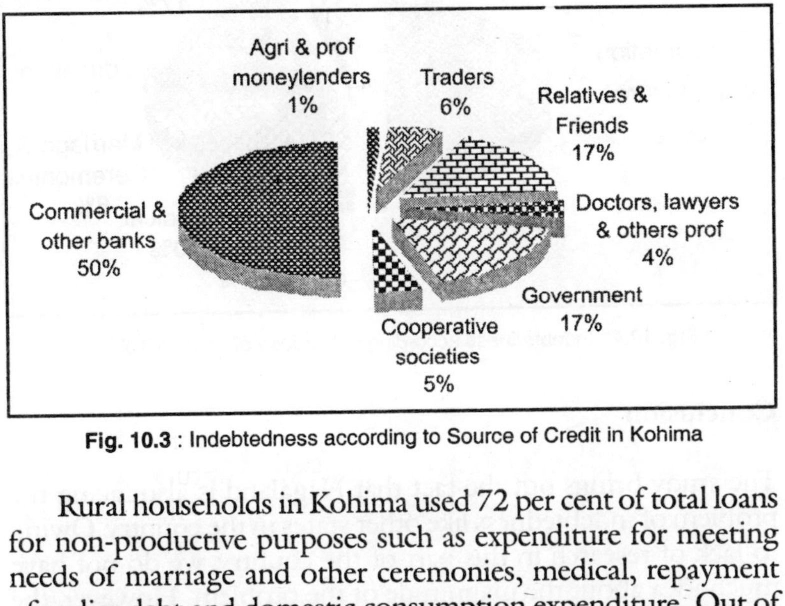

Fig. 10.3 : Indebtedness according to Source of Credit in Kohima

Rural households in Kohima used 72 per cent of total loans for non-productive purposes such as expenditure for meeting needs of marriage and other ceremonies, medical, repayment of earlier debt and domestic consumption expenditure. Out of this, about 50 per cent of loan was used for domestic consumption expenditure alone. This is not a good indication as the bulk of the credit is going towards unproductive purpose, thereby accumulating the debt in multiple proportions. The percentage used for the purpose of repaying of earlier debt was very less at about 7 per cent. Loan amount that went for productive purpose was only 28 per cent. Of this, about 17 per cent was utilized for non-farm business and only 3.4 per cent for agricultural development. About 7.4 per cent of productive loan was used for the purpose of education. This is a good trend as it would help raise literacy level which in the long run would build efficient human capital, which ultimately means higher productivity and production and hence higher rural income. In Fig. 10.4, indebtedness according to purpose of loan is shown.

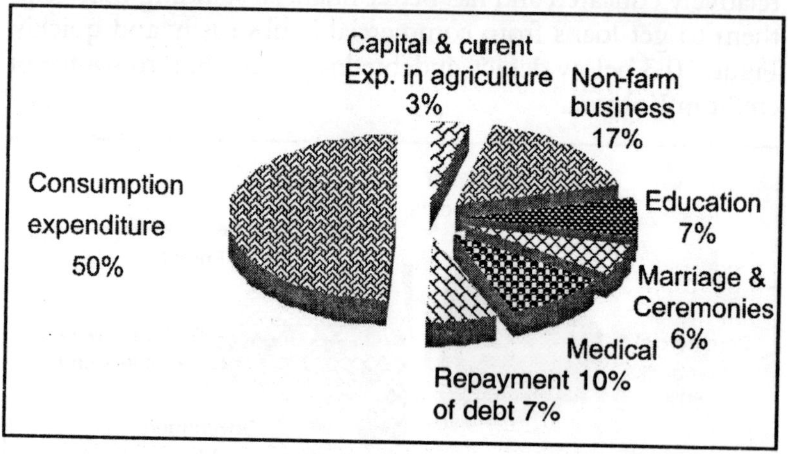

Fig. 10.4 : Indebtedness according to Purpose of Loan in Kohima

Conclusion

The study brings out the fact that Nagaland is also facing the problem of indebtedness like other states in the country. Owing to lack of research in this part of the country, we do not have much idea about the magnitude of the problem. However, the study reveals that people here are poor and living under debt. Shifting cultivation is a primitive method of agriculture and productivity in it by no means is comparable with settled cultivation. Rural credit delivery is not adequate and not used for productive purpose. Most of the loans are being used for domestic expenditure and purchasing electronic items, merry making etc. Repayment culture is yet to be developed in the

State. Non-repayment of loans has made commercial banks hesitant to lend credit to rural households. NEPED's intervention in the rural economy is changing life of rural people. Their Micro credit initiative that began in 2001-06 is helping farmers in transition to market economy. People are more receptive to new technologies and are now accessing banking systems. This would ultimately help upliftment of the living standard of the farm families. However, all depends upon the productive use and proper management of credit available to the households.

References

Gogoi, Jayanta Kumar (2004). Rural Credit Scenario in North East India, *Kurukshetra*, February, p.39.

Sivaloganathan (2004). Problems in the Recovery of Rural Credit, *Kurukshetra*, February, p.36.

Mandal, P.K. (1977). Nature of Rural Indebtedness, *Kurukshetra*, June.

Singh, Sukhpal (1996). *Dynamics of Rural Poverty*, (1st Edition) Anmol Publications, New Delhi. p.16

Ramachandran, V. K. and Swaminathan, Madhura (2000). *Does Informal Credit Provide Security*? International Labour Office, Geneva, October.

Pratapaditya Datta (1993). Agricultural Indebtedness and Sources of Finance – A Study in West Tripura District in *Agricultural Development in NE India – Constraints and Prospects*, (Ed.) by K. Alam, Deep and Deep Publications, New Delhi, pp.306-320.

Darling, M. (1977). *The Punjab Peasant in Prosperity and Debt*, Manohar, New Delhi.

Ao A Lanunungsang (1993). *Rural Development in Nagaland*, Har Anand Publications, New Delhi.

Adding Value to Shifting Cultivation in Nagaland (2007). *Nagaland Environmental Protection and Economic Development*, International Development Research Centre, New Delhi, February.

11 Infrastructure Facilities and Economic Development in Nagaland

Pranab Baishya and P. K. Deka

Introduction

Infrastructure development is a fundamental prerequisite for realizing the vision of progress towards peace and prosperity, and for creating an investment climate and market development in the North East. Expansion in the supply of basic infrastructure such as an efficient transportation network, telecommunications and power, etc. is extremely important for the development of the region. Apart from delivering essential services that improve the quality of life and livelihoods, these elements of the infrastructure are crucial for establishing a stable and peaceful society and hence for the progress and prosperity of the region.

The State of Nagaland was formally inaugurated on December 1, 1963, as the 16th State of the Indian Union. It is bounded by Assam in the North and West, by Myanmar and Arunachal Pradesh in the East and Manipur in the South and runs more or less parallel to the left bank of the Brahmaputra. It has a land area of 16579 sq. km. and is a predominantly hilly state. Nature has given the State abundant resources which are not exploited properly due to geographical locations, inadequate infrastructure facilities in the State. The population of Nagaland increased from 12.10 lakh in 1991 to 19.90 lakh in 2001. It has experienced the highest decadal growth of population in the country during 1991-2001 at 64.46 per cent as compared to the all-India growth rate of 21.34 per cent during the same period. The population density of Nagaland has increased from 73 persons per sq. km to 120 persons per sq. km. The sex ratio is 909 in 2001 as against 886 in 1991. Nagaland's Gross State Domestic Product for 2004 is estimated at $1.4 billion at current prices.

From a policy perspective, there is now a widespread consensus that contribution and productivity of Public Sector Units in the State is not significant due to the inadequate infrastructures. At the same time, a pure reliance on private production in an unregulated market is not likely to produce sound outcomes. Government has been actively engaged in finding the appropriate policy framework, which gives the private sector adequate confidence and incentives to invest on a massive scale, but simultaneously preserves adequate checks and balances through transparency, competition and regulations. Therefore, any study on regional development such as ours must make it a point to examine the existing status of infrastructure of the region in question with a primary object of suggested lines of development in the future.

As we have stated that the level of economic development of the State is still at infant stage and State's economy has remained backward in terms of all indicators of development. Lack of proper infrastructures and several man-made obstacles have hindered the development of the State's economy. Therefore, among the several constituents of the infrastructure of the economy of the State, we propose to discuss here the existing scenario of infrastructure facilities like transport and communication, power supply, financing and credit institution and facilities of education and public health. The present study tries to examine the following objectives:

- To examine the existing scenario of infrastructure facilities in Nagaland.
- To highlight the importance of infrastructure in the development of the State's economy.
- To make a comparative study of infrastructure facilities in Nagaland with neighbouring State of NER.
- To suggest measures for the development of infrastructure facilities of the State of Nagaland.

The prosperity of the State entirely depends upon the development of both agriculture and industrial production. However, both the sector needs the support of power, transport and communication facilities, credit and finances, machinery and equipment and also efficient manpower management, marketing facilities. All these services and facilities constitute collectively the infrastructure of an economy and the expansion and development of these services are essentially prerequisite for the increase in the production of the both sectors. In the words of Dr. V. K. R. V. Rao, "The link between infrastructure and development is not at once for all affairs. It is a continuous process; and progress in development has to be proceeded, accompanied and followed by progress in infrastructure, if we are to fulfil our declared objectives of a self-accelerating process of economic development." The following details of infrastructure facilities will give us a crystal clear picture of the present status of the State of Nagaland.

Transport and Communication

Roads are the only means of transport in the State, though having railed and air connectivity. The length of National Highway in the State is 471.17 km and the State Highway is over 1050 km. All the major towns are now connected by all weather roads. Efforts will be made to convert the roads leading to all industrial zones, industrial estates, Growth Centre, EPIP, etc. to sustain heavy vehicular traffic for transportation of raw materials and finished products. The present position of Road transport connectivity of Nagaland can be represented with the help of Table 11.1.

The railway network in the State is minimal. The length of broad gauge lines is 7.63 km, while that of the metre gauge lines is only 5.22 km and the total railway route length in Nagaland is only 12.85 km, whereas it is 2392 km in Assam and 62809 km in all India. Now, it is very clear that the cheapest mode of transportation (railway) can be considered as almost

Table 11.1 : Scenario of Road Transport

NH-61	**Traffic Volume (No/Day)-2000**	
Major Route	***District Served***	***Town Touched***
Kohima-Wokha-Mokokchung-Amguri	Kohima, Wokha, Zunheboto, Mokokchung	Kohima, Tseminyu, Wokha, Mokokchung, Changtongya, Tuli
NH-39	**Traffic Volume (No/Day)-10000**	
Major Route	***District Served***	***Town Touched***
Dimapur-Imphal Road	Dimapur, Kohima	Dimapur, Chiimukedima, Medziphema, Kohima
NH-39	**Traffic Volume (No/Day)-10000**	
Major Route	***District Served***	***Town Touched***
Army Byepass Near Zubza	Dimapur, Kohima	Dimapur, Chiimukedima, Medziphema, Kohima
NH-36	**Traffic Volume (No/Day)-12000**	
Major Route	***District Served***	***Town Touched***
Dimapur-Diphu Road (Assam Border)	Dimapur	Dimapur

State Roadway Length (km 1032.5)

Route	*Traffic Volume (No/Day)*	*District Served*	*Places Touched*
Chakabama-Mokokchung *Via* Chazuba Zunheboto	250	Kohima, Mokokchung, Zunheboto	Chakabama, Mokokchung, Chazuba, Zunheboto
Kohima-Meluri Road	300	Kohima, Phek	Kohima, Chakabama, Pfutsero, Chizami, Meluri
Mokokchung-Mariani Road	600	Mokokchung	Mokokchung, Khensa, Chungtia, Changki
Mokokchung-Tuensang Road	450	Mokokchung, Tuensang	Mokokchung, Chare, Longkhin, Tuensang
Namtola-Mon Road	500	Mon	Tizit, Mon
Tuensang-Mon-Naginimora Road	350	Tuensang, Mon	Tuensang, Tobu, Abei, Mon, Wakching, Naginimora

Source: Compiled from different years, Statistical Handbook, Govt. of Nagaland.

nil in the State. The only airport in the State is at Dimapur, which is also not convenient for the poor people and not having convenient flight service. Coming to National Highway, the density of national highways is higher in Assam and more have been added in recent years and road transport has been handicapped by inadequate development and poor maintenance. All-weather roads linking the scattered villages are a prerequisite for development of potential areas. This holds true for agriculture, social, industrial, entrepreneurial and mineral development. As many villages are still not covered by all weather roads, the villagers have been deprived of proper socio-economic development in education, primary health care, and ready access of farmers' products to the market.

Inadequate transport facilities in the State as well as its linkage with the rest of the country are revealed by the above fact that the only rail route in the State is of 12.85 kms. And the only airport is located in Dimapur for nothing. Recently central government sanctioned a project to link Dimapur with Zubza (near Kohima) which is in progress. The only retarding factor in the development and expansion of railway is of its hilly terrain. Therefore, it is becoming urgent need to link the entire State with roads.

The State has shown a steady growth in respect of postal service facilities. In 1987 there were only 255 post offices which have increased to 328 in 2005, out of which, rural area accounts for 92.68 per cent. In terms of per capita availability, one post office serves 3788 population in the State against 5462 of all India average. As special distribution of post office in Nagaland is concerned, 51.24 sq. km is served by one post office against 21.26 sq. km of all India average in 2000.

All the district headquarters are now well connected with 60 telephone exchanges as on March 2004 and the Tele Communication Department is in the process of expanding its network to cover all the recognized villages in the State, 1059 villages already connected during 2003-04. The State Government is also planning to set up Community Information

Centre in Block Headquarters and also open more new Telephone exchanges in backward area for training data base and application oriented end use. Internet facilities are available in Dimapur and Kohima. Lying of optical fibre cable to enable Video conferencing facility is available at Kohima and is expected to be commissioned soon at Dimapur. The three towns of Kohima, Dimapur, and Mokokchung have more than 50 per cent of these facilities. Whereas the telephone density is very low and the quality of services is still poor, especially in the other towns and in the rural areas. The rural coverage in districts other than Kohima and Dimapur is minimal or non-existent. Though Internet usage is growing, at present it is largely confined to the district headquarters and mainly in Kohima and Dimapur. Roughly there are hardly about 40 Internet cafes in the State. In an important project, the Government of India, in collaboration with the State Government, has set up community information centres (CICs) in all 52 blocks of the State. These centres provide Internet connectivity through V-Set at the block level.

Power

Power increases the productive capacity of the economy by several times. There is an acute power shortage in the State of Nagaland. The present peak demand of power in the State is only 79 MW and energy requirement is 264MU but the availability is 254MU as on 31-12-2006 with total deficiency of 10.0 the MU. With commissioning of more 132/66KV substations in Wokha and Tizit during the 2000, augmentation and System improvement in the peak demand is expected to reach 80 MW. Even after commissioning of the 75 MW Doyang HEP, 24 MW Likhimro HEP and 24 MW Thermal Power Station, the State will still be in shortage of power. Therefore, there is tremendous scope of investment opportunities in the Power sector. Nagaland has potential of more than 2000MW in hydel power generation. Despite the vast potential, the power generated within the State is quite insignificant. According to the Annual Administrative Report of the department of power, the total power generation was 3.21(MU) and the total purchase was 230 (MU) in 2000-01. Thus the State could generate only 1.39 per cent of the total power requirements. The State mainly purchases power from NEEPCO, NHPC and PGCI. The demand forecast says that the peak demand (MW) requirements as on 2011-12 will be 152MW and energy of 698MU.

Table 11.2 : Power Scenario of the State

As on 31.12.06	*Hydro*	*Thermal*	*Renewable*	*Total*
In MW	78.5	21.0	3.2	102.7

Source: Statistical Handbook, Govt. of Nagaland.

The bulk of the power in Nagaland is purchased from the North-Eastern Grid, which is expected to be power surplus, with large hydel projects coming on-stream in other states. The total existing installed State generation capacity is 29 MW, all based on hydropower. Current mean availability from this is about 90MU (2002 onwards). Under the central sector there is an operational 75 MW hydel plant, from which the State receives a share of 12 per cent of the generated power. The 24 MW Likimro Hydro Electric Project has been commissioned and a few minihydro projects are under construction, which will add about 3 MW to the existing generation. A thermal power plant is planned to be set up at Dimapur within the next two years.

Power generation, transmission and distribution are managed by the Nagaland Department of Power (DoP). The DoP's current financial situation is dire with a revenue collection of Rs. 19 crore against a power purchase bill of Rs. 36 crore (2001). The State suffers from high transmission and distribution (T&D) losses, estimated at 58 per cent. Due to old and overloaded T&D infrastructure, technical losses form a significant fraction. In this regard, it may be mentioned that the State Power Department does not have the facility to undertake an audit of power transmission or distribution. Consequently, no detailed projection or analysis of segment-wise demand is available in the State. However, an investment projection of Rs. 4,500 crore (US$ 900 million) has been made to raise the generating capacity of the State to 450 MW, based on a notional per capita consumption target of 1,000 units. The per capita electricity supplied is a mere 116 kWh/person/year in Assam. This is only one-fourth of the all India per capita generation of 479 kWh and one hundredth of per capita consumption in the United States which exceeds 12000 kWh. The gap is also large and is so in spite of large resources in Assam and the North-East.

Credit and Financial Institutions

Money is the life blood of economic development and the degree of monetization of an economy is a direct indication of the level of development attained by it. Now a principal test of the degree of monetization of the economy of a country or a region is the structure and the efficiency of the Financial and Credit institutions operating therein. At the National as well as State level, there are large number of financial institutions provide a variety of financial services for the promotion of infrastructure facilities which contribute to develop large, medium and small scale industries.

The State has a reasonable banking network. All the major banks have branches in Dimapur and Kohima, while other districts are served by the SBI and other State level banks. In order to provide adequate credit linkage to the industrial sector, the Nagaland Industrial Development Corporation Ltd. (NIDC) which is also acting as SFC shall be strengthened to cater to the needs of the entrepreneurs in the services of IDBI, SIDBI, NEDFi, NMDFC, NSDFC and commercial banks for channeling credit for industrial development of the State. In Nagaland, as on March 31, 2004 the number of scheduled commercial bank branches in Nagaland was 69 down from 70 as on March 31, 2000. The bank deposits were Rs. 1223 crore and bank credit was Rs. 206 crore. On March 31, 2004, as compared to the national average of 58.72 per cent the credit deposit ratio in Nagaland was as low as 16.84 per cent. The Financial institutions operating in Nagaland are NEDFi, IDBI, SIDBI and NABARD. Till March 31, 2005, NEDFi sanctioned a total of Rs. 1237 lakh to various projects located in Nagaland.

Table 11.3 : Branches of Scheduled Commercial Banks

Scheduled Commercial Banks	*2000*	*2001*	*2002*	*2003*	*2004*
Bank Branches	70	69	70	69	69
Bank Credit	118	124	132	161	206
Bank Deposit	770	890	1052	1231	1223
Credit Deposit Ratio	15.34	13.92	12.55	13.08	16.84

Source: Statistical Handbook, Govt. of Nagaland.

Table 11.3 reveals that the credit deposit ratio of Nagaland in 2004 stood at 16.84 crore compared to this the credit deposit ratio of the North East as a whole stood at Rs. 29.35 crore. On a low deposit base, this indicates a near absence of credit facilities for local business and enterprises. From the bankers' perspective credit recovery is an area of concern. In this concern, one of the first initiatives, taken by the Government, has been the enacting of a legislation to relax the transfer of land in the industrial zone at Dimapur. The possibility of involving village councils to help in credit recovery is being explored.

The industrial base of Nagaland can be considered to be still in a rudimentary stage and it would, therefore, be appropriate to promote such industrial projects, which have better chances of success. Due to the agrarian nature of the state's economy, potential for developing agro-based industries should be exploited on priority basis. In terms of natural resources, forest and mineral-based industries would deserve similar priority. It would, therefore, be necessary to set up industries based on raw materials from outside the state to cater to demand for particular products both inside Nagaland and other markets. In general, such activities could relate to high value-added and low volume items such as electronics. However, while selecting such projects, their comparative success prospects with respect to project viability and extent of benefits to local people would need to be examined carefully.

The following industrial infrastructures are available for setting up industrial units in the State. They are: Old Industrial Estate and New Industrial Estate at Dimapur and Infrastructure projects at the final stage of completion.

- Mini Industrial Estate at Tizit (Mon) and Kiphire (Tuensang).
- Growth Centres under 'No-Industry District' at Longleng and Noklak (Tuensang).
- Growth Centres under DIC schemes at Chuchuyimlang (Mokokchung), Baghty (Wokah) and Saring (Mokokchung).

Projects under implementation and expected to be ready for use by 2001-02 are:

1. Industrial Growth Centre, Ganesh Nagar, Dimapur (Under PM's new initiative).
2. Export Promotion Industrial Park (EPIP), Ganeshnagar, Dimapur.

The following areas in the State have been identified as Industrial Zones where industrial units set up will be eligible for the package of incentives provided under the industrial policy:

- Bhandari Subdivision
- Dimapur Subdivision
- Ghathashi area
- Industrial Growth Centre, Longleng

- Industrial Growth Centre, Noklak
- Mini Industrial Growth Centre, Viswema
- New Industrial Growth Centre, Ganeshnagar
- Tizit Subdivision
- Wazeho Area
- Tuli area
- Kiphire Subdivision
- Longnak/Longtho area

Besides the above, the Government will endeavour to notify some other similar zones in other potential areas such as Naginimara-Tiru and Jalukie valley for a balanced industrial development of the State. The Government will also set up IID Centres, Food Parks, IT Parks and chain of Cold storages, etc. in the State to provide all necessary industrial infrastructures to facilitate prospective investors/entrepreneurs to set up industries in the State. The all small and medium scale industries in the State which started operation, almost all are now out of order in respect to production. The Government of Nagaland with a view to develop industrial sector had set up a few medium scale industries (Dimapur Sugar Mill, Paper and Pulp Industry at Tuli, Ply Wood Factory at Tizit, Mini Cement Plant at Wazeho, Phek, Fruit and Vegetable Processing unit at Dimapur) but almost all these units have ceased to operate and caused a heavy loss. The basic reason for industrial backwardness of the State is the inadequacy of infrastructure. There is a need to pay attention to the development of industries in the large and medium sector by concentrating on the development of infrastructure of need.

Educational Infrastructure

Education plays a distinct role in the economic development of a backward region and provides adequate quantum of Manpower. In the State of Nagaland, the growth of general education especially with primary level has been phenomenal. In Nagaland, the primary stage of education is from class1 to 4 and upper primary stage is class 5-8. The secondary education stage is from class 9 to 10. Per capita expenditure on education is Rs. 1282.3 which is 14.55 per cent of the total budget expenditure of the State.

Table 11.4 : Number of Educational Institutions (Schools)

Year	*2001-02*			*2005-06*		
Types of Institutions	*Govt.*	*Private*	*Total*	*Govt.*	*Private*	*Total*
Primary	1309	190	1499	1311	190	1501
Middle	261	218	479	273	218	491
High	123	198	321	125	215	340
Higher Secondary	5	18	23	16	45	61
Total	1698	624	2322	1725	668	2393

From Table 11.4, it can be seen that the number of government sponsored primary schools has increased from 1309 during 2001-02 to 1311 during 2002-03 while the number of private primary schools has remained same at 190 during the same two periods. In case of government sponsored middle schools the number has gone up from 261 in 2001-02 to 273 in 2005-06. The number of privately sponsored middle schools has remained the same. In case of high schools, the number of government sponsored schools has increased from 123 to 125 and that of privately sponsored high schools has increased from 198 to 200 from 2001-02 to 2005-06. The number of government sponsored higher secondary schools has increased from 5 to 16 and that of privately sponsored higher secondary schools has also increased from 18 to 45 during the same year.

The total number of higher and technical educational institutions has increased from 56 to 57. These educational institutions include 1 university, 44 colleges of general education, 2 polytechnic schools, 3 law colleges and others. Apart from this number of institutions in the State, there is a burning need of more vocational and technical institutions of employment oriented course curriculum. Still in the State there is no engineering and management institutions. Looking at the present job market and unemployment situation in the State, it is felt that, if government will not take initiative to establish such institution, existing scenario will be more critical. There is need for at least one college each for medicine and engineering. At the moment, the Government of Nagaland nominates and sends students on stipend, annually, to various institutions in the country as per allotment of seats made by the Union Government. Other sectors like IT, biotechnology and environmental studies need to be built up, considering the inherent strengths of the State in these areas. The existing two government polytechnics (a third polytechnic is in the offing) need to be revitalised by inculcating the spirit and attitude towards work, introducing relevant trades, and by providing adequate support for physical facilities and equipment.

A knowledge-based economy would require, among other things, the following international quality telecommunication facilities; institutions for higher education, especially technical education; an open and democratic society, open to innovation; IPR protection and a financial sector that can fund high-risk projects. Nagaland has to invest a lot in each of these aspects. The quality and spread of the telecom infrastructure needs to be increased tremendously. Naga society has traditionally been a democratic society. However, it may need to become more open. The absence of a vibrant financial sector needs to be addressed urgently. Developed countries have made use of technology to improve the standards of living of their people. It has served them well as a tool for economic growth in two ways—it has enhanced efficiency in the production of goods and services and helped to bring out new and innovative products. In its march towards a developed Nagaland, the State will also need to use technology in a big way.

Health Status

Despite the challenges such as insurgency and conflict, the

indicators for health in Nagaland are impressive. The life expectancy at birth has been calculated at 73.4 years, way above the national average of 62.3 years, and much closer to the figures in developed countries. Infant mortality rate (IMR) at 42.2 per 1000 is also much better than the national average of 68 per 1000 live births. Similarly, under-five mortality rate, per 1000 live births, is 63.8 as against the national figure of 96. In terms of maternal mortality rate (MMR), the State's figure is less than 1 per 1000 live births, against the national average of 5.4, is much closer to the figures in developed countries at 6-8 range. However, the total fertility rate (TFR) of Nagaland, at 3.77, is a cause for concern. The last decadal growth rate (1991–2001) at 64.4 per cent, for instance, is the highest in the country, and 10-15 times higher than in developed countries. This poses a great demographic challenge for planners and policy makers in the State. As of March 31, 2000, over 60 per cent of the villages in Nagaland are still to be covered by any kind of basic health care such as dispensaries, etc. Based on population norms, as per 2001 Census, the State requires 25 CHCs, 100 PHCs and 666 sub-centres. Nagaland also requires improvements in secondary and tertiary health care. Specialised services are very limited and available only in Kohima, Mokokchung and Dimapur. The State has eight STD clinics, two TB hospitals, one mental hospital and DTCs for a population of 20 lakh. Most existing facilities are also ill-equipped and without access to modern diagnostic and therapeutic aids. There is only one CT scan machine in the whole State, at a private hospital. High-end investigations and immunology, as well as complicated cases of neurology, cardiology, cancer, etc., are all referred outside the State. This results not only in much inconvenience to the people but also tremendous financial losses to the State. Strengthening and streamlining the areas of strength of the communities, while at the same time, carrying out awareness and education programmes and building infrastructure are required. Nagaland has a rich tradition of herbal and ethno medicines with many indigenous medicine practitioners (IMPs). This is further bolstered by the presence of the State's rich biodiversity and availability of herbal plants. Official recognition and incentives could extend health care coverage to all.

Remedial Measures and Suggestions

The following remedial measures and suggestions can be considered for improvement of infrastructure facilities of the State, which can contribute to the sustainable economic development of the State of Nagaland.

1. The Government must provide funds for construction of roads in core areas. Toll free roads and express highways will have to be developed for strengthening the infrastructural base of the State.
2. Innovate to mobilise the large investments required for the infrastructure sector. Prepare a database of the available infrastructure and a comprehensive road map for building the infrastructure and plan public spending with a clear focus to execute this plan.
3. The State Government will have to actively promote foreign direct investment in the projects that involve and improve infrastructures like power, roads, social and health care facilities. Similarly, foreign direct investment shall be encouraged in manufacturing activities in thrust areas identified under this policy.
4. The caution to be exercised while embarking on the path of economic development is to ensure that the resources available are used efficiently and in a sustainable and planned manner for equitable economic growth within a reasonable time-frame.

   Some of the ***Suggestions*** to take the State on this path are given below.

1. Develop strategies to produce goods to take advantage of existing local markets and exploit the demand for indigenous products outside the State in order to reduce the trade gap, resource drain and to benefit from the income and livelihood opportunities thereof.

2. The limited prospects for expansion of Government activities necessitate the encouragement of private investment for accelerating economic growth in the State and also for creating employment opportunities.
3. The limited resources available with the State and the dependence on Central Government assistance limit the flexibility of the State to plan its own course of development. The State Government has to generate sufficient resources of its own in the near future.

Conclusion

To facilitate rapid and sustained economic development in the State through enhanced investment, an investor friendly environment, provision of infrastructure and institutional support, attractive incentive package and optimum utilization of existing resources in order to gainfully exploit emerging opportunities in the national and international markets and generate substantial income and employment avenues for the people of Nagaland. For which globally acclaimed condition necessary for is good governance system which is considered to be poor in the State. Nagaland is rich in natural resources, ideal for the growth of industries and therefore, there is imperative need for basic infrastructure on a more liberal scale so as to ensure smooth and sustainable development of the State.

The State should try earnestly to provide necessary infrastructure to facilitate the growth of industries and as a whole. The concept of Build-Operate-Transfer shall also be considered in identified areas of Power Generation, Road and Bridges, Warehousing and Industrial Infrastructure either in the Private Sector or Joint Venture with the State Government. Existing infrastructure shall be strengthened/upgraded to suit the ever increasing demands of the industrial sector.

References

NEDFI (2006) *Databank Quarterly,* January, Vol. 5, Issue I.

Government of Nagaland : *Statistical Hand Book* (2007) *of Nagaland*, Directorate of Economics and Statistics, Kohima.

——, *Statistical Handbook of Nagaland (2008)*, Directorate of Economics & Statistics, Kohima.

Government of India, *Economic Survey of India 2006-07,* Economic Division.

SECTION III

INSTITUTIONS, AGENCIES AND PERFORMANCE

12 Entrepreneurship in SMEs

A Study of Rural Manipur

Elangbam Nixon Singh

Introduction

"My son is now an 'entrepreneur'. That's what you're called when you don't have a job."
—Ted Turner, *Broadcasting Entrepreneur*

What is *Entrepreneurship*? Who are entrepreneurs? How are they different from non-entrepreneurs? Is entrepreneurship just another career option? Drawing from various research findings, people choose entrepreneurial careers because of the perceived greater economic and psychological rewards than regular employment. The definition of an entrepreneur has been evolved in last three centuries, from someone who bears risk by buying at a low price and selling at a higher price; to the creation of new enterprises of which the entrepreneur is the founder. Considerable effort has gone into understanding the psychological and sociological wellsprings of entrepreneurship; and some common characteristics like the need for achievement, locus of control, orientation towards intuitive rather than sensate thinking, and risk-taking propensity of entrepreneurs have been suggested. This begs the question: can these traits be generalized across countries and culture? In the current scenario, we have a broad spectrum of different countries with respect to the economic structure as well stage of economic status they are in. In India, small firms contribute considerably to economic growth and employ a very large number of people, second only to agriculture. The concentrations of these firms are mostly in the urban areas while rural areas have failed to seize the opportunities unleashed by economic reforms. Different models of rural entrepreneurship are being attempted by various government and private agencies to tap the potential of human sources as an engine of growth. However, little is known about the characteristics of rural entrepreneurs who take up entrepreneurship mostly because they do not have a better opportunity and only incidentally due to their interest. Empirical literature analyses the characteristics of entrepreneurs, which found direct relationships between the need for achievement, locus of control and risk taking propensity with success in most cases. Again, the entrepreneurial characteristics required to launch a business successfully are often not those required for its growth and even more frequently not those required to manage it once it grows to considerable size. In other words, the role of the entrepreneur needs to change with the business cycle as it develops and grows.

Rural Entrepreneurship and Economic Development

Indian economy is purely based on agriculture. Over 75 per cent of its population depend for their livelihood on agriculture. But the capacity of agriculture to absorb additional labour force is limited. According to 2001 Census, 43.37 per cent of the total secondary sector work force is in the rural secondary sector including household manufacturing and construction activities. Despite rural migration to towns and cities, rural unemployment remains a serious problem. A great deal of the rural workers, artisans, craftsmen, has to be, by necessity, self-employed. This is where rural entrepreneurship will have to play an important role in the economic development of a region.

In fact, entrepreneurship is effectively required for improving the economic condition of rural people, generate their income to lift the quality of life and above all, prevent migration to towns in search of income and employment.

In view of the facts mentioned above, there is an urgent need for developing rural industrialisation and entrepreneurial activities will have to promote rural industries.

Small and Medium Enterprises — Concept and Significance

The "Micro, Small & Medium Enterprises Development Act, 2006" which became operational from October 2, 2006, been changed the earlier concept of 'Industries' to 'Enterprises'. As per this Act, enterprises have been classified broadly into:

1. Enterprises engaged in the manufacture/production of goods pertaining to any industry; and
2. Enterprises engaged in providing/rendering of services. Manufacturing Enterprises have been defined in terms of investment in plant and machinery (excluding land and buildings) and further it has been classified into:

   (a) Micro Enterprises – investment up to Rs. 25 lakh;
   (b) Small Enterprises – investment above Rs. 25 lakh andupto Rs 5 crore;
   (c) Medium Enterprises – investment above Rs.5 crore and up to Rs. 10 crore.

The Service enterprises have been defined in terms of their investment in equipment (excluding land and buildings) and further classified into:

(a) Micro Enterprises – investment up to Rs. 10 lakh;
(b) Small Enterprises – investment above Rs. 10 lakh and up to Rs. 2 crore;
(c) Medium Enterprises – investment above Rs.2 crore and up to Rs. 5 crore.

It defines 'Medium Enterprises' to facilitate achievement of economies of scale. It provides statutory basis to purchase preference policy for goods and services provided by micro and small enterprises. It also strengthens the legal provisions to check delayed payments to micro and small enterprises. The Act provides statutory basis to the National Board for Micro, Small and Medium Enterprises. The cumbersome two-stage registration process of SSI has been substituted with an optional filing of memorandum by Micro, Small and Medium Enterprises. The Act aims at facilitating the promotion and development of small and medium enterprises in a competitive way. It seeks to empower the Central Government to notify programmes, guidelines or instructions for facilitating the promotion and growth of small and medium enterprises. One of its primary objectives is to make provisions for ensuring timely and smooth flow of credit to small and medium enterprises.

The most significant aspect of small industry development is that this sector has stimulated economic activity of a far reaching magnitude and has created a sense of confidence among a huge number of small entrepreneurs about their strength and validity. These industries meet the twin needs, *viz.*, solution of unemployment problem and checking the economic concentration in the hands of a few. They encourage self-sufficiency, self-reliance and co-ordination. Not only they are beneficial to re-location of available resources and their proper utilisation but also they help to eradicate poverty in the rural sector.

The SMEs (Small and Medium Enterprises) are the hub of many economic activities in a developing country like India. The role played by these industries in the economic activity of advanced industrialized countries is also very significant. The socio-economic transformation of India cannot be achieved without paying adequate attention to the development of this labour intensive and capital sparing sector. Since independence, these industries have made an all-round effort to boost the Indian economy. The traditional village and cottage industries provide a vital means of livelihood to village artisans. At the same time, these labour-intensive industries can play a crucial role in the equitable distribution of national income.

Industrial Scenario of Manipur

Manipur is an industrially backward State. Economic reforms have failed to revive the down trend in industrialization. Manipur has practically no large scale industry which can produce a commodity in a large scale. The few small scale industries that are functioning are also not functioning optimally due to lack of availability of resources and the appropriate environment. The share of manufacturing in real Net State Domestic Product (NSDP) declined from 4.16 per cent in 1980-81 to 3.37 per cent in 1995-96. The growth rate of this sector in the 1990s was insignificant. The share of the tertiary sector started dominating the economy without any significant relationship in the commodity producing sectors of the economy. Private sector employment constituted only 3 per cent of organized sector employment. It is worthwhile to mention here that unemployment level reached 5,84,830 persons in Manipur as on 30th April, 2007 (Employment Exchange, Imphal). It was 5, 83,653 persons as on 31st March, 2007. The rate of increase per month was 1,177 persons. Out of the total, 4,21,623 were male and 1,63,207 were female candidates searching for jobs. Eventhough International Monetary Fund (IMF) studies categorize this state with 23 lakh people (2001 census) as one of the fastest growing states in India, its per capita income has persistently fallen short of all India level.

Imphal East and Imphal West Districts — A Profile

The Imphal District is an offshoot of the then one district State of Manipur. Now, there are 9 (nine) Districts in Manipur, *i.e.*, 5 Hill Districts and 4 Valley Districts. The Imphal District has a total area of 1,201 sq. km.

The Imphal District was bifurcated into 2 (two) Districts as Imphal West and Imphal East Districts with effect from 18th June, 1997. The Imphal East District has 4 (four) Sub-Divisions, namely (i) Imphal East-I (Porompat), (ii) Imphal East-II (Sawombung), (iii) Keirao Bitra, and (iv) Jiribam Sub-Division and 5 (five) S.D.C. Circles. Likewise, the Imphal West District has 4 (four) Sub-Divisions, namely (1) Imphal West – I (Lamphelpat), (2) Imphal West–II (Wangoi), (3) Lamsang Sub-Division, and (4) Patsoi Sub-Division and 10 S.D.C.

Circles. Besides, Imphal East District have 3 (three) Community Development Blocks, viz., (i) Imphal East – I, (ii) Imphal West–II and (iii) Jiribam and Imphal West District have 2 (two) of the same, *viz.*, (1) Imphal West–I and (2) Imphal West–II for the implementation of development schemes.

Need of the Present Study

The development of the Indian economy has lead to a rise in unemployment mostly because of the mismatch between creations of employment and the addition to labour force. Therefore, expansion of avenues for industrial employment within rural areas is one of the major ways diversifying the rural economy. The rural non-farm sector has the potential to equalise the country side with the towns as well as the promise of becoming the most dynamic part of the economy.

In view of the above, the paper seeks to analyse the socio-economic origins of rural entrepreneurs of Imphal East and Imphal West Districts of Manipur.

Objectives of the Study

The specific objectives of the study are as follows:

1. To enquire into socio-economic origins of the rural entrepreneurship in SMEs in the Imphal East and Imphal West Districts of Manipur.
2. To analyse the problems and prospects of rural entreneurship in the said two districts.
3. To recommend some possible suggestions for the growth and development of rural entrepreneurship in Manipur.

Research Design

The sampled entrepreneurs are taken from registered small scale industries of rural areas of Imphal East and Imphal West districts of Manipur but those with 5 years' existence and particularly sick units have been completely ignored. The study was conducted in between August and October, 2005. It was also ensured to give representation to different types of industries. Altogether 36 and 28 units were randomly selected from Imphal East and Imphal West districts respectively, with a view to facilitate meaningful comparision among them.

The basic data for the study has been collected through field study using the following tools:

(i) Questionnaires.
(ii) Personal interviews with the sampled entrepreneurs.

Findings of the Study

The information collected from the field study were summarised as findings of the study as follows:

1. *Generation of Entrepreneurs*

It has been found that 51 out 64 sampled rural entrepreneurs (79.7 per cent) were first generation entrepreneurs, followed by 12 second generation (18.8 per cent) and 1 third generation entrepreneurs (1.6 per cent).

District-wise, first generation formed 93.8 per cent of all rural entrepreneurs in Imphal East and second generation 6.2 per cent whereas first generation constituted 65.6 per cent in Imphal West district followed by 32.8 per cent second generation and 1.6 per cent third generation rural entrepreneurs.

It can thus be concluded that majority of the first generation rural entrepreneurs are from Imphal East district while majority of the second generation and third generation are from Imphal West district.

2. *Age of Entrepreneurs*

The highest percentage of the rural entrepreneurs (45.3 per cent) entered into entrepreneurship at the age of 21-30 years. The average age of the entrepreneurs in this group worked out to be 25.48 years. Only 7.8 per cent of them entered at the age group of 51 years and above (average age 58.83 years).

3. *Earlier Occupation of Entrepreneurs*

Twenty of the total 64 sampled rural entrepreneurs (31.25 per cent) were having professional background related with the type of industry they have chosen. Fourteen (21.9) were found to be associated with some other business. Moreover, 4.7 per cent entrepreneurs (3 out of 64) and 15.6 per cent (10 out of 64) were employed in government service and agriculture respectively, prior to entering industry. It was 26.6 per cent (17 out of 64) who were either unemployed or students before starting their own units.

4. *Type of Industry Preferred*

Table 12.1 shows the types of industries preferred by the rural entrepreneurs covered by the study.

Table 12.1 : Type of Industries Chosen

Type of Industry	*Number of entrepreneurs*	*Percentage*
Food based	3	14.1
Metal based	10	15.6
Handloom and handicrafts	1	1.6
Plastic and Rubber based	7	10.9
Wood based	8	12.5
Printing and Stationery works	6	9.4
Automobile and Engineering works	19	29.7
Others (Arts, Perfumery, Detergents etc.)	4	6.3
Total Units	**64**	**100.00**

Source: Field Survey.

As can be observed from the above, the highest percentage of the rural entrepreneurs started automobiles and engineering units (29.7 per cent) followed by metal based units (15.6 per cent) and food based units (14.1 per cent).

5. Form of Organisation Chosen

It can be seen from Table 12.2 that private limited company and partnership form of organisation were preferred by the rural entrepreneurs in the ratio 1:3. As regards to sole proprietorship form of organisation, it was preferred by 81.3 per cent of the entrepreneurs selected for the study.

Table 12.2 : Form of Organisation Preferred

Type of Industry	*Number of Entrepreneurs*	*Percentage*
Private Ltd. Co.	3	4.7
Partnership	9	14.1
Sole Proprietorship	52	81.3
Total Units	64	100.00

Source: Field Survey.

Problems of Rural Entrepreneurs in Manipur

An attempt is made here to analyse the major problems faced by the rural entrepreneurs from time-to-time. The problems may be relating to raw-materials, marketing, power, labour, finance, technical and managerial assistance etc. Above all, unutilised capacity of a unit is an index of all its problems.

- *Under-utilization of Installed Capacity:* On enquiry, it is found that only 5 units, 2 from Imphal East district and 3 from Imphal West district, reported 100 per cent installed capacity utilisation. Including these 5 units, 45.3 (29 out of 64) per cent had unutilised capacity to the extent of less than 25 per cent. On the other hand, only 1.6 per cent (1 out of 64) had reported unutilised capacity of 75 per cent and above.

  On further enquiry as to the main cause of underutilisation of capacity, it has been found that power scarcity and slackness of demand of products are the main causes of it. Lack of raw-materials is also another reason for underutilisation of capacity.

- *Problems of Raw-Materials:* Sixteen of the 64 sampled units complained scarcity of raw-materials as number one problem. Another 15 units suffered from high prices as against 10 units whose number one problem is the problem of transport. It is encouraging to know that 23 units had no problems regarding raw-materials.
- *Problem of Marketing:* It can be noted that competition from small as well as large firms is number one problem for the majority of the units (23 out of 64). The number one problem is slackness in demand of products for another 10 units. Other problem like seasonal demand, lack of godown facilities etc. are faced by 15 units as against 16 units who have no marketing problems.
- *Problem of Power:* Uncertainty of power supply was suffered by 41 units out of 64 units as number one problem. It was the scarcity of power for 12 units. It is alarming that none of the units are free from power problems and as such they incurred high costs for running their units by generators.
- *Problem of Labour:* It is worth mentioning that only 27 entrepreneurs (42.2 per cent) complained about the problems of labour. Majority of them suffered from absenteeism of labour (31.3 per cent) followed by problem of training which was reported by 5 units (7.8 per cent).
- *Problem of Finance:* Fifty four out of 64 sampled rural entrepreneurs (84.4 per cent) faced problems relating to finance. Twentynine entrepreneurs had difficulty in mobilising the necessary working capital (45.3 per cent) as against 20 entrepreneurs who were in shortage of fixed capital (12.8 per cent). Other important problems include high rates of interest, red-tapism in government agencies etc.
- *Problems of Technical and Managerial Assistance:* Only 28 entrepreneurs faced problems relating to technical and managerial assistance. Ineffective consultancy services provided by the government agencies, lack of

skilled workforce and expensive consultancy services provided by private agencies were some of the important problems faced by the sampled entrepreneurs covered by the study.

Evaluation

After the socio-economic origins of thc sampled rural entrepreneurs and their major problems are analysed, next the attention is drawn towards its evaluation and suggestions.

(a) *Entry into Entrepreneurship*: The time and age at which the entry is made into entrepreneurship are the important factors to be examined.In the present study, it is found that 21-30 years is the most appropriate age group to start an industry.

(b) *Earlier Occupations of Rural Entrepreneurs:* It has been found that more than those employed in agriculture or government service, people with professional background were attracted towards industrial entrepreneurship. A sizeable number of entrepreneurs were unemployed or students prior to starting the industrial units. Thus, entrepreneurship is not confined to any particular occupation. What is required is the presence of entrepreneurial spirit and zeal.

(c) *Type of Industries Started:* Engineering and automobile units followed by metal based units are most commonly preferred by the rural entrepreneurs covered by the study.

(d) *Forms of Organisation Preferred*: Sole proprietorship is widely preferred in rural areas. But it does not mean that private limited companies and partnership firms are not common.

(e) *Problems of Entrepreneurs:* Under-utilization of capacity due to scarcity of power, scarcity of raw-materials, competition from small as well as large firms for marketing products, uncertainty of power supply, absenteeism of labour, shortage of working capital, and ineffective consultancy services provided by the government agencies were some of the major problems being faced by the entrepreneurs. These problems need to be properly attended and concerned authorities can play a meaningful role in this regard.

Suggestions

The government must provide efficient and effective consultancy services to the entrepreneurs. Some of the tips are listed below:

- Unhealthy competition among the small units as well as large units should be discouraged as far as marketing problems are concerned. The state government needs to be active in this regard. As a sign of encouragement to local entrepreneurs, government departments should procure products produced by these entrepreneurs.
- Raw-material banks needs to be opened up in Manipur as this state is infamous for long *bandhs*, strikes and economic blockades. Scarcity of raw-materials and its high prices as a result of it, the main problem is of raw-materials.
- Both the Central and State Governments should give wide publicity so as to reach the information to all the rural entrepreneurs about policies, incentives, schemes, programmes, etc., relating to small scale industries.
- As far as possible, in order to reduce the competition from the sectors, the small scale industrial units should operate in the areas reserved for them. Similarly, more number of items should be reserved for the exclusive production of the small scale sector.
- Law and Order problems needs to be tackled properly by the Government so that there will have a conducive atmosphere for the entrepreneurs to run their businesses without any hindrances.

- It is a common understanding that all who want bank loans are not necessarily genuine entrepreneurs or businessmen. There are some who want to get loan merely to divert it for non-productive purposes. It may not be difficult for banks to identify such persons. But while doing so, banks should not discourage genuine entrepreneurs.
- The commercial banks and financial agencies may establish more small scale industrial specialised branches at least one in every district headquarters to cater the financial needs of small entrepreneurs.
- Timely and adequate finance depending up to the operational cycle of the activity must be available to the entrepreneurs.
- Banks need to re-think about their loan giving policies to the entrepreneurs. Shortage of working capital is the main factor responsible for slow commencement of an industrial unit. So, proper handling of this problem is very important.
- The rural entrepreneurs should develop a proper industrial plan before starting a unit. Undertaking of feasibility study either by him or through outside agencies can be very helpful in this regard.
- The rural entrepreneurs should take proper training through the government and non-governmental agencies before starting a unit, this enables the entrepreneurs to protect their units from sickness.
- The rural entrepreneurs should employ latest techniques of production, skilled labour so as to improve the quality of the products and marketing.
- Urban background is not a pre-condition of industrial entrepreneurship.
- Previous experience or employment in the industry should form a basis for selecting the right type of industries.
- For starting an industry, the availability of enough

finance is the most important factor. Without it, the idea to start business or industry will always remain a simple wish.

- One should have some basic and essential managerial skills in the functional areas like finance, production and marketing for entering into industrial entrepreneurship.
- The small scale industrial units should maintain proper books of accounts. Statutory obligation should be imposed on the units to maintain and prepare their books of accounts by professional accountant.

Conclusion

It need not be repeated that rural entrepreneurs can play a decisive role in giving a qualitative and qantitative content to rural economy in particular and national economy in general. What is not forthcoming is the contribution of rural entrepreneurs. Provision of adequate credit, adequate supply of raw-materials, and marketing arrangements for products etc. should be taken up simultaneously.

The prevailing law and order problems in Manipur need to be properly tackled, otherwise it may send wrong signals to the prospective entrepreneurs who may risk their hard earned resource. Extortion by unlawful organisations adversely affects industrialisation. Industrialists cannot work with commando protection. Without the participation of local and rural entrepreneurs, a region cannot develop socially and economically.

References

Batra, G.S. and Daugal, R.C. (2000): *Entrepreneurship and Small Scale Industries* New Delhi, Deep & Deep Publication Pvt. Ltd.

Bhattacharya, S.N. (1986): *Development of Small Scale and Cottage Industries* New Delhi, Metropolitan Book Co.

Cashin, P. & R. Sahay (1996): "Regional Economic Growth and Convergence in India", *Finance and Development*, IMF, March.

Desai, Vasant (2000): *Small Scale Industries and Entrepreneuship*, Mumbai, Himalaya Publishing House.

Desai, Vasant (2002): *Dynamics of Entrpreneurial Development and Management* Mumbai, Himalaya Publishing House.

Gangadhara Rao, N. (1973): *Entrepreneurship and Growth of Enterprise in Industrial Estates*, New Delhi, Deep & Deep Publications.

Government of Manipur (2003): *Manipur Today,* Directorate of Information and Public Relation (DIPR).

Khanka, S.S. (2002): *Entrepreneurial Development*, New Delhi, S. Chand & Company Ltd.

Mali, D.D. and Bundopadhyay, R. (1993): *Small Industry Development in North East India: Status and Strategy*, New Delhi, Omsons Publications.

13 Small-Scale Industries
A Boon of Economic Development

L. Rome Singh

Introduction

Small-scale industries have been deemed as one of the most important powers for providing better economic opportunities for the people of developing countries, like India. Small-scale industries are grouped under the general heading of village and small industries (VSI), cover a wide variety of activities. The sector is split up into eight sub-sectors, namely, *khadi*, village industries, handlooms, sericulture, handicrafts, coir, small-scale industries and power looms. Of these, the first six sub-sectors contribute traditional industries and the last two, the modern small-scale industries. Power looms are considered as Modern Small Scale Industries, which use modern technologies and are mostly rural and semi-urban in character.

The small sector is again identified in terms of fixed capital investment. All industrial units with a capital investment (on plant and machinery) of not more than Rs. 1 crore is treated as small scale units. The investment limit for units in the hosiery and handloom sub-sectors has been raised to Rs. 5 crore. For ancillary units (*i.e.* those supplying components, etc. to large scale industries and export oriented units), the limit of capital investment is also Rs. one crore. There are also the 'Tiny Sector' Industrial units with an investment of up to Rs. 25 lakh belong to this sector. Capital investment covers only investment in plant and machinery. Nevertheless the ceilings of these investments were being found changed from time-to-time.

Small-scale industries can be launched at any place, any time with a small capital investment if the industrialist or entrepreneur or management thinks it fit. They provide immediate large-scale employment, they offer a method of ensuring a more equitable distribution of the national income and they facilitate an effective mobilization of capital and entrepreneurial skills which might otherwise remain unutilized. Some of the problems that unplanned organization tends to create will be avoided by the establishment of small-scale industries of production all over the country. The small is no doubt, beautiful. In India the cottage and small industries should, therefore, be developed and given priority importance because the development suits to the peculiar conditions in which India finds herself.

Virtually, small-scale industries should be assigned top priority in any programme of economic development, especially in a developing economy like India. Although we are rich in minerals, we are yet to exploit them fully; we have abundant skilled labour and extensive un-employment and yet we suffer from scarcities of skilled technical labour and our predominantly agricultural economy has made us neither self-sufficient on the food front nor provided agriculturists with sufficient income for a respectable standard of life.

Tendency of SSIs towards Economic Development

The importance of small-industries has materialised vividly after globalization. Small Scale Industries (SSIs) are the backbone of Indian Economy. Though this sector involves low capital and a short gestation period, employment potential is very high. The SSI sector accounts for 80 per cent of industrial employment. Small scale sector is able to provide employment to 26 persons for every Rs. 1 lakh of fixed investment whereas it is only 4 persons in case of the large scale sector. This sector had provided employment to more than 18 million people which was only 40.5 lakh during the year 1974-75.

The extent of small scale sector's contribution to the national economic developments is inereasing increasing in the levels of output, productivity, employment generation, exports and happiness of the rural masses. The development of modern large scale industries with their highly sophisticated techniques of production and tremendous efforts of improving the quality, technique, design, grade, standardization etc., have contributed its role to the further decline of cottage and small scale industries. This is a fact that the small scale industrial sector has been assigned an important place keeping in view the potential of this sector in employment generation, dispersal of industry in rural areas and enhancement of exports.

The small-scale industries play a vital role in economic development of the country as a whole. Development of medium and large scale industries cannot bring their existence in the country in the absence of small scale industries. They are subsidiaries to large scale units and resulting to say that small-scale industries are the key industries with a view to bring industrial estates more in the country. It can provide employment opportunities for both educated as well as un-educated youths to some extent. Giving employment to additionally increased population, small-scale industries can directly or indirectly assist towards the development of the status of the people, especially the weaker sections of the country. In view of the meagreness of capital resources, there is no possibility in the short-run for creating much employment through the factory industries. Now consider the household or cottage industries. They require very little capital. About six or seven hundred rupees could get *an artisan family started*. small seale industries in the villages. With any given investment, employment possibilitres would be ten or fifteen or even twenty times greater in comparison with corresponding factory industries. Many ills of urbanizations, which inevitably follow the establishment of large-scale industries, can be avoided by setting up of small industries. Mahatama Gandhi had rightly said that "Salvation of India lays in the development of cottage industries."

Small-scale industries play a strategic role in the progress of a country. These industries, by and large, represent a stage in economic transition from traditional to modern technology. The transitional nature of this process is reflected on the diversity of these industries. Some small-scale units use simple skills and machinery, while many other units use modern and sophisticated technology. The challenge of economic growth is to accelerate the productivity of agriculture and industry by improving their techniques of production. So far as industries are concerned, this will involve the adoption of a progressively superior technology, particularly in semi-urban and rural areas.

Objective and Methodology

The present study is being carried out to see the economic development potentialities through small-scale industries of the country. In order to mould this article a meaningful one only secondary data were collected by referring related journals, books, and annual publications of central as well as state governments. To analyse and evaluate the objective of the present study, statistical tools and techniques like correlation of coefficient and mean are used.

Review of Related Literature

In order to make this article a meaningful one, author have required a review of available related literature. Mention may be made here that, A.N. Agrawal's book "*Indian Economy Problems of Development Planning*" (2003) dealt with economic laws, concepts, the need of economic development as a whole. Vasant Desai's book on "*Small–scale Enterprises – Organisation and Management*" (1999) revealed about the growth and need of congenial atmosphere of an enterprise with sound profit motive. S.P. Gupta (1995) wrote about the collection, classification, analysis, presentation and interpretation of data in the presence of applicable tools and techniques of statistics. Rajan Kumar and Subhashchander's article "Financing of fixed assets in small-scale industries : A study of the Textile Industry in Punjab" described about the ways and procedures of financing fixed assets in small-scale industries of India in general and Punjab in particular.

Rationale of Small-Scale Industries

Small-scale industries had been contributing significantly in economic development of the country by increasing the quantum of gross national product, gross domestic product, net national product of the country. To estimate these aspects of national income, the estimation of products produced, employment as well as exports of SSIs can be taken into consideration. It will be witnessed by the performance of SSIs in India by reflecting on production, employment and exports which are being reproduced below:

Table 13.1 : Performance of Small-Scale Industries (SSIs) in Terms of Units, Production, Employment and Exports for Eleven Years

Year	*Regd.SSI Units (in lakhs)*	*Un-regd. SSI Units (in lakhs)*	*Total Units (in lakhs)*	*Production (Rs. in crores)*	*Employment No. (in lakhs)*	*Export (Rs. in crores)*
1994-95	11.61(-)	67.99(-)	79.60(-)	122,210 (-)	191.40(-)	29,068(-)
1995-96	11.57 (-0.34%)	71.27 (4.82%)	82.84 (4.07%)	1,48,290 (21.34%)	197.93 (3.41%)	36,470 (25.46%)
1996-97	11.99 (3.27%)	74.22 (9.16%)	86.21 (8.30%)	1,68,413 (37.80%)	205.86 (7.55%)	39,278 (35.12%)
1997-98	12.04 (3.70%)	77.67 (14.23%)	89.71 (12.70%)	1,89,178 (54.79%)	213.16 (11.36%)	44,442 (52.88%)
1998-99	12.00 (3.35%)	81.36 (19.66%)	93.36 (17.28%)	2,12,901 (74.20%)	220.55 (15.22%)	48,979 (68.49%)
1999-2000	12.32 (6.11%)	84.33 (24.03%)	97.15 (22.04%)	2,34,255 (91.68%)	229.10 (19.69%)	54,200 (86.45%)
2000-01	13.10 (12.83%)	88.00 (29.43%)	101.10 (27.01%)	2,61,289 (113.80%)	239.09 (24.91%)	69,797 (140.11%)
2001-02	13.75 (18.43%)	91.46 (34.51%)	105.21 (32.17%)	2,82,270 (130.97%)	249.09 (30.14%)	71,244 (145.09%)
2002-03	14.68 (26.44%)	95.42 (40.34%)	110.10 (38.31%)	3,11,993 (155.29%)	261.38 (36.56%)	86,013 (195.90%)
2003-04	15.54 (33.85%)	99.68 (46.60%)	115.22 (44.74%)	3,48,059 (184.8%)	273.97 (43.14%)	N.A. (-)
2004-05	16.90 (45.56%)	101.70 (49.58%)	118.60 (48.99%)	4,07,630 (233.54%)	282.80 (47.75%)	N.A. (-)

Notes: N.A. (*i.e.* Not Available)
Figures in the bracket indicate the percentage increased.
Taking 1994-95 as based year.
Source: NSIC (National Small Industries Corporation). Imphal

It is obvious from the above table, that the number of small-scale industries during the period of 1994-95 was 79.60 lakh consisting of both registered as well as un-registered units (*i.e.* 11.61 lakh registered and 67.99 un-registered SSIs) production during the same year was Rs. 1,22, 210 crore while employment and export recorded to the tune of 191.40 lakh and Rs. 29,068 crore respectively. However, 16.90 lakh registered and 101.70 lakh un-registered altogether 118.60 lakh SSIs were being found in 2004-05. The production has gone to Rs. 407,630 crore during the year giving employment to 282.80 lakh during the same year. It can now be dictated that number of small scale industries that are prevalent in the country has increased from 79.60 lakh to 118.60 lakh which could show 48.99 per cent increased in total units over the previous 11 years. Production too increased from Rs. 1,22,210 crore to Rs 4,07,630 crore which marked 233.54 per cent increase in production. Employment can also be seen an increasing changing scenario from 191.40 lakh to 282.80 lakh *i.e.,* 47.75 per cent incremental change during these 11 years.

There is a close relationship among total units, production, employment and exports which are ingredient of national income calculation. Whenever, there is increase in total units that is reflected on production, employment as well as exports by increasing their respective monetary values. To measure the quantum of correlation, the following calculation of correlation co-efficient is required.

Table 13.2 : Calculation of Co-efficient of Correlation

Year	*Total Units (X) (in lakhs)*	*$(X-\bar{X})$ x*	*x^2*	*Employment (in lakhs) (Y)*	*$(Y-\bar{Y})$ y*	*y^2*	*xy*
1994-95	79.60	-18.50	342.25	191.40	-41.72	1740.55	771.82
1995-96	82.84	-15.26	232.86	197.93	-35.19	1238.33	536.99
1996-97	86.21	-11.89	141.37	205.86	-27.26	743.10	324.12
1997-98	89.71	-8.39	70.39	213.16	-19.96	398.40	167.46
1998-99	93.36	-4.74	22.47	220.55	-12.57	158.00	59.58
1999-00	97.15	-0.95	0.90	229.10	-4.02	16.16	3.82
2000-01	101.10	+3.00	9.00	239.09	+5.97	35.64	17.91
2001-02	105.21	+7.11	50.55	249.09	+15.97	255.04	113.54
2002-03	110.10	+12.00	144.00	261.38	+28.26	798.62	339.12
2003-04	115.22	+17.12	293.09	273.97	+40.84	1668.72	699.18
2004-05	118.60	+20.50	420.25	282.80	+49.68	2468.10	1018.44

$\Sigma x=1079.10$ $\Sigma x=0$ $\Sigma x^2=1727.13$ $\Sigma y=2564.33$
$\Sigma y=0$
$\Sigma y^2=9520.66$ $\Sigma xy=4052.98$

$$\text{Here } \overline{X}=\frac{1079.10}{11} \text{ and } \overline{Y}=\frac{2564.33}{11}$$
$$=98.10 \qquad =233.12$$

$$\therefore r=\frac{\Sigma xy}{\sqrt{\Sigma x^2\times\Sigma y^2}}$$
$$=\frac{4052.98}{\sqrt{1727.13\times 9520.66}}$$
$$=\frac{4052.98}{41.55\times 97.57}$$
$$=\frac{4052.98}{4054.03}$$
$$=(+)\ 0.999$$

Therefore, the calculated value of the co-efficient of correlation (r) is (+) 0.999 and further the value signifies that there is a highly positive correlation in between the number of units and employment. It can interpret in such a way that whenever increases in total units, it can lead to increase in employment too and will boost production as well as exports which can facilitate the development of Indian Economy.

Conclusion

Small Scale Industries had been become an important segment of the economy contributing substantially in the form of production, employment and exports. It has continued to play a vital role in the fulfilment of socio-economic objectives. When people search for a means which can earn money with a meagre investment, small-scale industry can emerge as a powerful means and people having the idea of launching the same should enjoy this ample opportunity. Small-scale industries contribute 40 per cent of the total industrial output and about 45 per cent of the total export earnings of the country. It further indicates that the need of the time is to give more and more emphasize on small scale industries by deeming it as a priority sector with an aim to accelerate the progress of the economic development of the country.

References

Agrawal, A.N. (2003): *Indian Economy: Problems of Development Planning*, New Delhi: Wishwa Prakashan.

Desai, Vasant (1999): *Small Scale Enterprises -Organisation* and *Management*, Mumbai: Himalaya Publishing House.

Gupta S.P. (1995): *Statistical Methods*, New Delhi: Sultan Chand & Sons.

Government of India, Ministry of Industry, Small Industries Service Institute, Industrial Estate, Takyelpat Imphal. *State Profile of Manipur 2002-2003*.

Government of Manipur, Directorate of Economics & Statistics. *Economic Survey Manipur, 2005-2006*.

14 People's Participation in Rural Development
Some Issues

Manoj Kumar Singh

Introduction

In any development scheme, people's role matters, because it is for their welfare that such programme are implemented (Sundram, 2002). People's participation is a central feature of present thinking about rural development. There appears to be an increasing consensus that participation is essential for any effective development and from this pre-supposition that arises the questions of how best it be operationalized on the assumed grounds that more of it is beneficial. In what activities, in what manner and shape, it can be participated and be maximized? Can participation be perceived in this way, as an ingredient to be injected into targeted groups as though they were ill and, as though, this was somehow the panacea? Can participation even be institutionalized? Or legalized? Or must perhaps be for ever on the margins of official policy prescriptions and in that way provide a vehicle for countervailing explanations and organizations that are so necessary in the struggle against entrenched orthodoxy.

In these latter terms, participation provides a potentially powerful tool, together with communication, education and conscientisation, etc. Present study concerns with participation rooted in a complex historical context. People's participation has been developing since the beginning of rural development in all the Asian and African countries that have emerged free from the colonial powers. The paper lays emphasis on same issues/as parts of peoples' participation in rural development.

What Constitutes Rural Development

Before we look into the various aspects of people's participation in rural development, there is need for a definition of what constitutes rural development which would indicate the scope, the limitations and the manner in which people could participate in their development. Rural development, in general, is a strategy designed to improve the economic and social life of people in a rural settlement and, in particular, it focuses on the rural poor comprising the small scale farmers, tenants and the landless. Since rural development is intended to reduce poverty, it must be clearly designed to increase production and raise productivity.

Rural development recognizes, however, that improved food supplies and nutrition, together with basic service such as health and education, cannot only directly improve the physical well-being and quality of life of the rural poor, but can also indirectly enhance their productivity and their ability to contribute to the national economy. It is concerned with the modernization and modernization in rural society, and with its transition from traditional isolation to integration with the national economy (World Bank, 1975).

What is People's Participation?

People's participation in a broader sense, signifies their total involvement with development agencies in deciding the programmes and activities, fixing up of priorities, taking initiative and carrying out the projects as partners by the contributing of their ideas, interest, material, labour and time.

The scope of people's participation depends upon the nature of the activity, the duration of its execution, its technical nature, the clientele it covers, whether it is an individual project or concerns with the total or some segments of the community, its location, the amount of funds it involves and, above all what the development agency stipulates about the kind of participation at different stages of activity and the quantity and quality of participation it expects from the people.

Of late, several terms have come into development terminology in respect to involving people for their betterment. Terms like people's participation popularly known as participation/community participation, citizen's participation and so on are in current use. It signifies almost the same thing that people as partners in their development. Participation is a comprehensive concept embracing all the facets and phases of development beginning with people's initiative and unto their sustaining the activity.

In view of the nature of rural development programmes, some of them have been initiated by the development agencies. The participation of people could be diverged as follows:

1. Responding to the programme, accepting the process and adopting technology and innovations,
2. Extending more support,
3. Participation in decision-making, co-operating in implementation,
4. Contribution of money, material and labour in executing the programme,
5. Taking initiative, mobilizing people and resources, and
6. Performing leadership role and ownership of the projects.

People's participation is bringing people together functionally. It is physical, psychic and emotional involvement of the clientele with the development activities. It is the training and organizing the community for self-reliance, responsiveness and leadership. Process-wise, people's participation is dousing people from periphery to the centre of action, widening their sphere of thinking, contacts and contributions. It is bringing people from relatively total isolation to mutual interaction.

Objectives of People's Participation

People's participation in rural development is an education

proceeds. It is a training for development involving people in the projects, making them their own. It creates a sense of possession and ownership.

- People's participation is to develop self-reliance, self-confidence, competence and managerial capacity.
- People's participation trains people to take initiative, accomplish and sustain their activities.
- People's participation is to build up and reinvigorate communities and generate social action.
- People's participation is to enable people to discover their strength, increase their aspiration level, mobilize and channelize their resources for productive purposes.

In the nut shell, the purpose and process of people's participation is the involvement of human resource development (HRD) in executing any activity. It is the development of human and inner material resources with stimulus and support external to the community development. Unless we create this culture of people's participation, democracy will not grow and development of rural sector is incomplete.

Why Should People Participate?

There is no controversy as to whether there should be people's participation in the development programmes designed to meet the basic needs of the people. There is a body of philosophy and a set of assumptions behind people's participation in rural development. We may briefly look into them.

1. The whole philosophy of rural development is based on one very simple and apparent assumption that the government machinery, however, big and efficient it might be; is grossly inadequate by itself to achieve the economic and social revolution needed for ensuring a better and richer life for the vast masses of humanity

living in the rural areas. The rural development personel were to function merely as "catalytic agents". The idea was that a programme started as a government programme with people's participation should gradually and eventually shape itself into people's programme with government's participation.

2. Communities can develop their own capacity to deal with their problems.
3. People participate in giving direction to social change in their communities. Change which is brought about by sharing of an effort and social participation, possesses democratic vitality and is also realistic self-imposed changes have permanence as compared to those imposed from outside and above.
4. Holistic approach is better than fragmented approach, because the life of a community is itself a whole and any attempt to tackle one aspect of the whole is bound to affect others.
5. People must learn participative skills in democracy because, unless they themselves share responsibilities and participate in fulfilling them, they do not strengthen the democratic will, weaken if not perish, unless the supper tiny institutions are created. The basic plank of community development is the growth of the democratic idea. Democracy does not function unless there is a decentralization of power to be shared very widely at various levels of the social strata.
6. People need help in solving their new problems. External help provides stimulus to inner resources of the community. Communities are like infants who need a proper support while they learn to walk. This is rational for agency functioning and agency support.
7. The tendency of sub-groups; developing themselves as separate entities inside a community, produces social tension and has, therefore, to be channelized and their energies to be diverted to common initiatives.

8. The barriers that prevent active participation by individuals in the direction of social change inhibit personal development. The process of community development is, therefore, to be so organized that the community functions for the community; they promote the growth of individuals.
9. The process of urbanization has destroyed the feeling of belonging to a community and it is necessary to revive this feeling in rural area where the masses of agricultural populations of the developing nations dwell. The contractual relations of an urban society do not work well in a rural society. The problem of developing and maintaining common and shared values, which form the basis of cohesion in a community, is made vastly more difficult by industrialization.
10. Beneficiary or target community consists of people who are adults and thinking human beings. They are also intelligent and pragmatic in their own way just as the patron or the helping agency.
11. If given the opportunity, people can organize and draw out solutions to the problems.
12. The community is in the best position to understand its own problems in all their dimensions and complexity.
13. The best resources for their progress and development are that themselves who, assisted and supported, could be the ritual and effective inputs for their own growth and development.
14. Outside assistance, support and expertise are only secondary though important resources provided within time bound frame.
15. The role of the community cannot be substituted or taken away, however grant may be the vulnerability of the community.
16. The apparently most helpless community can be an active factor in helping itself.
17. People always have their own wisdom to rectify the mechanism of doing so appears to be.

Peoples' Participation — Some Problems

Though people's participation in rural development is necessary; there are several problems associated with such participation. We have to first decide at what stage in the planning process it is desirable. It is also necessary to understand the value. If they put forward a list of demands based on narrow local perspectives, the ultimate gains may not be impressive; even the collection of data for the people may suffer from personal or group bias under the present setup. The participation of the rural poor in the development process can be speeded up only when the poor become conscious of their rights and privileges and subsequently build up strength to achieve justice for themselves in the sharing of benefits of development.

The major obstacles to popular participation are absence of a strong commitment on the part of the government; unhelpful attitude of the civil servants; monopoly of local organizations by the localities; division among the rural poor themselves.

The rural society in India is a heterogeneous in character. The rural population, to a great extent, differs in economic and social status. Generally, the richer section shows an attitude of indifference to programmes meant for the economically poorer sections. The implementation of anti-poverty programme may also create a climate of tension, given the rural power structure. The organization of beneficiaries has to have capacity to work out strategies to ease such tensions.

Enabling and Facilitating People's Participation

People's participation in rural development has short-term and long-term goals. We need to have trust and faith in the ability of the people in rural communities, provide them with the opportunity for participation, however, humble and insignificant it may be. Respect their ideas and views; channelize and integrate of their life. Even at the cost of repetition, it may be mentioned that the process of working with people demands understanding, appreciation, respect, patience and, above all, wisdom on effective methodology for channelizing people's participation is through community organization and, cooperative development. Participation shows the ethos and the pattern of behaviour on the part of the people. We may think of several core and marginal factors in a contextual sense either facilitating or inhibiting participation.

Role of a Development Agency

The onus of providing space, encouraging and facilitating people's participation lies on the part of development agency. The development agency may have to indicate, open up, solicit and encourage people to participate in large number of programmes at different stages in the process of development activity. It may be a school lunch programme, adult literacy, an approach road or provision of drinking water facilities.

Working with the People

In order to involve people, we should work with the people. It is the field level functionaries in the field of rural development agriculture, livestock, public health and medicare, education, etc., who are supposed to have more close and frequent contact with the community. People's participation depends to a large degree on how the field level personnel manage the involvement of the people in the development activities. Involving people and securing their participation depends on the attitude, patience, skills, wisdom, commitment and leadership on the part of the development personnel working with people is an art and it is human relations and it is an essential part of human development.

The following measures may be taken to mobilize people to join the mainstream of development (Bajpai, 1995):

- Measures should be taken to understand the group

dynamics and heterogeneous character of society. It is necessary to understand how a community views a particular problem;

- Special attention must be given to identify the resources of the people and to educate them to understand their needs and problems;
- It would be better if individuals and household development plans were drown up and people motivated to take active part in their own development;
- People must realize that the ultimate responsibility of supporting the programme lies with them only and for which they have to work consistently and collectively towards the mobilization of resources; and
- Monitoring should be People-centred feature of the programme in order to avoid any in desirable incidents. Attempts should be made to stabilize various interest groups and people's organizations.

Conclusion

People's participation is a necessary component in rural development. Its essence lies with the proper coordination of individuals and groups efforts, in fully utilizing the potential of the local institutions, the higher levels statutory bodies, the village cooperatives, the village school and other associate organizations such as farmers forums, youth clubs, women's clubs, and in proper harmonization of individual needs with group needs and group needs with national needs.

References

Sundaram, I. Satya, (2002): *Rural Development*, Himalaya Publishing House, Mumbai, p. 518.

World Bank, (1975): 'Rural Development Sector' Policy Paper, Washington, D.C., World Bank.

Setty, Desingu E. (1970): 'Community Development and Extension in India." *Gandhigram*, Gandhigram Rural Institute, pp.7-9.

Mishra, S.N and Sharma, Kushal (1985): 'Ensuring People's Participation in Rural Development Programmes, *Kurukshetra*, January, 1985, p. 7.

Dhillon, D.S. and Hansra, B.S. (1995): "People's Participation in Rural Development Programmes". *Kurukshetra,* January, 1995, p. 8

Bajpai, P.K. (1995): "Peoples Participation in Development", *Mainstream*, July 1, 1995, p. 11.

15 Impact of SGRY on Socio-Economic Development of Rural Community in Nagaland

M. Yangar, K.K. Jha and Amod Sharma

Introduction

Relatively higher growth of population as against food production has a serious implication on the nation's economy and the society as a whole. Creation of increased avenues of employment opportunities with food security has been an important objective of developmental planning in India. The Government of India aims to bring employment through wage and self-employment into a larger focus with the goal of reducing unemployment and underemployment to a negligible level and of providing food security against hunger. The ever-increasing population and hence the excess labour force has led to an increase in the volume of unemployment and, now, it has emerged as a serious concern *vis-à-vis* with the food shortage. To combat the twin threats of food level insecurity and unemployment, the Government of India has introduced various schemes that are predominantly self-reliant and self-sustainable in nature.

In view of the above facts, the Government of India launched a new scheme, the Sampoorna Grameen Rozgar Yojana (SGRY) on 25th September, 2001 to provide food security through wage employment and building durable assets and infrastructure for the rural communities. In Nagaland, SGRY was implemented in the year 2002. In the scenario of declining growth rate of employment, increasing number of unemployed, 193.2 million poor people (BPL) living in rural areas, and India being home of nearly 25 per cent of world's hungry population despite considerable food surplus, the SGRY assumes importance. By implementing such schemes, it is assumed that food shortage is contained and unemployment is reduced to a negligible level. Such schemes are also initiated for the socially and economically marginalized communities, in addition to providing a source of sustenance during times of lean harvesting seasons and natural calamities.

Objectives

In order to assess the achievement of SGRY a research study was undertaken with following:

1. To study the socio-economic and personal characteristics of the selected respondents.
2. To study the impact of SGRY on the rural community in the selected area of study.
3. To ascertain the association of selected independent variables with the dependent variable impact of SGRY.
4. To know the problems faced by SGRY beneficiaries.

Research Methodology

Selection of State

The present study was conducted in the State of Nagaland having a rural population of 16,35,815 out of the total population of 19,88,636 (Anonymous, 2001). In this State, a non-working population of 1,138,654 (Anonymous, 2003) indicates that a major proportion of the population is un-employed and need wage employment which can be provided under the SGRY scheme.

Selection of District

There are 11 districts in Nagaland. Out of these districts,

Dimapur district was selected purposively since it consists of the largest number (189) of villages in Nagaland with 2,06,122 non-workers out of the total population of 3,08,382 (Anonymous, 2001).

Selection of Block

Dimapur district consists of four rural development blocks, namely Medziphema, Niuland, Kuhuboto, and Dhansiripar. Medziphema block was selected purposively for the study because it is one of the largest blocks of Dimapur district consisting of 66 villages where the SGRY programme was being carried out successfully.

Selection of Villages

Medziphema block consists of a total number of 66 villages. Ten per cent of the total number of villages from Medziphema block were selected randomly comprising Pherima, Medziphema, New Socünoma, Khaibong, Sirhima and Jharnapani villages.

Selection of Respondents

After a formal consultation with the BDO of Medziphema block, a complete list of the households and the SGRY beneficiaries from the selected villages was obtained. From this list, about 100 respondents were selected through proportionate random selection procedure, which included 16 from Pherima, 32 from Medziphema, 16 from Sirhima, 16 from New Socünoma, 12 from Khaibong and 8 from Jharnapani village.

Selection of Variables

Independent variables selected for the present study included Age, Education, Family size, Annual income, Social participation and Mass media information sources. Impact of SGRY on beneficiaries was selected as the dependent variable.

Tools and Techniques of Data Collection

Primary data were collected from the selected respondents with the help of a pre-tested structured schedule by conducting personal interview. Secondary data were collected from government records, journals, books, etc. The collected data were analysed by using relevant statistical tools like calculation of mean, standard deviation, frequency, percentage and correlation coefficients.

Findings

Socio-economic Characteristics of the Selected Respondents

Age: It was revealed from Table 15.1 that majority (69 per cent) of the respondents belong to the middle age (in line with the findings of Padaria *et al.*, 1999, Prakash *et al.*, 2003) followed by young age (16 per cent) and old age (15 per cent). It was observed that the respondents belonging to the middle age category formed the single largest segment. This may be attributed to the fact that most middle aged people were in need of wage employment during lean agricultural period or off seasons.

Table 15.1 : Distribution of the Respondents based on their Age

N = 100

Sl. No.	*Category*	*Frequency*	*Percentage*	*Mean*	*SD*
1.	Young	16	16	43.24	11.54
2.	Middle Aged	69	69	—	—
3.	Old	15	15	—	—
	Total	**100**	**100**	**—**	**—**

Education : Table 15.2 revealed that the maximum number of respondents had education up to primary and middle school level (26 per cent each), followed by high school (25 per cent), college level (16 per cent) and illiterate (7 per cent). It could be inferred that the educational level of the respondents was very satisfactory since only 7 per cent were found illiterate and the rest were all literate.

Table 15.2 : Distribution of the respondents based on their educational levels

N = 100

Sl. No.	*Category*	*Frequency*	*Percentage*
1.	Illiterate	7	7
2.	Primary School	26	26
3.	Middle School	26	26
4.	High School	25	25
5.	College	16	16
	Total	**100**	**100**

Size of Family: Table 15.3 revealed that the majority (68 per cent) of the respondents had medium size of family followed by small size (20 per cent) and the only 12 per cent of them had big size family. It was observed that respondents belonging to medium sized families were more aware of SGRY and the percentage of unemployment was found higher in this segment.

Table 15.3 : Distribution of the Respondents Based on their Size of the Family

N = 100

Sl. No.	*Category*	*Frequency*	*Percentage*	*Mean*	*SD*
1.	Small	20	20	5.17	2.21
2.	Medium	68	68	—	—
3.	Big	12	12		—
	Total	**100**	**100**	—	—

Annual Income: Table 15.4 revealed that the mean annual income of the respondents was Rs. 34,729.75. Majority (77 percent) of the respondents were in the medium category of annual income (Rs. 25,285.16 to Rs. 44,174.34) followed by high category (more than Rs. 44,174.34) as evident in case of

14 per cent of them and the low category (less than Rs. 25, 285.16) as in case of 9 per cent of the respondents. These findings differed from the findings of Kumar and Kaptan (2004) who reported that the number of middle and higher income families were nearly the same.

Table 15.4 : Distribution of the Respondents Based on their Annual Income

N = 100

Sl. No.	*Category*	*Frequency*	*Percentage*	*Mean*	*SD*
1.	Low < Rs 25,285.16	9	9	34,729.75	9,444.59
2.	Medium (Rs. 25,285.16 to Rs. 44,174.34)	77	77	—	—
3.	High > Rs. 44,174.34	14	14	—	—
	Total	**100**	**100**	—	—

Social participation: It was evident from Table 15.5 that majority (77 per cent) of the SGRY beneficiaries had medium level of social participation followed by 14 per cent of them having high level of social participation. Only 9 per cent of them had low level of social participation. Therefore, it may be inferred that the majority of the selected respondents were socially active.

Table 15.5 : Distribution of the Respondents Based on their Social Participation

N = 100

Sl. No.	*Category*	*Frequency*	*Percentage*
1.	Low	9	9
2.	Medium	77	77
3.	High	14	14
	Total	**100**	**100**

Utilisation of Mass Media Sources: Table 15.6 reveals that the Newspaper was most often used as mass media source of information as reported by 38 per cent of the respondents, followed by Radio and TV as reported by 25 per cent and 13 per cent of them respectively. TV was used sometimes by majority (77 per cent) of the respondents followed by Radio and Demonstration as reported by 72 and 47 per cent of the respondents respectively; whereas exhibition was the least (13 per cent) used source of information in this category. Majority (87 per cent) of the respondents never attended or participated in Exhibitions, 53 per cent of them never had access of Demonstration and 10 per cent of them never used TV for obtaining required information. Thus it may be inferred that Radio was the most popularly used source of mass media being used by 97 per cent of the respondents.

Table 15.6 : Distribution of Respondents Based on their Frequency of Contact with Mass Media Sources

N =100

Sl. No.	*Mass Media Sources*	*Most Often*		*Sometimes*		*Never*	
		Frequency	*Percentage*	*Frequency*	*Percentage*	*Frequency*	*Percentage*
1.	Demonstration	0	0	47	47	53	53
2.	Exhibition	0	0	13	13	87	87
3.	TV	13	13	77	77	10	10
4.	Radio	25	25	72	72	3	3
5.	Newspaper	38	38	30	30	32	32
6.	Folders, Bulletin/Leaflets	0	0	21	21	79	79
7.	Magazine	32	32	49	49	19	19

Impact of SGRY

It was evident from Table 15.7 that beneficiaries experienced some distinct benefits from the SGRY programme. Majority (52 per cent) of the respondents experienced increase in annual income, followed by increase in purchasing power as reported by 24 per cent of them. Increase in family's health and nutritional level was experienced by 21 per cent of them, increase in the educational status of the children was experienced by 10 per cent of them and increase in social status was experienced by only 4 per cent of the respondents. Sixty per cent of the beneficiaries reported that there was a marked improvement in the overall development of the community after implementation of SGRY.

Table 15.7 : Distribution of Respondents Based on Selected Dimensions of Impact Assessment

N =100

Sl. No.	*Dimensions of Impact Assessment*	*Yes*		*No*	
		Frequency	*Percentage*	*Frequency*	*Percentage*
1.	Increase in annual income	52	52	48	48
2.	Increase in wage employment	52	52	48	48
3.	Increase in the educational status of the children	10	10	90	90
4.	Increase in social status	4	4	96	96
5.	Increase in purchasing power	24	24	76	76
6.	Increase in family's health and nutritional level	21	21	79	79
7.	Improvement in the overall development of the community	60	60	40	40

Association of Selected Independent Variables with the Dependent Variable Impact of SGRY

Table 15.8 reveals that the variable education had positive and highly significant relationship with the dependent variable impact of SGRY. Thus it may inferred that higher is the level of education greater is the quantum of impact on the beneficiaries. The variable family size had negative and highly significant relationship with the dependent variable. Thus it may be inferred that lower is the size of family higher is the chance of impact of such rural development programmes on the target community. Further, the variable mass media sources also had positive and significant relationship with the dependent variable inferring that more exposure of the mass media sources may be helpful in promoting greater impact on the community.

Table 15.8 : Association of Selected Independent Variables with the Dependent Variable Impact of SGRY

Sl. No.	Variables	Correlation coefficient 'r'
1.	Age	0.115^{NS}
2.	Education	0.379^{**}
3.	Family Size	-0.314^{**}
4.	Annual Income	-0.002^{NS}
5.	Social Participation	0.129^{NS}
6.	Mass Media Sources	0.221^{*}

** – Significant at 1 per cent, * – Significant at 5%, NS – Non-significant

Problems Faced by SGRY Beneficiaries

It was evident from Table 15.9 that the majority (88 per cent) of the respondents experienced that lower wages were being paid to the beneficiaries under SGRY as against the recommended wages. Fifty four per cent of the respondents reported that the average number of days of wage employment provided under SGRY were also less because the average days of employment were only 13 days in a year. This finding is in line with the findings of Singh (1999). Twentey eight per cent of them reported that they faced unemployment problem during agricultural lean period/off seasons as the implementation of the scheme coincided with the cultivation period of the region and 12 per cent of the respondents expressed that wages were not paid in right time.

Table 15.9 : Distribution of Respondents Based on Selected Dimensions of Problems

N = 100

Sl. No.	Dimensions of Impact Assessment	Yes		No	
		Frequency	Percentage	Frequency	Percentage
1.	Non-availability of wage employment during agricultural lean period/off seasons when wage employment is required	28	28	72	72
2.	The number of days of wage employment provided is less	54	54	46	46
3.	The wages paid under the scheme is less	88	88	12	12
4.	Non-payment of wages in time	12	12	88	88

Conclusion

Based on the findings of the study, it was observed that majority of the SGRY beneficiaries experienced the benefit in terms of increase in annual income increase in wage employment period, increase in purchasing power, increase in health/nutritional status and overall development of the community well-being. The variables – education, utilization of mass media sources and family size were found useful in influencing the level of impact of SGRY on the selected beneficiaries. The most important problem being faced by majority of the respondents was experienced in terms of lower rate of wage payment under SGRY as against the recommended rate.

References

Anonymous (2001): *'Annual Administrative Report'*, Department of Rural Development, Nagaland, Kohima.

Anonymous (2003): *'Statistical Handbook of Nagaland'*, Government of Nagaland, Kohima.

Kumar, C.R. and Kaptan Sanjay, S. (2004): 'Changing Face of Rural Marketing', *Kurukshetra*: 4-7.

Padaria, R.N. *et al.* (1999): 'Training Needs of Arid Farmers', *Agriculture Extension Review:* 7-10.

Prakash, Vinod *et al.* (2003): 'Adoption Extent of Rice Growers Regarding Rice Production Technology', *Rajasthan Journal of Extension Education,* XI: 55 – 56.

Singh, S. (1999): *'Impact Assessment of Wage Employment Programmes in Selected Areas of Bihar*. National Institute of Rural Development, Hyderabad.

16 Rural Development in Nagaland

A Study of KOMUL

Abhijit Chakraborty and **Pranay Jyoti Goswami**

Meaning and Definition of Cooperative

A cooperative is a form of business organisation that is owned and democratically controlled by its shareholders/members. A cooperative is also known as a 'mutual organisation'. The organisation is run for the mutual benefit of its shareholders/ members. It is established so its shareholders/members may purchase goods or use services of the organisation, rather than being established for the purpose of earning profits for investors.

Basically, it is a non-profit organisation, but can be made a profit organisation if members wish. If it is a non-profit, the organisation is formed by a group or organisation who themselves own and control it for their own benefit as services are offered to them. Usually the dairy farms, farmers, grocers, etc. forms the cooperative.[1]

Cooperative Movement in India

The Cooperative Movement in India was formally introduced with the promulgation of Cooperative Societies Act in 1904. The National Cooperative Union of India (NCUI), the apex organisation of the Indian Cooperative Movement traced back its origin in 1929 and reorganised as Indian Cooperative Union, renamed later as All India Cooperative Union in 1954 and re-christened as National Cooperative Union of India in 1961.[2]

History of Dairy Cooperative in India

In the forties, the dairy industry was dominated by one firm – *Polsons*. It was established by a rather enterprising gentleman named Polson who also discovered that Kaira District in Gujarat, which is again at present the centre of focal point for the development of Amul for the people in India as well as of the World. One of Polson's businesses was to supply milk to Bombay. As Kaira district was an abundant source of milk, Polson had chosen to procure it from there. Polson had arranged a number of contractors who collected the milk and thereby Polson made a handsome profit. The contractors too managed to earn large margins by overquoting the farmers. Realising that its farmers in the Kaira district in Gujarat were being exploited by middlemen and this exploitation was put an end to by the start of dairy cooperative movement. The growth of Dairy Cooperative was favourable due to the following factors:

1. It responded to the farmers financially as well as with services.
2. It is owned by farmers who have a stake in its success.
3. It has been managed by capable professionals and dedicated scientists, technologists and workers.

Today, in India, there are 75,000 dairy cooperative societies, spread all over the country with a membership of 10 million. The farmer in the village is now assured of a better future, thanks to these cooperatives. Today three biggest "companies" in the dairy business in the country are:

1. The Gujarat Cooperative Milk Marketing Federation (GCMMF).
2. The Kaira District Cooperative Milk Producers' Union Limited.
3. The Mehsana District Cooperative Milk Producers' Union.

The First Step: Formation of Kaira Union

Realizing this unequal balance of wealth, farmers turned to Sardar Vallabhbhai Patel for advice. He advised them to stop selling milk to Polson and formed a cooperative of their own. Farmers of Kaira followed his advice and the Kaira District Cooperative Milk Producers' Union (AMUL) was born, in 1946. By good fortune, they could get as Chairman – Shri Tribhuvandas Patel, an equally remarkable man. He understood the concept of cooperation and people. His integrity and the modest experiment in Kaira had not only become a success, people began to recognize it as such. Farmers learnt and implemented this concept in their own districts and started their own cooperatives. The result was that the district milk producers unions of Gujarat were formed and it owns the Gujarat Cooperative Milk Marketing Federation which markets the milk and milk products manufactured by its owners.

In 1964, the then Prime Minister Shri Lal Bahadur Shastri came to inaugurate cattle feed factory owned by Amul near Anand and expressed his wish to "transplant the spirit of Anand in many other places". He wanted the Anand model of dairy development replicated in other parts of the country.

The Next Achievement: Operation Flood

In the late sixties, the Board drew up a project called Operation Flood (OF) – meant to create a flood of milk in India's villages with funds mobilized from foreign donations. Producers' cooperatives, which sought to link dairy development with milk marketing, were the central plank of this project. Operation Flood which started in 1970 concluded its third phase in 1996 and has to its credit these significant results:

- The enormous urban market stimulus has led to sustained production increases, raising per capita availability of milk to nearly 200 grams per day.

- The dependence on commercial imports of milk solids are done away with modernization and expansion of the dairy industry and its infrastructure, activating a milk grid.
- Marketing expanded to supply hygienic and fair priced milk to some 300 million consumers in 550 cities and towns.
- A nationwide network of multi-tier producers' cooperatives, democratic in structure and professionally managed, has come into existence. Millions of small producers participate in an economic enterprise and improve the quality of their life and environment.
- Dairy equipment manufacture has expanded to meet most of the industry's needs[3].

Geographical Location of Nagaland and its People

Nagaland lies approximately between 25.6° North and 27.4° North latitude and between 93.20° East and 95.15° East latitudes situated extremely north-east of the country. Nagaland is bounded by Arunachal Pradesh in the North, Assam in the West, Manipur in the South and Myanmar in the East. The population of Nagaland in 2001 Census has been 1,990,036.

Almost three-fourth of the working population in Nagaland is engaged in the primary sector. Like the other states of the North East, Nagaland is predominantly an agrarian economy with agriculture and its allied activities contributing about 30 per cent in 1998-99. Rice is the staple food and occupies about 70 per cent of the total cultivated area consisting about 75 per cent of the total foodgrain production. Nagaland has been identified as a potential area for development of food processing industries in its geo-climatic conditions. The agriculture and allied sectors in Nagaland offer good inputs for development of a host of industries which could include floriculture, horticulture, rubber plantation and allied industries, sericulture, tea cultivation and processing, bamboo shot preservation, mushroom cultivation and processing, piggery, poultry, etc. Due to inadequate industrial infrastructure, lack of mineral resources and transportation, the industrial growth is limited in Nagaland. Despite vast endowment of natural resources, Nagaland is considered as one of the most industrially backward states of the country. The industrial structure of Nagaland may be classified, based on resource uses into agro-based industries, mineral based industries, forest based industries and other industries.[4]

Birth of KOMUL

The concept of dairy cooperative is a new concept in the mind of the rural people. The Cooperative movement and its economic venture came into existence only after attainment of Statehood of Nagaland in the year 1963. The first ever initiative on dairy activity was taken by the State Rural Dairy Project during 1974 which set up 2000 LPD chilling unit at Dimapur. Dr. Akho Yhokha was the founder managing director and armed with a Ph.D. from Nottingham University, UK, set up his office in a dilapidated building on the outskirts of Dimapur, with no proper road connectivity. People laughed at him as he walked to his work through flooded drains. 'Nagaland is no Gujarat' and '…Nothing works in Nagaland, will this work?' his critics hurled at him. Dr. Yhokha's response was, 'Give us a chance'. And he and his team, with a meagre daily collection of only 100-200 litres, and a mini plant, refused to give up. They quietly went on establishing more cooperatives. By 1989-90, the daily milk collection reached 1000 litres. The skeptics now began to turn around. The State Government began to take more active interest and initiative. With the start of the 8th Five Year Plan in 1992, the Central Government gave a one-time grant to set up the Union's Central Dairy Plant, at Dimapur with an installed daily capacity of 10,000 litres. During 1998-2000, Nagaland Dairy Industry was declared one of the top 10 fastest growing dairies in India. On 26th January, 2003, Dr. Akho Yhokha was honoured with the Governor's Medal.[5]

Inspired by the growth and success story of Dimapur dairy cooperative, Department of Animal Husbandry and Dairying, Ministry of Agriculture (Nagaland), took initiative and with the financial aid, established two milk plants, one each in Dimapur and Mokokchung respectively with the aim 'to promote dairying and related sustainable economic activities to facilitate the emergence of a dignified and equitable society in rural Nagaland through value based democratic institutions'. The creation of a milk union at Dimapur was initiated in the name of KOMUL (Kohima District Cooperative Milk Producers' Union Limited) at Dimapur, was started in the year 1985-86 (Operation Flood II project). As North-East was then declared as economically not viable for dairy cooperative, Operation Flood Project initiated by National Dairy Development Project was withdrawn from the State of Nagaland. As KOMUL had made some efforts and mobilized the rural mass to inculcate the cooperative values, Nagaland Dairy Development Board (NDDB) re-considered and initiated another project, named IDDP (Integrated Dairy Development Project) so that KOMUL could remain functional. The proposal was approved and KOMUL started operating under IDDP.[6]

After a span of 16 years of the success story of KOMUL, the State Government decided to set up a State Level nodal agency under the nomenclature of the "Nagaland State Dairy Cooperative Federation Ltd." It was registered as the State Apex body on the line of "Anand Pattern" under the Cooperative Act (Assam Cooperative Act, 1949) during 2001-02. The NSDCF Ltd. with its headquarters at Kohima co-ordinates and monitors the overall dairy development activities in the State including the District Milk Unions/Societies affiliated to it. However, the District Milk Unions maintain their functional autonomy as per the provisions of the byelaws.[7]

KOMUL today handles about 5000 litres of milk per day. A fleet of milk vans traverses a total of over 500 km twice daily just to collect milk. Its diversified products are sold all over Nagaland and in neighbouring states as well, especially Assam, through a dozen dealers and 150 retailers. KOMUL has over 3300 registered farmer-members and 106 primary level Dairy Cooperative Societies (DCS). Among them are 18 women's societies. Sample survey of the Department of Veterinary and Animal Husbandry, Nagaland (2003) indicated a bovine population of 5.25 lakh. Out of which 4.51 lakh are cattle, with 0.33 lakh buffaloes and 0.40 lakh of Mithuns. There are approximately 70,295 indigenous milch population and 1, 27,910 crossbred cows. An estimated 54,000 metric tonnes of milk produced with per capita availability scaling about 83.33g/h/d. [8]

A Brief Profile of Different Dairy Cooperative Unions in Nagaland

With the creation of Dimapur District, the original name has been changed to Dimapur District Cooperative Milk Producers Union Ltd. but the brand name, KOMUL has been retained.

During the second phase of IDDP (1998-2002), six districts were covered. These included Kohima, Dimapur, Phek, Wokha, Zunheboto and Mon. Thus, except the Tuensang district, all the seven districts have been covered by IDDP in Nagaland. However, the project is concentrated in Dimapur while training and motivational programmes are initiated in other districts. Table 16.1 gives the Dairy Plant and Chilling Plant that exists as on 2003-04.[9]

Table 16.1 : Different Dairy/Chilling Plants in Nagaland

Sl. No.	*Dairy/Chilling plants*	*Capacity*	*Status*
1.	Central Dairy Plant, Dimapur	10 TLPD	Functional
2.	Mini Dairy Plant, Kohima	2 TLPD	Functional
3.	Mini Dairy Plant, Mokokchung	2 LPD	Functional
4.	Milk Chilling Plant, Wokha	1 TLPD	Functional
5.	Milk Chilling Plant, Pfutsero	1 TLPD	Functional
6.	Milk Chilling Plant, Zunheboto	1 TLPD	Under Construction
7.	Milk Chilling Plant, Mon	1 TLPD	Under Construction

Activities of the Union

The undulating nature of the topography and the resultant poor communication facilities coupled with the unique socio-cultural scenario cooperatives have greater advantages in running an economic enterprise. This is because of the higher economies of scale that results when we work in unison.

The number of cooperatives has been steadily rising with organisation of two more cooperatives. Consequently, business has improved significantly with 5 per cent growth in sales turnover over the previous year. Table 16.2 shows the growth and development of Dairy Cooperatives (DCs) and the membership from 1995-96 to 2004-05.

Table 16.2 : Growth of DCS and Membership from 1995-96 to 2004-05

Year	*No. of DCS*	*Total membership*
1995-96	50	1141
1996-97	55	1478
1997-98	58	1594
1998-99	61	1888
1999-2000	65	2128
2000-01	68	2730
2001-02	75	3067
2002-03	76	3108
2003-04	78	3158
2004-05	80	3220

Fig. 16.1 shows that there is steady growth of dairy Cooperatives over these years.

There has been significant growth of membership but the growth seems to remain more or less constant from 2001-2005 eventhough there was growth of dairy cooperatives. Though Fig. 16.1 shows the growth of dairy Co-operatives from the period (1995-98 to 2004-05) but the true picture of the Unions as on 2007 is 106 primary level Dairy Cooperative Societies (DCS) as on 31 March, 2007 but significant contribution in the dairy co-operatives is felt in the three districts of Nagaland. Table 16.3 shows the data collected from three districts provides

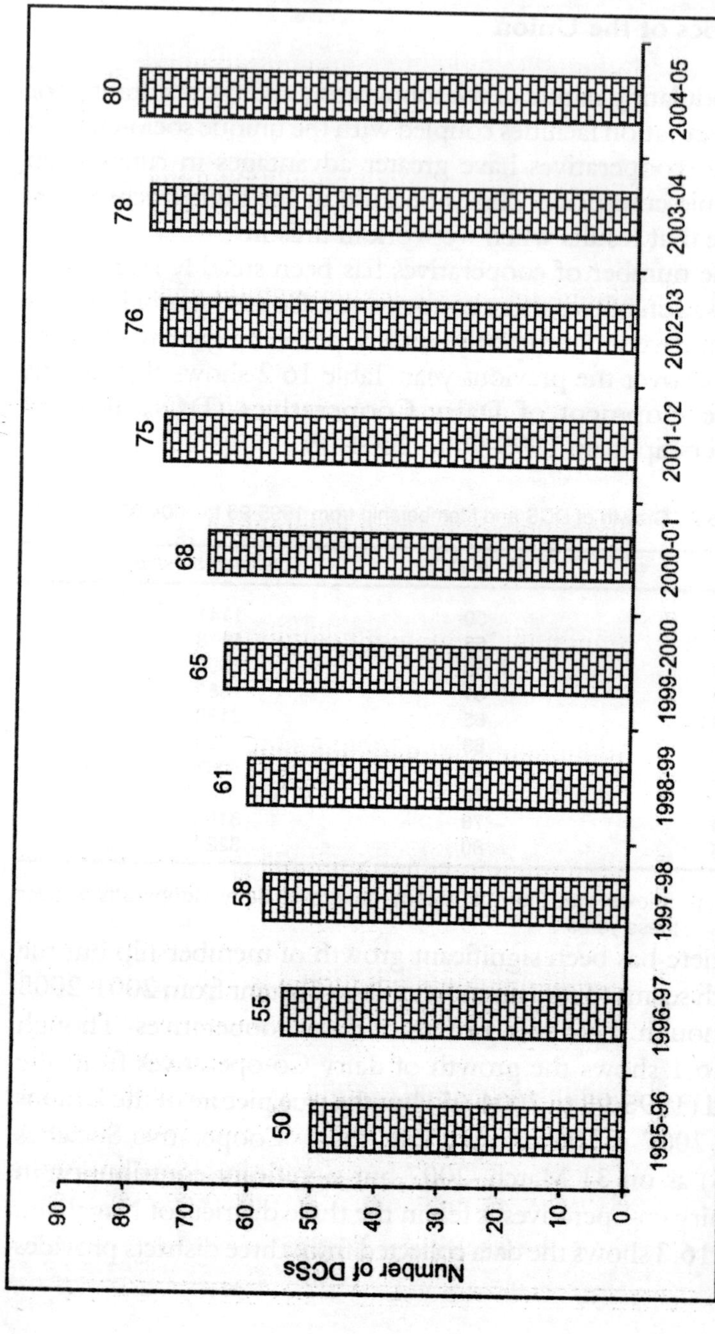

Fig. 16.1 : Growth of Dairy Cooperatives (1995-96 to 2004-05)

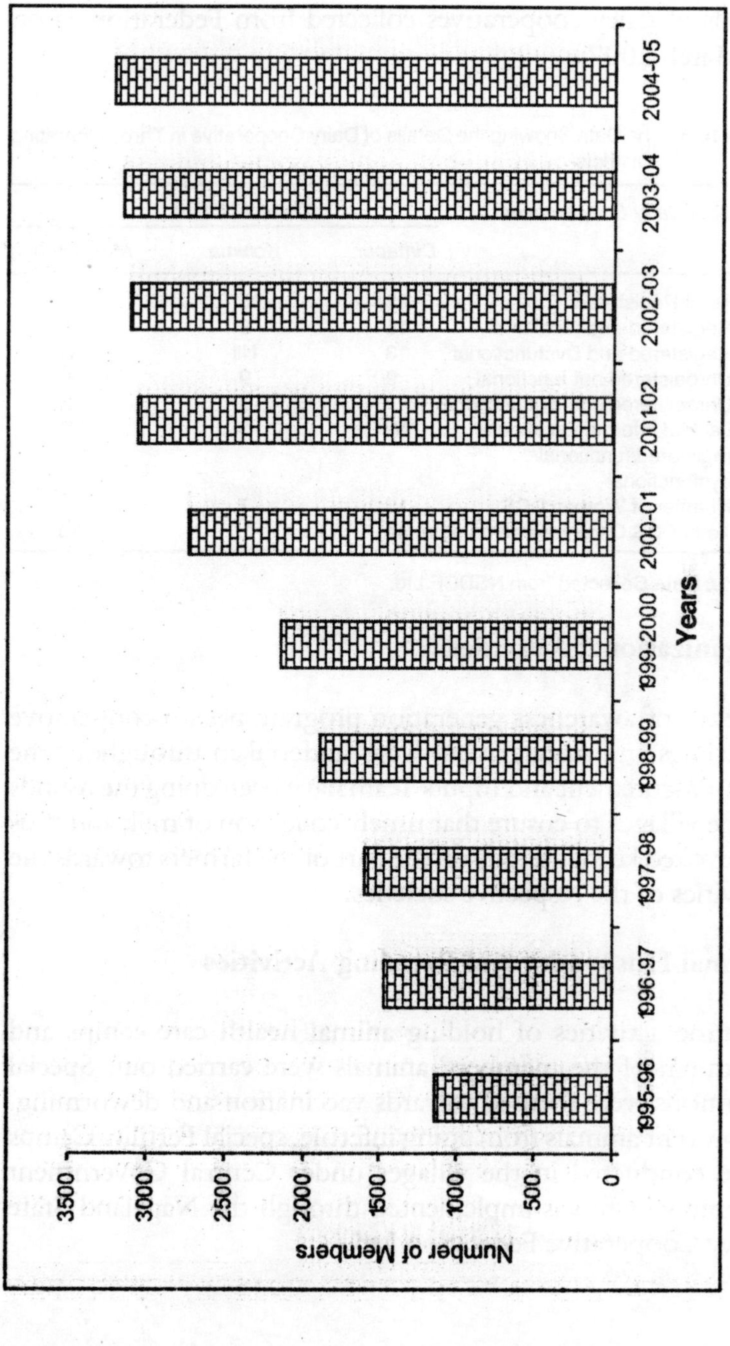

Fig. 16. 2 : Growth of Membership (1995-96 to 2004-05)

details of dairy cooperatives collected from Federation as on 31 March 2007.

Table 16.3 : The Data Showing the Details of Dairy Cooperative in Three Operating Districts

	Details of Dairy Cooperatives	*District Unions*		
		Dimapur	*Kohima*	*Mokokchung*
1.	Total Registered	28	5	10
2.	Registered and functional	15	5	6
3.	Registered and Dysfunctional	13	Nil	Nil
4.	Unregistered but functional	9	9	4
5.	Unregistered and dysfunctional	7	3	Nil
6.	Lack of information about registered/functional/ dysfunctional	Nil	3	Nil
7.	Number of Women DCS	13	7	7
8.	Total DCS Organised as on date	44	15	10

Source: Data Collected from NSDCF Ltd.

Organizational Activities

A series of awareness generation programmes on cooperative principles and management were undertaken throughout the year. Procurement and Inputs Team have been doing the rounds of the villages to ensure that timely collection of milk and thus has evoked keen interests on the part of the farmers towards the activities of the respective societies.

Animal Husbandry and Breeding Activities

Routine activities of holding animal health care camps and treatment of the members' animals were carried out. Special attentions were focused towards vaccination and deworming. To prevent animals from going infertile, special Fertility Camps were conducted in the villages under Central Government scheme which was implemented through the Nagaland State Dairy Cooperative Federation Ltd.

Even after two decades of the Union's existence, large number of farmers are maintaining low yielding animals. As a result, the farmers' attention towards dairying is divided since this alone cannot sustain their families. To do away with this malady, the farmers were linked with the banks for availing loans to procure high yielding animals from outside the State. At the same time, Artificial Insemination (AI) facility is delivered at the farmers' doorsteps at affordable costs through a special programme sponsored by the State Dairy Federation. The Secretaries of the DCS are imparted training on AI and Veterinary First Aid at the Training Centre of the State Dairy Federation from time-to-time.

Fodder Development

Non-availability of fodder during the winter months have been forcing many farmers to dispose their animals and look for other alternative means of livelihoods. To do away with this problem, fodder seeds which are suited to the soil and the season were distributed free of cost to the farmers. A total of 23 quintals of fodder seeds were thus distributed during the year.

Cattle Feed Production

The traditional feeding practices which entail feeding of self-compounded feeds have led to nutritional deficiencies in many animals belonging to the farmers. This has led to a host of problems which includes infertility, low yields, other metabolic disorders and even deaths of the animals. The net result is that the farmers suffer heavy economic losses. To convince the farmers of the advantages that could be derived through use of balanced feed, experiments were conducted by feeding the concentrate feed produced at the Cattle Feed Production Plant of the Union through use of experimental and control animals at many locations in the villages. During the year the Union's cattle feed plant has sold over 150 metric tonnes of cattle feed.

The existing system of delivering the feeds through the milk procurement vans at the farmers' doorsteps and deducting the cost from the milk bill have proven to be quite helpful to the farmers.

Milk Procurement

The sustained awareness generation campaigns have started to pay huge dividends in all aspects of milk production and procurement. Members have started desisting from the age old practice of adding water to milk with the expectation of earning an extra rupee. The futility of this practice has been realised by the farmers now. This is manifested from the fact that the per litre price received by the farmers have increased significantly. Union has also registered a perceptible increase in the quantity of milk procured during the year as is evident from Table 16.4.

Table 16. 4 : Milk Procurement and Marketing Performance

Year	*Procurement (in lakh litres)*	*Marketing (in lakh litres)*
1995-96	3.50	3.60
1996-97	4.65	4.72
1997-98	4.70	5.00
1998-99	6.98	10.50
1999-2000	8.97	11.15
2000-01	11.07	14.87
2001-02	10.00	11.40
2002-03	10.80	12.18
2003-04	11.20	14.28
2004-05	11.25	14.36

Production and Product Mix

Union's persistent effort towards increasing the range of milk and developing new products have yielded positive outcome in the form of addition of Flavoured Milk. Ghee has become a regular feature now and is packed in attractive HDPE packing. To maintain quality standards and enhance the keeping quality

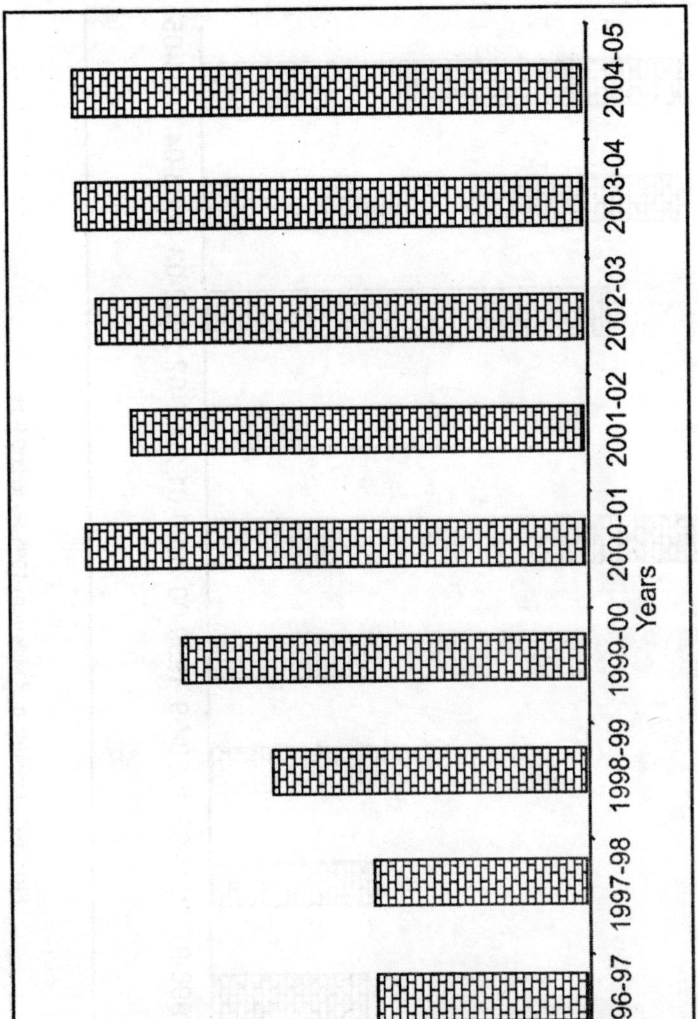

Fig. 16.3 : Total Milk Procurement from 1995-96 to 2004-05

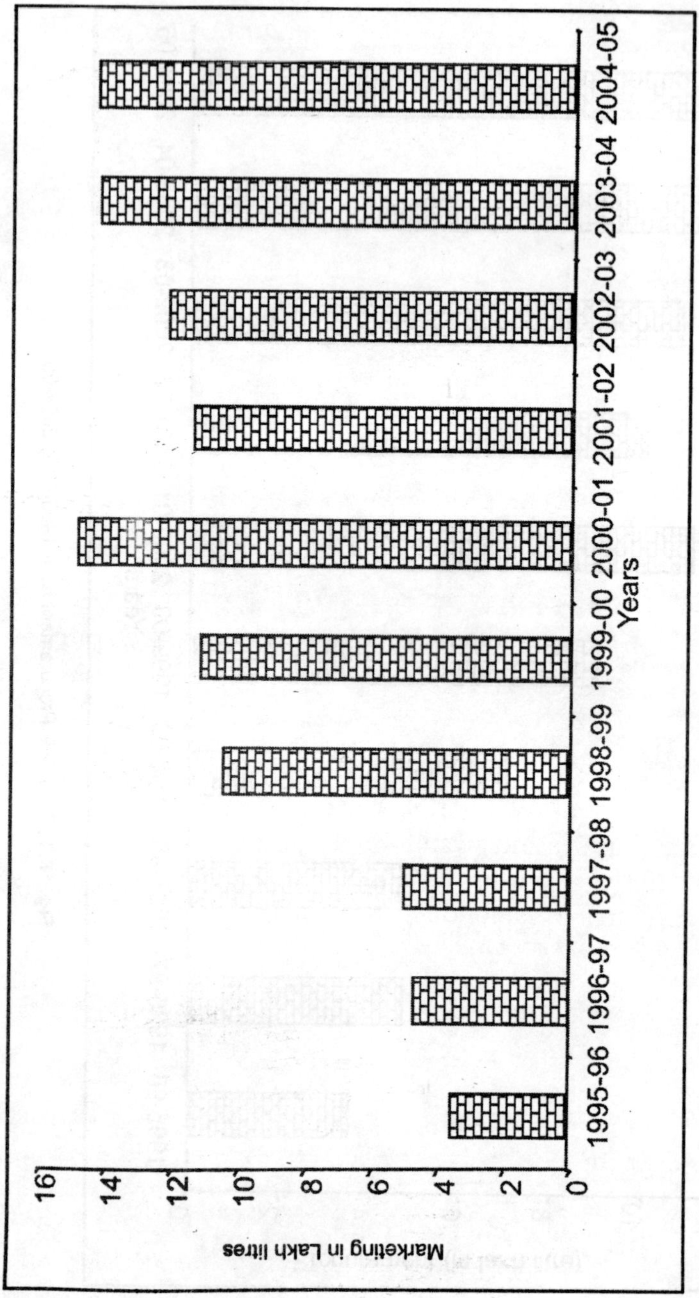

Fig. 16.4 : Marketing of Milk from 1995-96 to 2004-05

of products, the Quality Control Laboratory was upgraded by equipping it with all mandatory Laboratory Equipments.

Marketing

Despite expansion of marketing network, the visibility of the products and outlets was very limited. During the year 2004-2005, intensified advertisement drive was conducted through Wall paintings, Danglers, Panaflex Hoardings, etc. in order to improve upon the aesthetics and ensure hygienic handling of products, insulation of all milk vans and carriage of milk in crates were made mandatory. Insulated Boxes were provided to all the Retail outlets for safe storage of milk and products.

As part of sales promotion programme, visits of schoolchildren to the Dairy, Retailers' and Dealers' meet were carried out at regular intervals. The Union also participated and exhibits its products in events like Trade Fairs, Exhibition, *Melas*, etc.

Training and Skill Upgradation

Trainings, awareness campaigns and skill upgradation programmes have become an integral part of the operation. A series of trainings and awareness programmes were conducted during the year within and outside the state. Some of the important trainings conducted during the year are given in Table 16.5.

Dairy Cooperatives and Economic Development

The growth of Indian economy can be partially viewed by the progress of the dairy industry. Millions of small farmers isolated in various parts of the country have gained the strength to sustain their livelihood. The cooperatives have started to provide gainful employment and brought farmers close to the market. In the beginning of the dairy Cooperative in India, farmers were at

Table 16.5 : Trainings Conducted During 2004-05

Sl. No.	*Name of the Programmes*	*No. of Participants*	*Place*
1.	Orientation programme, Officer cadre	1	KOMUL, Dimapur
2.	Fertility camp	482	11 different DCSs
3.	Women farmers' induction programme	74	KOMUL,Dimapur
4.	Animal Health Camp	47	Bhagatbil
5.	DCS Secy training	14	KOMUL,Dimapur
6.	Workshop on Managerial Skill of KOMUL Employees	14	Conducted by NESCOM at KOMUL
7.	Farmers' Orientation-*cum*-Awareness camp	468	At Millennium DCS
8.	Dairy Animal Management	179	At 12 different DCSs

the mercy of the middlemen. Today, with about 100 lakh farmer producers, Indian dairy farmers have been shown the way to prosperity and health. The ideal conditions for long term growth in procurement have been created. The factors are:

- Modern technologies in animal breeding and feeding have been adopted by a significant number of farmers.
- Modern consumer processing and marketing facilities have been created all over the country.
- Technical input services including animal insemination, balanced cattle feed/bypass proteins feed, better fodder varieties and emergency veterinary health services – have not only helped in raising and sustaining milk production but have also ensured a better quality of life in the villages.

Besides creating urban employment in dairy plants, marketing, transport and distribution, these dairy cooperatives have helped to provide farmers with a sustainable rural employment programe. A majority of the cooperative members are landless, marginal or small farmers who contribute their produce of milk at the cooperatives. For these contributors, the income derived from milk provides their only regular cash flow, transforming dairying into an economic activity. The village cooperative is a clean well lit and orderly place. The villages have gone through a similar transformation ever since the cooperatives began to operate. Thus when people of a village see cleanliness, sanitation, hard work and discipline in the cooperative and thus they know that the cooperative serves them well. It probably inspires them to bring more of these qualities into their lives.

The women members of our dairy cooperatives visit our dairies. They are shown the mysteries of artificial insemination under a microscope. Their knowledge of conception in animals helps them to better understand their own lives and thus they have to begin to control their family as desired by the Government.

The efficacy of the modern medicine has helped poor villagers to find that a veterinarian can cure an animal that would have otherwise died. When they see their income from milk increases as their animals improve, and the farmer produces better feeds as they ensure better housing and care, they learn to have confidence and hope on the system of cooperation. Now they can take control of their own destinies.

Dairy cooperatives are giving a fresh lease of life to farmers in drought-prone areas. Milk production and unexploitative marketing through the cooperatives is providing an assured source of income to farmers helping them sustain themselves against recurring drought. The migrating population is settling down. About Rs. 2,000 crore is being paid to the farmers in their villages daily morning and evening which constitutes a large portion of their income. Operation Flood has, therefore, emerged in India as the largest rural employment scheme. It has been able to modernize the dairy sector to a level from where it can take off to meet not only the country's demand for milk and milk products in the next century but can also exploit global market opportunities. India has provided that the right policy options which are now exercised to overcome some already visible signs of market disorder in the post-liberalization period. Among them are:

- Over-capitalization in the private dairy sector
- Ineffective enforcement of standards of processing, hygiene and quality
- A near absence of any monitoring mechanism to enforce market discipline.

These threats need to be countered to protect the long-term interests of milk producers, their organizations, as well as of the consumer.

When producers have such structures at their command, they have the means to ensure that the fruits of science and technology reach all those who benefit. It is only when such structures exist that farmer develops confidence in getting an assured remunerative price for their produce. This, in turn stimulates investment in productivity. Further, farmers also demand the delivery of services and inputs they need to realize returns on their investments. One big lesson learnt is that farmers must be respected and trusted. Though they may not be educated, or even literate, but they possess common sense and even wisdom. Frequently, they have shown the ability to rise above narrow self-interest to act together in pursuit of long-term goals and the common good.

The expansion of India's dairy industry since the early 1970s was the result of the successful implementation of Operation Flood (OF) by the National Dairy Development Board (NDDB). The National Dairy and Development Board (NDDB) was founded in 1965, with the mission of organizing poor milk producers, thereby transforming dairying into an instrument for the economic development of India's rural people. Operation Flood followed the success story of "Amul" and developed the principles based on Amul, called as Anand principle (based on the first such cooperative set up in 1946), intended to keep the milk cooperative in the private sector. Thus the cooperative dairy development scheme followed by OF based on complete 3-level marketing system owned and operated by 6.1 million individual small-scale dairy farmers. Some 57,000 village-level Dairy Cooperative Societies own 172 Milk Producers' Unions, which in turn control 22 State-level federations. These principles call for adherence to a:

- three-level, farmer-owned structure,
- professional management which reports to farmer controlled,
- boards of directors,
- right to hire and fire staff (no patronage appointments, or bureaucrats as managers),
- right to set producer and consumer prices, and
- right to file bankruptcy.

Operation Flood serves 6 million producers directly (60 per cent of which are marginal or small farmers or landless producers), and many more producers have benefited in various ways from the policy changes. Therefore, it can be safely assumed that a dairy cooperative is an institution which can usher in economic development in the states and to the country as a whole.[10]

Apex Dairy Cooperative Organisation

National Cooperative Dairy Federation of India (NCDFI), based at Anand (Gujarat), is the apex organisation for the cooperative dairy sector. Its members include federal dairy cooperatives of states and union territories. Primary objective of NCDFI is to facilitate the working of dairy cooperatives through coordination, networking and advocacy.

Important activities of NCDFI include: coordinating sale of milk and milk products of its members to the Ministry of Defence and other para military organizations, and marketing of frozen semen doses produced by Sabarmati Ashram Gaushala and Animal Breeding Centre.[11]

Conclusion

It is true that several encouraging attempts have been made by KOMUL over the years for the development of the economic status of the rural mass but the growth and development of KOMUL depends on the role of the Federation, dairy union and different dairy cooperatives. Different factors which may hamper the growth and development of the Union and dairy cooperatives are as follows:

1. Financial constraints of the farmers.
2. Non-availability of the fodder is another factor.
3. Lack of understanding between Union and Cooperative.
4. Lack of leadership quality amongst the members of the farmer's family.
5. Lack of awareness among the members of the co-operatives in relation to the management of the Union and the development and maintenance of the cooperative society.
6. Extend of Government support.
7. Extend of training and support by the Union.

Notes

1. *http://www.legal-explanations.com/definitions/cooperative.htm*
2. *http://www.ncui.net/*
3. *http://www.indiadairy.com/ind_profile_factsheet.html*
4. *http://72.14.235.104/search?q=cache:s6KdH-g3ZqgJ:www.censusindia.gov.in*
5. Tables Published/SCST/ dh_st_nagaland.pdf- Tribal population of Nagaland
6. Chasie, Charles, *The Road Less Travelled and Interviews,* Katalyst, Nagaland Human Development Report-2004.
7. *Evaluation Study on Integrated Dairy Development Project*, Pro-

gramme Evaluation Organisation. Planning Commission, Government of India, ttp://planningcommission.nic.in /reports/ peoreport/ peo/peo_iddp.pdf

8. *Dairy Development in Nagaland: A Saga of Progress* – Souvenir-National Project for Cattle & Buffalo Breeding Under Department of Animal Husbandry & Veterinary, Government of Nagaland.
9. Souvenir, Dept. AH & Vety., Govt. of Nagaland & Nagaland State Dairy Co-operative Federation Ltd.; 2003-04.
10. Annual Report of Dimapur District Cooperative Milk Producers' Union Ltd. Dimapur : Nagaland-2004-2005.
11. Karmakar, K.G & Banerjee, G. D. *Opportunities and Challenges in the Indian Dairy Industry, Technical* Digest- Issue 9, 2006.
12. *http://www.indiadairy.coop/appl/index.html*

17 Performance Evaluation of National Rural Employment Guarantee Scheme (NREGS) in North East India

A Study of Manipur

Rajmani Singh, Ksh. Ranjan Singh and Th. Surjit Singh

Introduction

India is one of the fast growing economies with a population of more than one billion. With this growing economy, rural unemployment is one of the most visible faces of poverty and social unrest in India. Lack of access to productive assets, financial resources and inadequate infrastructure for microeconomic development is the major cause of rural poverty along with high level of illiteracy and poor health. It is also true that 48 per cent of population in India do not get two meals a day. As per 2001 census, rural population was 741.66 million (70 per cent) out of 1027.01 million. The National Sample Survey Organization [NSSO] has estimated that poverty declined by mere 0.74 per cent during 2004-05. The survey also revealed that Indians below poverty line were 22.15 per cent in 2004-05. People in 45 per cent of villages don't work for more than 6 months in a year and 20 per cent do not get work opportunities in any form. It has been established that the rural-urban divide has been widening. The worsening disparity in the last decade is to a good measure the result of deceleration in agricultural productivity which, in itself, is a matter of concern in rural employment generation.

Over the last few decades a plethora of poverty alleviation programmes in various forms has been implemented in the country and a huge amount of social and financial investment has been made to achieve the sole aim and objective of poverty eradication. Most of the programmes were based on top-down approach and did not consider needs and requirements of the people and also the pace of rural development is far behind the expectation. The main reason behind the slow pace of development in rural economy is unable to reach benefit towards the direct beneficiaries at the grassroots level which is rightly pointed out by the former late Prime Minister Rajiv Gandhi, "that hardly 10 paisa is benefited out of Re. 1 spent for rural development project". Thus, it is true that unless we change the strategy of top-down to bottom-up strategy for rural economy in one side and mindset of the people on the other, we cannot lessen the burden of poverty nor can we solve the problem of unemployment.

Various centrally sponsored schemes of area based and beneficiary oriented programmes were undertaken by the government over the last few five year plans such as Training of Rural Youth for Self-Employment (TRYSEM) 1979, National Rural Employment Programme (NREP') 1980, Integrated Rural Development Programme (IRDP) 1980, Development of Women and Children in Rural Areas (DWCRA) 1982, Rural Landless Employment Guarantee Programme (RLEGP) 1983, Council for People's Action and Rural Technology (CAPART)1986, District Rural Development Agency (DRDA), 1993, Prime Minister Rojgar Yojana (PMRY)1993, Swarna Jayanti Gram Swarojgar Yojana (SJGSY) 1999, Jawahar Gram Samridhi Yojana (JGSY) 1999, Pradhan Mantri Gram Sadak Yojana (PMGSY) 2000, Sampoorna Grameen Rojgar Yojana (SGRY) 2001, National Food for Work Programme 2004, Bharat Nirman Programme 2005, National Rural Health Mission 2005, National Rural Employment Guarantee Scheme (NREGS) 2006, and so on. After successfully implementing all of the above centrally sponsored schemes for the upliftment of rural economy, the pace of rural development of the region remains standstill. Few of the schemes have already closed and few of the schemes have merged with the newly launching rural development programmes. One of the main reasons behind the slow pace of rural development in India in general and north eastern region in particular is lack of effective and efficient utilization of fund allocated for the development, lack of transparency from the policy makers and also lack of people's participation at the grassroots level.

National Rural Employment Guarantee Scheme (NREGS)

To eradicate the rural poverty and unemployment, the Government of India enacted the National Rural Employment Guarantee Act (NREGA) which, indeed, is a revolutionary and historic landmark in independent India because it provides at least 100 days of employment for desiring rural households through Gram Panchayats. The enactment of the legislation marks a paradigm shift from the earlier programmes in ensuring to the unemployed rural household a legal right to get at least 100 days' wage employment. The National Rural Employment Guarantee Act, 2005, was passed unanimously in the Lok Sabha on 23rd August, 2005. It came into force in 200 districts on 2nd February, 2006.The two rural development programmes of Sampoorna Grameen Rojgar Yojana (SGRY) and National Food for Work Programme (NFWP) are being subsumed within the NREGS in 200 districts identified in the initial stage and is due to be extended to the whole of rural India within five years. The objectives of the Act *inter alia* include creation of durable assets and providing employment opportunities in the rural areas, thereby curbing the problem of migration to the urban areas in pursuit of employment and boosting the rural economy.

In one year of NREGS 1.47 crore households were provided with employment against the demand from 1.51 crore households in 200 districts of the 27 States in the country. Of the 53.65 crore person-days of employment generated 21.13 crore were the women and of about 5.81 lakh works taken up,

2.34 lakh were completed. The programme had a total available fund of Rs. 9,856.92 crore and the total expenditure was Rs 5,033.48 crore, which forms 51.07 per cent of the available funds. While 64 per cent of the 5.81 lakh works taken up were water based, road construction 23.2 per cent and other works like land development accounts 12.7 per cent.

The NREGS is way behind yielding desired results. Not only the scheme could not provide employment to all eligible, in many cases the labourer did not get the stipulated rate of wages too. According to a recent survey, in 2006-07, only 6 per cent of households registered in the scheme in the country got 100 days of employment as prescribed by law. The lackluster attitude of the government machinery to implement the scheme properly was evident as the survey showed that 4 out of 14 states – Bihar, Orissa, Gujarat and Haryana — did not even constitute State Employment Guarantee Council though more than a year has passed.

The NREGS was formally launched in February 2, 2006, in 200 districts of the country. An additional 130 districts were notified under Phase II with effect from May 15, 2007. From April 1, 2008, all 605 rural districts in the country were covered under Phase III of the scheme. The allocation for the NREGS for 2006-07 was Rs. 11,300 crore (200 districts) and Rs. 12,000 for 2007-08 (330 districts) and Rs 20,000 crore for 605 districts from April 1, 2008. However, against this allocation, only Rs 8,800 crore was actually spent in 2006-07 and this year the expenditure is likely to touch Rs. 10,000 crore at the most. During 2007-08, the Union Government made budgetary provision of Rs. 12,000 crore for the NREGS. The total amount available with the states up to March, 2008, including the balance from the previous year, was Rs. 19,028 crore. The total expenditure reported till March 2008 was Rs. 15,678 crore.

Thus, it will provide an employment to 2.10 crore rural households in 200 districts in 2006-07, creating 90.5 crore man-days. Of this, over 60 per cent are belonged to schedule castes and schedule tribes. Also, 40 per cent of those employed were women.

NREGS in North East India

National Rural Employment Guarantee Scheme was first launched in the region on the same date along with 200 initial district selected for the country on 2nd February 2006. Out of total 200, 16 districts from North East India have been covered to get the benefit of this scheme. Further 23 districts in the second phase and another 47 districts in the third phase have been covered under this scheme. Thus, today all the every districts of the North East India are under the grips of NREGS.

Table 17.1 : NREGS Districts in North East India

Sl. No.	*States*	*Phase-I*	*Phase-II*	*Phase-III*	*Total*
1.	Arunachal Pradesh	1	2	13	16
2.	Assam	7	6	14	27
3.	Manipur	1	2	6	9
4.	Meghalaya	2	3	2	7
5.	Mizoram	2	2	4	8
6.	Nagaland	1	4	6	11
7.	Sikkim	1	2	1	4
8.	Tripura	1	2	1	4
	Total North East India	16	23	47	86 (76)
	All India Total	200	130	275	605(593)

Source: Ministry of Rural Development, Government of India.

Table 17.1 represents the NREGS districts in North East India under phase-I, phase-II and phase-III respectively. Out of 200 rural districts identified for first phase in India, 16 districts from North East India have been selected of which Assam have 7 districts (Bongaigaon, Dhemaji, Goalpara, Karbi Anglong, Kokrajhar, Lakhimpur and North Cachar Hills). 2 districts each of Mizoram (Lawnglai and Saiha) and Meghalaya (South Garo Hills and West Garo Hills) and rest one district each of Tamenglong, Mon, Upper Subansiri, North District and Dhalai in Manipur, Nagaland, Arunachal Pradesh, Sikkim and Tripura respectively. In the second phase another 130 districts have been extended of which 23 districts from North East India have been selected for the scheme. In the third phase another 47 districts of the region have been covered under the NREGS schemes. Thus, all together 86 districts have been covered in North East India.

Table 17.2 : Financial Performance under NREGS in North East India during 2007-08, Phase-I and Phase-II

(Rs in lakhs)

States	*OB as on 1st April of the year*	*Fund Release by the Centre*	*Misc. Receipt*	*Total Funds*	*Total Cumulative Expenditure*	*%age of Exp. Against Total Funds*
Arunachal Pradesh	—	105.38	—	105.38	—	—
Assam	15377.26	35091.87	7047.58	57516.71	10887.64	18.93
Manipur	—	1088.13	—	1088.13	—	—
Meghalaya	509.14	3687.12	23.13	4219.39	2109.91	50.01
Mizoram	1211.10	652.96	4.50	1868.56	1517.76	81.23
Nagaland	140.33	2166.59	—	2306.92	36.14	1.57
Sikkim	710.98	—	—	710.98	94.58	13.3
Tripura	711.89	12451.45	637.37*	13800.71	2479.49	17.97
NE Total	18660.70	55243.50	7712.58	81616.78	17125.52	20.98

*(i) Rs. 421.77 lakhs release of last year but received during current year.
(ii) Rs. 185.60 lakhs release from State Government during current year.
(iii) Misc. received Rs 30.00 lakhs.
Sources: www.nrega,nic.in

Table 17.2 shows the Financial Performance under NREGS in North East India during 2007-08 under Phase-I and Phase-II. It has been observed that except Mizoram and Meghalaya other states of the region were not able to utilize the sanctioned funds and released fund for the purpose. As a result the entire North East India account only 22.98 per cent of the total fund could utilized. Mizoram could utilize 81.23 per cent of the total allocated fund under the scheme followed by Meghalaya with 50.01 per cent.

The implementation of third phase of NREGS has given a new dimension to North East States in the same line with other states and Union territories of the countries. All the districts of the region are now under the schemes and showing a ray of development from this scheme unlike the other centrally sponsored scheme after independence.

NREGS in Manipur

The NREGS is implemented for the first time in Tamenglong district under phase-I in 2006. Now it is implemented in all the nine districts of Manipur including Tamenglong district. As per census report there are 2,391 villages in Manipur of which Senapati district cover 625 villages, Churachandpur district cover 546 villages, Chandel 361, Imphal East 204 villages, Ukhrul 198 villages, Tamenglong 171 villages, Imphal West 134, Thoubal 103 and Bishenpur having 49 villages. Some of the villages in the hill areas are notoriously inaccessible and equally disturbed.

The Manipur Information Centre at New Delhi has recently informed that out of 86,458 households, who demanded employment under the National Rural Employment Guarantee Act (NREGA), 64,458 households were provided employment during 2007-08. Official sources at the Ministry of Rural Development said that all 20,024 households, which demanded employment in Tamenglong and 44,434 households in Churachandpur district, were provided employment during the period.

Of the Rs. 2553.06 lakh allotted under the programme for Manipur, Rs. 2078.48 lakh was spent during the period, in which Tamenglong got Rs. 652.87 lakh, Churachandpur Rs. 1765.68 and Chandel got Rs. 134.51 lakhs. Total works under the programme were 1232 of which only two have been completed. During the period, 15.34 lakh man-days were generated in the State, sources said.

Problems in Implementation of NREGS

Among the numerous irregularities and ways of manipulating master rolls and wages detected by the CAG report as the problems in implementation of NREGS in the country. Manipur in particular and the region in general is no exception. In spite of several controlling measures and inspection at different levels, problems were encountered at different stages. Following are the few selected problems in implementation of NREGS in the State and more specifically in the region is given below :

- Lack of proper planning and management in implementation of NREGS. Block level committee and village level committee or Gram Sabha were unable to prepare proper long-term planning, labour budget, accounting and record keeping due to lack of appropriate knowledge on planning, budgeting and accounting.
- Distribution of job cards to non-registered is the main problem encountered while implementing NREGS in Manipur. For instance in Henglep TD block of Churachandpur district, the Deputy Commissioner detected 337 excess job cards and later it has been cancelled. Further, fraudulent withdrawal from the NREGS funds by cheating job card holders and without taking up actual physical works has been detected at Singngat block of Churachandpur district in Manipur.
- CAG report 2008 stated that in Manipur, "No written applications for work were on record. Work was provided on verbal consent of workers."
- It is also found that in Churachandpur district on many instances, unidentified persons collected job cards from the villagers and took away the wages to be distributed to NREGS workers.
- Engaging of JCB for works so as to allow deduction of wages of the job card holders while there was a total ban on contractors and labour, replacing machinery in place of manual works under the NREGS.

- One of the Block Development Officers also alleged that the village chief had withdrawn the whole amount worth of Rs. 2,55,200 for the work to be taken up at a Jatropha plantation under NREGS without carrying out the actual works.
- Most of the NREGS works were not on the priority list given in the NREGA and also most of the funds for NREGS were utilized for road connectivity and plantation in the hills and cleaning of ponds and drains in the valley in lieu of giving more attention on the durable assets creation.
- NREGS demand active community participation for ensuring transparency and public accountability which is very much lacking in the state like Manipur and other states of the region.
- It is also observed that there is no real social audit process taking place in any location in any of the NREGS districts nor is there any system to do so.

It is evident that both the number and quality of human resources deployed so far are completely inadequate and more than 90 per cent of the workers are women which make difficult for shouldering the complex and manifold responsibilities of NREGA scheme implementation in the State.

A web-based Management Information System (MIS) has been put in place to record and make available, *via* the Central Government NREGA website, consolidated district-wise, block-wise and village-wise data pertaining to registrations, employment, funds, works, etc. contradictory to this, in Manipur only Imphal West district has a web based management information system.

Suggestions for Improvement of NREGS in Manipur

From the above analysis, following recommendations can be made for improvement of NREGS particularly in Manipur and North East India in general which include:

- Deployment of full time professionals dedicated to NREGA at all levels, but most crucially at the block level, which is at the cutting edge of implementation.
- For smooth payment and removal of delay, adequate amount of funds should be allocated and also services of post office and bank must be taken to prevent from misuse and diversion of funds sanctioned for the purpose.
- Durable assets generation activities must be undertaken as per the nine different priorities list given under the NREGA mandatory.
- More effort must be undertaken to strengthen the village-level planning and decision-making by revamping current operational structures. For this, village communities must be consulted for implementation of any NREGS works on priority basis as per the Act.
- NREGS workers must be covered under the rural poor category of the Janashree Bima Yojana (JBY) which is jointly launched by Government of India and LIC of India in 2000.
- For effective and more transparency in implementation, the guidelines of the ministry must be adopted by the State and regularly inspected. As per the guidelines given in the Act, 2 per cent of works are to be inspected by a State-level officer, 10 per cent by a district officer and 100 per cent by a block officer and these guidelines must be strictly implemented in the State.
- The NREGA gives a central role to social audits as a means of continuous public vigilance. The process involves public verification of 11 stages of NREGS implementation, from registration of families to evaluation of work. Social audits must be held twice a year at the Gram Sabha level for all works done in the preceding year.
- An important feature of the NREGS, compared to other

government schemes, is its emphasis on transparency. The NREGA operational guidelines prescribe detailed formats for monitoring both physical and financial performance. Based on these formats, State Governments must compile and send in their reports.

- A web-based Management Information System (MIS) has been put in place to record and make available, *via* the Central Government NREGS website, consolidated district-wise, block-wise and village-wise data pertaining to registrations, employment, funds, works, etc. Till date only Imphal West district is having the system. All the remaining eight districts must be equipped with the system to implement the scheme effectively.

Concluding Remarks

From the above discussion on the performance of NREGS at national level, regional level as well as state level, it can be concluded that National Rural Employment Guarantee Schemes is considered as one of the distinct rural development programmes introduced by the Government of India till date with full of aspirations and expectations. The NREGS has been considered the most powerful initiatives ever undertaken by the government for transformation of rural livelihoods in India. The main reasons behind this are its transparency, accountability, social audit, local people involvement, durable assets generation, 100 days job guarantee, unemployment allowance and so on. But the pace of success rate is far behind the expectation. The Ministry of Rural Development is claiming 33 per cent success rate after one year of its implementation. However, to realize the expectation of NREGS and its potential, it must focus on raising the productivity of agriculture in India's most backward regions, *i.e.*, North East India. Here the dedicated effort and firm commitment of the local people, officials associated with different levels of NREGS, respective State Governments, North Eastern Council, Ministry of DONER and Central Government particularly Ministry of Rural Development is highly essential. Without this, the agenda for rural development will remain as unfinished agenda like other rural development programmes.

References

Singh, Rajmani *et al.* (2007): 'Growth and Development of Rural Urban Settlements in Manipur', Paper presented in two days regional seminar on Habitation Pattern in Manipur. Organized by Department of Geography, Manipur University on 23rd and 24th March.

The Sangai Express, 11th July 2004.

The Sangai Express, 9th December 2003.

Office record of the Directorate of Employment Exchange, Government of Manipur.

Census of India 2001 Series 14, Manipur.

Ved Prakash Memorial Lecture, delivered by Prof. M.S. Swaminathan in New Delhi on May 21st 1999.

18 Khadi and Village Industries in Arunachal Pradesh

Its Impact on Socio-Economic Development

Ram Krishna Mandal

Introduction

The main principle of Gandhian approach is to set up a system of village self-sufficiency. In this regard, the hypothesis of M.K. Gandhi was establishment of 'Gram Swaraj' in the country side which means the complete independence of the Indian villages. The ultimate goal of Gandhian planning was to make Indian villages fully independent. Mahatma Gandhi often used to say that the real India was to be found in the villages, not in the cities and towns. This sector has not only continued to play a vital role in fulfillment of socio-economic objectives but also offers an excellent opportunity for industrial self-employment.

It was Mahatma Gandhi, who pioneered the revival of the age-old self-sufficiency (*Gram Swavalamban*) and leased a new life and glory to the concept of *Swadeshi*. According to Gandhi, the law of *Swadeshi* was the *Swadharma* of the *Gita* interpreted in terms of one's physical environment. Gandhi advocated Khadi as the necessary and most important corollary of the principle of *Swadeshi* in its application to society, he warned that "it is the greatest delusion to suppose that the duty of Swadeshi begins and ends with merely spinning some yarn and wearing Khadi made from it. In *Swadeshi*, there is no place for ill-will. It is a doctrine of self-less service and has its roots in the purest *ahimsa*, love" (R. Chowdhury, *Gandhi's Ethical Ideas,* 2007).

The aim and objective of the Khadi and Village Industries (KVI) in the State is to promote the industrial activities in the State and thereby to provide employment opportunities to the rural and urban and to improve the economic conditions of the people. About 94 per cent population of Arunachal Pradesh lives in the rural belt making agriculture the main occupation. The world is moving towards natural and eco-friendly products. More and more people are becoming conscious of responsibility towards the environment and ecology and products like plastic, etc. are highly looked down upon and greater demand is being generated for bio-degradable and eco-friendly products. The KVI Sector produces a wide range of exclusive products which are having distinct characteristics. Most of the projects of KVIC are local resource based and eco-friendly and which is very much suitable for a place like Arunachal Pradesh.

Khadi Industries have played a pioneering role in restoring the lost glory of the time tested for self-employment model, the model of just distribution of wealth, the model that generates maximum number of employment, the model that employs local resources and local talent to produce for masses. As we know, the advent of the British in India saw an emergence of a new politico-economic policy, which aimed at annihilating the traditional industry and handicrafts to find an outlet for its own products in the Indian market. The shear discrimination and oppressive policy totally led to destruction of the Indian handicrafts *vis-à-vis* the village self-sufficiency. It was Mahatma Gandhi, who pioneered the revival of the age-old self-sufficiency (*Gram Swavalamban*) and leased a new life and glory to the concept of Swadeshi. Initially, Khadi and village industry was entirely a non-governmental effort under the inspired guidance of Gandhi. In 1923, he founded the All India Khadi Board, an integral part of the Indian National Congress. In 1925 he formed an autonomous organization called 'All India Spinner Association' (AISA). In 1935, for the promotion of other village industries he set up 'All India Khadi and Village Industries Association' (AIVIA). To Gandhi, Khadi and Village Industries are absolutely inter-dependent and so later the AISA and AIVIA were merged into a single entity under the banner of 'Akhil Bharat Sarva Seva Sangh'. After Independence, the Government of India set up the All India Khadi and Village Industries Board in 1953. This Board, aimed to function in close cooperation with the State Governments and the Akhil Bharat Sarva Seva Sangh plagued with procedural handicaps. It was then decided in 1955 to replace this Board by a statutory body. Accordingly, the Khadi & Village Industries Commission (KVIC) came into being in 1957.

The broad objectives of the KVIC are: (i) The social objective – of providing employment, (ii) The economic objective – of producing salable articles, and (iii) The wider objective – of creating self-reliance amongst the people and building up a strong community spirit.

Rural industrialization is important not as a means of generating employment opportunities in the rural areas with low capital cost and raising the real income of the people, but because it contributes to the development of agriculture and urban industries. Without rural industrialization, it would be considerably more difficult to solve the problem of agricultural unemployment and widespread under-employment. Rural industrialization promotes rural industry.

According to Khadi and Village Industries Commission, "rural industry or village industry is the one which is located in the rural area and produces any good or renders any service with or without use of power and in which the fixed capital investment per head of an artisan or a worker does not exceed Rs. 50,000 (fifty thousand)" (Dr. N. K. Trikha, 2005). The definition of village industry has been recently modified by the government so as to enlarge its scope. Accordingly, any industry located in rural areas, village or town with a population of 20000 and below and an investment of Rs.10 million in plant and machinery, is classified as a village industry.

Rural industry embraces different kinds of village and small industries. All the village industries have been grouped into seven major categories as follows:

1. Mineral based industry,
2. Forest based industry,
3. Agro based industry,
4. Polymer and chemical based industry,
5. Engineering and non-conventional industry,
6. Textile industry (excluding khadi), and
7. Service industry.

Need for Rural Industrialization

Developing industries in the rural areas is essential because: (i) Rural industries are labour intensive, (ii) By providing employment, these industries have also high potential for income generation in the rural areas, (iii) These industries encourage dispersal of economic activities in the rural areas and thus, promote balanced regional development, (iv) Rural industries also and help protect and promote art and creativity, *i.e.*, the age-old rich heritage of the country. Rural industries being environment-friendly lead to development without destruction.

Programmes of Rural Development

The Government has initiated a number of policy initiatives through various central ministries for over-all promotion of village and small scale industries. Some of the important policies are:

1. Progressive allocations made in the five year plans,
2. Policy of reservation,
3. Price preference (up to 15 per cent) and purchase preference policy for marketing small scale industrial products,
4. Technical assistance through industrial extension service centres,
5. Provision of built up factory accommodation in industrial estates,

6. Supply of machines under the hire purchase system,
7. Subsidy on power consumption,
8. Provision of raw material,
9. Policy of priority credit, and
10. Entrepreneurship Development Programmes conducted by various National Institutes and support to State level institutes.

The Centre and State Governments in India have also sponsored various employment generation and poverty alleviation programmes for development of rural industries. Some of them are as follows:

(1) Prime Minister's Rozgar Yojana (PMRY)

The PMRY was launched on 2nd October, 1993 with the objective of providing employment opportunities to educated unemployed youth through setting up of small-scale enterprises in rural and urban areas. The loans under the scheme are available to all educated unemployed youth between 18-35 years (18-45 years for women) who have passed 8th standard examination for undertaking all economically viable activities including agriculture and allied activities. This scheme also provides for preference to weaker sections and women. The PMRY has been allocated Rs. 196.65 crore in 2005-06 budget. It has a tenth plan target of setting up 11 lakh micro enterprises providing employment to 16.5. lakh persons.

(2) Swarnjayanti Gram Swarozgar Yojana (SGSY)

SGSY which was initiated on April 1, 1999, is a credit-*cum*-subsidy programme. It aims at establishing a large number of micro enterprises in rural areas. The beneficiary families may be individuals or groups (SHGs). In order to give an impetus to the group, a revolving fund of Rs.25,000 is provided from banks. In addition, for individual, subsidy is also provided at

30 per cent of the project cost subject to Rs. 7,500. In respect of SCs /STs and disabled persons subsidy is 50 per cent of the project cost subject to a maximum of Rs.10,000. For groups of swarozgaris the subsidy is 50 per cent of the scheme cost, subject to per capita subsidy of Rs.10,000 or a total of Rs.1,25,000 whichever is less. Within the target group, special safeguards have been provided to vulnerable sections by way of reserving 50 per cent benefits for scheduled castes/scheduled tribes, 40 per cent for women and 30 per cent for disabled persons. It is envisaged that 50 per cent of the groups formed in each block should be exclusively for women.

Today, in the country, two lakh SHGs are linked with banks under this scheme. The number will be increased to 2.5 lakh in 2005-06. The Swarnjayanti Gram Swarozgar Yojana (SGSY) has been allocated Rs.862.24 crore from the total central plan outlay for 2005-06.

(3) Rural Employment Generation Programme (REGP)

The Government through Khadi and Village Industries Commission is implementing this programme for the promotion and development of Agro and rural industries. The revised target for the Tenth Plan under the REGP is to generate 25 lakh additional employment opportunity and Rs. 369.95 crore has been provided for the rural employment generation programme in 2005-06 budget in the country.

Under this scheme, the KVIC provides margin money assistance at the rate of 25 per cent of the project cost up to Rs.10 lakh and for projects above Rs.10 lakh and up to Rs.25 lakh, rate of margin money is 25 per cent of Rs.10 lakh plus 10 per cent on remaining cost of the project. In the case of SC/ST/OBC/women/ physically handicapped and other special category, the margin money grant is 30 per cent of the project cost up to Rs.10 lakh and for projects above Rs.10 lakh and upto Rs.25 lakh, is 30 per cent of Rs.10 lakh plus 10 per cent of the remaining cost of the project. Under this scheme the beneficiary's contribution is 10 per cent of the project cost. In the case of SC/ST and other weaker sections, beneficiary's contribution is 5 per cent of the project cost.

(4) District Rural Industrial Project (DRIP)

The National Bank for Agricultural and Rural Development is implementing this programme. The main objective of the project is to generate sustainable employment opportunities through coordinated efforts in financing rural non-farm enterprises, creation of essential infrastructure and also enabling promotional agencies to take up entrepreneurial development, technology upgradation, raw material supply, marketing assistance and other common services with an area covering the entire district. The emphasis in the project is on provision of timely and adequate credit support.

The State Khadi & Village Industries Boards have come into existence in response to advice of the All India Khadi & Village Industries Board which was required by the Government Resolution of January 14, 1953 to work "in close cooperation with the State Government". Today there are 33 States and Union Territories Khadi & Village Industries Boards in the country.

The Arunachal Pradesh Khadi & Village Industries Board (APKVIB) was created by a State Act. The Board was initially under the administrative control of Department of Industries lately on bifurcation of this department and on creation of Department of Textile & Handicrafts it was placed under latter's administrative control. This Board like any other State Boards was positioned to promote the KVI sector and to act as a replica of KVIC at the State level. The Board is a promotional body with no income of its own as it does not undertake any commercial operation but generally channelizes and monitors utilization of central sector developmental funds provided by KVIC. The broad objectives are similar to that of the KVIC within the jurisdiction of the state of Arunachal Pradesh.

However, the State Government has to bear its establishment and administrative expenses. The APKVIB Act was amended in 1998 and also framed its Rules and Regulations in this year. The Board got its first developmental fund from the KVIC in year 1991-92.

The tribal communities were extremely self reliant; they constructed their own inter village path, build their own cane bridge, devised their own indigenous equipments to husk or grind rice and millets, weaving their own cloths, ornaments and jewels, hats, cooking vessels, weapons. This shows the exceptional similarities of Gandhian concept of self-reliance in the tribal communities of the State. However, there was hardly any development. The economy and the society at the dawn of independence were primitive. But, now the days are fast moving far from culture of self-sufficiency in this tribal soil. Thus, in the context of changing scenario, the study aims at making a study that the KVI sector is relevant in the tribal soil of Arunachal Pradesh.

In view of this, the paper attempts to address the objectives:

(i) To investigate the development of Khadi and Village Industries and employment scenario,
(ii) To find out the major problems faced by Khadi and Village Industries, and
(iii) To find the probable solutions of the problems in the State.

Development of Khadi and Village Industries and Employment Scenario in the State

The nodal agency for implementation of KVI programmes in the State is APKVIB. The Arunachal Pradesh Seva Sangh runs Human Resource Development Programme in the MDTC including Khadi spinning and weaving. The KVIC's State office headed by Assistant Director with 9 other supporting staff has been implementing REGP and other programme. The APKVIB is in a shocking position now in the State that it devoids the attention of the authority. The Chairman is appointed casually. There is no regular or full time CEO. The post of vice-chairman is non-functional and creates unnecessary strains on hard earn resources. State Government's funding is abysmally very meagre with no long-term plan on anvil. Indifference of the state authorities coupled with lack of institutional in built capacity has resulted *inter alia* a low treatment by KVIC in sharing developmental funds. The Board has ended up by distributing KVIC funds without further follow up/monitoring. The KAVIRC observes, 'although these Boards were supposed to be replicas of the KVIC at the State level, but in reality they have not gone beyond the disbursement of KVIC funds. The Boards have even not efficiently and properly performed their primary functions' (Report of KAVIRC, 1987). 'Organizational weakness, lack of trained manpower and technical expertise, inadequate support from the state government are some of the reasons for inability of the Board in making any significant impact' (Majumdar, 2000). The number of units of KVI established in different years is shown in Table 18.1.

Table 18.1 : No. of Units of KVI Established in Different Years

Year	*No. of Units*
1999 - 2000	9
2000 - 01	60
2001 - 02	23
2002 - 03	16
2003 - 04	14
2004 - 05	20
2005 - 06	19
2006 - 07	30
Total	191

Source: The Arunachal Pradesh Khadi and Village Industries Board.

The year-wise employment generation, total investment and per capita investment are shown in Table 18.2.

Table 18.2 : Year-wise Employment Generation

(Rs. in lacs and employment in No.)

Year	*Employment*	*Total Investment*	*PCI*
1991-92	107	26.70	0.250
1992-93	98	24.62	0.251
1993-95	222	55.48	0.250
1995-97	160	132.79	0.830
1999-2000	100	41.52	0.415
2000-01	378	187.21	0.495
2001-02	168	95.79	0.570
2002-03	190	103.83	0.546
2003-04	78	67.78	0.869
2004-05	137	99.64	0.727

Source: The Arunachal Pradesh Khadi & Village Industries Board.

Per capita investment (PCI) falls down from 1995-97 and moves up marginally from 2003. The PCI has been near stabilized from 1999-2000 to 2002-03. Then suddenly jumps up and again in 2004-05 falls considerably. Again the year-wise employment generations in different industries are shown in Table 18.3.

Table 18.3 : Industry-wise Employment Generation

Year	*Khadi*	*Mineral based*	*Agro based*	*Chemical based*	*Engineering & NCE*	*Textile*	*Forest based*	*Service Industry*	*Total*
1991-92	10	–	2	–	33	42	20	–	107
1992-93	10	–	23	–	24	36	2	3	98
1993-95	2	16	52	8	37	18	89	–	222
1995-96	–	–	19	38	46	18	39	–	160
1997-99	–	–	–	–	–	–	–	–	Nil
1999-00	–	22	16	–	34	–	22	6	100
2000-01	–	–	79	–	98	66	57	78	378
2001-02	–	24	48	–	46	–	32	18	168
2002-03	–	36	14	–	78	18	20	24	190
2003-04	–	–	–	–	38	26	14	–	78
Total	**22**	**98**	**253**	**46**	**434**	**224**	**295**	**129**	**1,501**

Source: The Arunachal Pradesh Khadi and Village Industries Board.

With the impact of globalization and development of education, the number of job-seekers is increasing drastically. The Khadi and Village Industries in the State are playing a significant role in employment generation.

Problems

The KVI are not commercially viable due to (i) lack of interest of weavers as minimum wages prevailing in the states are much higher than wages payable to Khadi Spinners and Weavers as per Khadi cost chart provision, (ii) lack of raw materials, (iii) lack of working capital or timely finance, (iv) lack of marketing facilities, (v) lack of capacity utilization, (vi) lack of technical know-how, (vii) devoid of organizational strength, (viii) competition on Khadi (hand spun & hand woven) from power loom (machine spun and machine woven) and hand loom(machine spun and hand woven), (ix) lack of entrepreneurial knowledge, (x) lack of power, (xi) lack of transport facilities, etc.

Let us discuss some major constraints.

1. *Market*

The KVI sector is not accessible to the modern means of marketing. In modern market economy, the buyer and seller are able to get in touch with one another so that the exchange of goods and services for money takes place between them. This can also be done through E-mail, internet, telephone, courier, speed post and ordinary mails. It is undisputedly accepted that success of an industry depends on market of its products. It has no well organized market outside this State and even inside the State. It has no world-wide Website and no advertisements through electronic or print media. Only entrepreneurs are given opportunities to participate to various exhibitions etc. which are also due to intrinsic reasons not availed to full extent.

2. *Inner-line System*

Inner-line System that was introduced in 1873 still exists even in the present changed scenario. This restricts the free movement of Non-Arunachalees to the State. A Non-Arunachalee who wants to cross beyond the Inner-line has to get the IL Pass issued for a limited period with certain conditionality as it is viewed that the territory is located at strategic-point from the stand point of defence. Besides, the Government of India feels it necessary to protect the tribal and their land and forest, who has a vivid socio-economic and cultural dimension, from the Non-Arunachalees' hunger of grabbing.

Globalization refers to a process of increasing economic integration and growing economic inter-dependence between the contemporary world economies. It is associated not only with increasing cross-border movement of goods, services, capital, IT, and people but also with an organization of economic activities which crosses national boundary. To get the good effect of globalization in the State it needs first cross state flows among the States of India. In fact the Inner-line system posing as a major hindrance for free flow of industrial environment.

The N.E. Region is isolated, landlocked which shares only 2 per cent of its border with the rest of the country and rest with Bhutan, Bangladesh, Myanmar and the Tibetan region of China. For most of this international border has been artificially created. The result has been the elimination of the region's trade, commerce and other linkages, which existed in the pre-independence days. These N.E. States are very close to the dynamic South-East and East Asian economics. It is imperative to develop a coherent policy linking this area (Dr. G. Sachdeva, JNU).

3. *Entrepreneurial Lack*

In the N. E. Region, the unemployment problem has become a paradox because the unemployment in the region is growing, not because there is lack of opportunities, but because the unemployed youths have failed to take advantage of the opportunities available. It is an accepted fact that the availability of entrepreneurship is the most important determinant in the process of industrialization. The government in its efforts to create entrepreneurship provides for various monetary and non-monetary incentives like the development of an infrastructure, assistance in marketing and procuring raw-materials, providing finance or granting subsidies on investment. Various state and central organization has accordingly been created to cater to the needs of entrepreneurs.

It can be argued that that lack of entrepreneurial skill of the local people and their deficient interest to invest and innovate has contributed in preventing the evolution of modern economic system in the State. One example of their lacking interest in setting up enterprises is that those tribal boys/girls who go for craft training do not want to have their own business but like to join as craft teachers in government organizations (Krishna, 2000). The mindset of the tribal is not to establish their own enterprise but to venture either in politics, contract business, or government services to earn "*easy money*". This mindset can be termed as *psychological barrier* which has emerged very strongly in the present socio-economic context of the State. Some tribal people within a very short period of time have experienced income and wealth inequalities to a high degree. Very few of them have been found to become very rich overnight and enjoy luxurious life and prefer conspicuous consumption which has been adversely affecting the rest of the society. The income inequalities in the tribal society are very strong. Some are very rich and some are stark poor. The presence of high degree of corruption at all levels and existence of underground economy is also a deterrent to state economy (Mandal, 2006).

4. *License Issuing System*

The outsiders who want to venture business in the State are to obtain licence in the name of some Arunachalees who get rent from the concern businessman for the licence. These trading people earn money and mostly siphon off in their respective home because they don't get the right to buy property for independent business. This status largely refrain the private investors incoming and opening up ventures in A.P. Institutional credit for trade and industries are available to the local people but they lack entrepreneurial skills and show hardly any interest in industrial activities. Therefore, like IL permit, the ***Licence issuing system of the government has discouraged*** the opening up of KVI units in the State.

5. *Lack of Dignity of Labour*

The contemporary Arunachalee, mostly, oblivious of their age-old pride of dignity of labour and even for petty household works they depend on migrated labour. This has quietly up-rooting the habit of doing productive works on self-help basis and making them dependent on others. This is contrary to the entrepreneurial trait.

6. *Power*

Power is one of the major infrastructures for the growth of industrial activities of any size. 'Arunachal has a huge potential for the development of hydroelectric power because of its many rivers. The State has the potential to supply one-third of total hydroelectric requirement of the country. The per capita consumption of electricity in Arunachal was 86.9 kWh in 2001-02 against the all-India average of 335 kWh (APHDR'2005, 45). In addition to water resource, the State has oil, natural gas and coal resources that can be used in the production of electricity. The Government of India has taken initiative for large scale production of hydropower. Such initiative will also have the spin-off benefits like employment avenues, increase in consumption of industrial products, roads, schools, banks, health care, postal facilities, and training centres etc. In 1971-72 only 37 villages were electrified. By March 2001 this has rose to 2,506 out of 3649 villages. The State having untapped estimated hydropower potential of 49,000MW, may emerge as powerhouse of India when this potential is fully harnessed (*Source*: Departmant of Power, GoAP).

7. *Transportation*

The service of transportation is a prerequisite for economic development. The road density in the State is very low. In 2001, the road density was 17.36 km per 100 sq. km of area as against the national average of 82 km per 100 sq. km. The main reasons for this low density are: the difficult topography and undulating terrain, the late start of development process, and the high cost of construction in the inaccessible and remote areas (APHDR, 2005, 44). The states does not have lateral roads connecting districts, since roads run vertically connecting places in Assam with districts or sub-divisions in A.P. This has not only resulted in high transportation costs but also affected by disturbed law and order situation and insurgency problem of Assam. The State at all has no railways except 1.26 km metre gauge railway line laid in 1989 connecting Bhalukpong with Indian railway map. This is a major handicap.

8. Banking Scenario

KVI comes under the priority sector *vide* RBI's circular No.RPCD.PLNFS.BC.84/06.0612/93-94 (*Source* RBI). The REGP is only scheme in common to be offered as rural industrialization tool. Under this major assistance has to come from bank as loan. In 2000-01, there were only 99 bank offices with an average of 9.07 offices per 1,00,000 population and availability of finance is not widespread in Arunachal yet. The credit-deposit ratio is only 17.25 per cent which is lowest among the N.E. States and is considerably lower than the national level (58.53%) (APHDR, 2005). There are vast areas where either there is no bank or a single man branch which is obviously not equipped to go beyond the normal banking transactions.

9. Vocational Training/Education

The State Government has a network of 88 craft centres, earlier called Cottage Industries Training and Production Centres (CITPC) Lack of modern tools-equipments, poor physical infrastructure, shortage of competent training instructors, outmoded curriculum and training methods, neglect of skill upgradation, low stipend offered to trainees etc. are some of the reasons for the suboptimal performance of the craft centres (Majumdar, 2000).

The dropout rates in Arunachal at the primary and upper primary level in 2003 were 20 per cent and 36 per cent respectively (APHDR, 2005). After primary school, vocational streams should be available to train the boys and girls in the local context so that they find education is relevant and employment oriented. Arunachal Pradesh is below the national level of female literacy (NPHDR, 2001). This is a case of Gender disparity contrasting women empowerment.

Probable Solutions

The following may be few suggestions to consider in order to strengthening the KVI in the State.

1. The State KVIB needs to be strengthened in different ways. It is in awful condition. The sector needs to be rejuvenated in totality. A carefully drawn holistic plan is the only panacea.
2. The sector needs advertisement for its product through all modern media. Initially, the free web-space provided by the KVIC in their website (www.kvic.org.in) for the state KVICs should be filled with information.
3. The State Government and the KVIC should implement the good recommendations made in the Anindo Majumdar Report, 2000.
4. Priority to develop border trades with Bhutan, China and Myanmar to be given.

5. A comprehensive techno-economic survey of the entire territory of A.P. should be done to find out potential area of activities under this sector.
6. Modernizing the government run craft centres is need worthy. Incorporation of innovative training streams on the basis of potentiality study. Setting up of inter-face with existing good technical and managerial institutes like SFRI, NERIST, IIE may be considered.
7. Complete financial support and its proper utilization in any probable unit should be shouldered by the government. KVIC at its special dispensation should do it. Identification of non-REGP villages and devising alternative scheme for these localities will be generous step in this direction.
8. Implementation and execution of KVI schemes and programmes should be left to APKVIB the local KVIC may perform mainly the supervisory and liaisoning role with GoI, KVIC head office etc.
9. The flow of relevant information relating to VSI (village and small industries) should be regularly circulated to keep the entrepreneurial world abreast with the recent trends. The department of Industries may launch a periodical bulletin.
10. The bank and FI should play more constructive role in lending credit support to good proposals. The A.P. Industrial Development and Financial Corporation needs to be revived. The monitoring machinery needs to be strengthened including detection of sick of industrial units and draw up a nursing plan for their rehabilitation.
11. Tourism/eco-tourism may be encouraged which will have ripple effect on the VSI. Nearing to the Eco-tourist spot, Gram-Udyog Darshan Park may be established to showcase the treasure-trove.
12. The State should strive hard to be self-sufficient in raw material, technical know-how, machines/tools and a well knitted marketing network.

13. A single item can be identified which could be synonymous with the name of the state. Escort services are given to V.I. unit in graduating it to a SSI unit.
14. The existence of IL System appears to be irrelevant in present global scenario and therefore authority may contemplate twice on its continuation.
15. Sustainability of any project depends upon fulfillment of certain basic requirements. Systematic approach, training to entrepreneurs, technology, quality control and marketing support etc. if all these will be taken care adequately, the KVIC can play an exemplary role in the process of Socio-Economic Development in Arunachal Pradesh.

Conclusion

The KVIC's funding policy need flexibility to the context of the State socio-economic situations. The State Government may display needed wisdom to reciprocate with KVIC to augment the efforts. The APKVIB needs a complete overhauling. The door be kept opened so that the autonomy that granted by the provision of the Act is realized unfettered for the benefit of the people. But again it should be under the scanner of social audit. The Chairman of APKVIB should not be a political man or should be a man of neutral, so that he cannot use its benefit for realizing the political mileage. It will be more befitting to the occasion if the Development Commissioner or Commissioner of Industries is made *ex-officio* chairman. A full time Chief Executive Officer is to be appointed for a sufficiently long tenure to work under direct control of chairman. This key post has to be held by an officer having proven track record of integrity, adequately qualified in the fleid of rural development and an aptitude for working in the unglamorous social sector. The Board should have a separate budget in the plan and non-plan document and should be released in form of statutory grants on time and not to depend on lump sum grant in aids.

Adequately reasonable service conditions will attract good professionals to serve in the Board.

Employment is the surest way to enable the vast numbers of people living below the poverty level to raise them above it. KVI is capable of offering employment opportunities at the place of residence to a large section of population. This has the capacity to correct regional imbalances by initiating industrial activities on dispersed basis in the most neglected, backward inaccessible areas like most of the areas of North East States where perhaps large scale sector is unable to penetrate. KVI is a key to rural development and rural prosperity.

References

Report of the Khadi and Village Industries Review Committee, under the Chairmanship of M. Ramkrishnayya, Ex-Chairman, NABARD & Ex-Deputy Governor, RBI, year 1987.

Human Development Report, 2005 of UNDP.

Samiran Das, Amal Prava Das (1986) '*A Biography*' translated by Hiranmoyee Devi, Publisher H. Devi.

Information from various records of Department of Industries, Government. of Arunachal Pradesh.

Compilations of Statistics/Reports of A.P. Khadi and Village Industries Board, Itanagar.

Arunachal Pradesh Human Development Report 2005, Department. of Planning, Government. of A. P.

Report of High Power Committee on KVI, 1994 under the Chairmanship of P.V. Narasimha Rao, then Prime Minister of India.

Publication of National Institute of Rural Development on Rural Industrialization 1999, NE Regional Centre, Guwahati.

Mandal, R. K. (2005): *Arunachal Economy: Socio-Economic Transformation,* Champion Publisher and Distributor, Itanagar, pp.90-91.

Mandal, R. K. (2006): "Constraint of Economic Development in Arunachal Pradesh with Special Reference to Globalization and Inner Line System", *Artha Beekshan*, Vol.15, No.3, Kolkata.

Mandal, R. K. (2006): "Arunachal Economy as Emerging Power House", *Journal of Global Economy,* Vol. I, No. 4, October-December, p. 223.

Mandal, R. K. (2005): "Emergence of Marketing of Handloom and Handicrafts Products of A.P." paper presented in the Annual Conference of NEEA, October, 2005.

Majumdar (2000): *The Khadi and Village Industries Sector in Arunachal Pradesh*, published by KVIC, Govt. of India Report under their Fellowship Programme.

Sachdeva, G. (2008): *Introduction to the North East*, NE Yellow Pages 2005–06.

National Human Development Report, 2001.

Various issues of *Jagriti*, a monthly journal of KVIC.

Kamalakannan, K. (2008): 'Rural Industrialization and Poverty Alleviation', *Kurukshetra,* Vol. 54, No. 52, New Delhi.

19 Structure and Scenario of Agriculture in Nagaland

Raju Das

Introduction

The State of Nagaland was formally inaugurated on December 1, 1963, as the 16th State of the Indian Union. It is bounded by Assam in the West, Myanmar (Burma) on the east, Arunachal Pradesh and part of Assam on the North and Manipur in the South. It runs more or less parallel to the left bank of the river Brahmaputra. It has a land area of 16579 sq. km. and is a predominantly a hilly state. The State consists of eleven Administrative Districts, inhabited by 16 major tribes along with other sub-tribes. Each tribe is distinct in character from the other in terms of customs, language and dress.

The average rainfall is between 175 cm and 250 cm. Most of the heavy rainfall is during the 4 months from June to September. The rain during April to May is low. Strong winds blow from the North West in February and March. By and large, the climate is pleasant in the State.

The State of Nagaland is rich in natural resources. The people are basically agrarian. About 84 per cent of the total population is dependent directly or indirectly on agriculture. The State is comparatively backward and neither agriculture nor industries could make any significant headway. Of late, some structural changes are noticeable in the State. Modern methods of agricultural practice, growth of small business enterprises and urbanization are the features of modern Nagaland.

Urbanization and the growth of trade and small industries have reduced the significance of the agriculture sector in

Nagaland. The fundamental issue is that going by the distribution of main workers in Nagaland, cultivators account for 72.65 per cent of the total main workers of Nagaland. This seen in the light of the Sector contribution to the SDP means that 72.65 per cent workers of Nagaland contribute only 27.18 per cent to the Gross State Domestic Product. The other 72.82 per cent of the GSDP is generated by 27.35 per cent of the population. This comprises a large extent by salaried State Government employees.

With this background in mind, the paper is the modest attempt on the part of the author to study the structure and scenario of agriculture in the state of Nagaland.

Land Utilization Pattern in North East and Nagaland

Out of total geographical area of 255.09 lakh ha in the North East India, area under forest is 164.3 lakh ha (64 per cent). Arunachal Pradesh has the highest area (93.79 per cent) under forests followed by Mizoram (61.98 per cent). In Manipur forest area is sharply declining. Net sown area (NSA) in the region has increased from 31.61 lakh ha in 1977 to 38.05 lakh ha in 1995-96. The proportion of net sown area to total area is as low as 15 per cent as against 46.6 per cent for all-India average. Although the mono-cropped area dominates the region, the gross cropped area has increased from 39.41 lakh ha to 54.3 lakh ha due to newer area under cultivation and introduction of newer crops. There are a few exceptions like Arunachal Pradesh and Mizoram, where only 2.68 per cent and 3.09 per cent of the total reporting area are respectively cultivated, primarily on account of adverse conditions, difficult terrains and barren land. The cropped area in Manipur, Meghalaya and Nagaland is 8.32, 9.02 and 12.40 per cent respectively. Table 19.1 describes the pattern of land utilization in Nagaland.

Land Holding Pattern

Total operational land in the N.E. India is 53.4 lakh ha. The

Table 19.1 : Area under Different Land-uses in Nagaland

(in Hectares)

Sl. No.	Classification	2001-02	2002-03	2003-04	2004-05	2005-06
1.	Geographical area	1657900	1657900	1657900	1657900	1657900
2.	Reporting area for land utilization	1585525	1581720	1582534	1583862	1581892
3.	Forest	862930	862930	862930	862930	862930
4.	Not available for cultivation	66690	67340	74893	76129	75444
5.	Land put to non-agri. Uses	66690	67340	74893	76129	75444
6.	Barren and uncultivable land	NA	NA	NA	NA	NA
7.	Other uncultivable land excluding fallow land	184430	181470	179370	178370	176784
8.	Fallow land	161015	157210	160223	157412	157847
9.	Net area sown	309660	312770	305138	309021	30887
10.	Total cropped area	357310	363420	369927	380256	38679
11.	Area sown more than once	476500	50650	64789	71235	77910
12.	Net irrigated area	64400	64490	67500	66900	67350
13.	Gross irrigated area	73900	74290	77684	82660	106150

Source: Statistical Handbook of Nagaland, 2007.

highest operated area is 31.6 lakh ha in Assam and the lowest (0.8 lakh ha) is in Mizoram. Nagaland has the unique characteristic of having size of operational holdings at 6.8 ha, which is higher than the North-East India's average (1.59 ha) and also of the all-India level (1.6 ha).

Agriculture in Nagaland

Almost three-fourth of the working population in Nagaland is engaged in the primary sector. Like the other States of the North-East region, Nagaland is predominantly engaged in agriculture and its allied activities. Rice is the staple food and occupies about 70 per cent of the total cultivated area, consisting about 75 per cent of the total food grain production. Nagaland has been identified as a potential area for development of food processing industries in its geo-climatic conditions. The agriculture and allied sectors in Nagaland offer good inputs for development of a host of industries which could include floriculture, horticulture, rubber plantation and allied industries, sericulture, tea cultivation and processing, bamboo shot preservation, mushroom cultivation and processing, piggery, poultry, etc. Table 19.2 describes the production of principal agricultural crops in Nagaland during the last 5 years with effect from 2002-03 to 2006-07.

Table 19.2 : Production of Principal Agricultural Crops in Nagaland (2002-03 to 2006-07)

(in Metric Tonnes)

Crops	*2002-03*	*2003-04*	*2004-05*	*2005-06*	*2006-07*
Jhum Paddy	111100	128000	133500	134100	16000
T.R.C. Paddy	11440	122000	128250	129000	10352
Maize	80000	80260	83500	92880	10834
Bajra	4000	5000	4000	3130	Nil
Jowar	4000	5000	4000	820	750
Small Millets	13000	8000	6460	16000	1725
Wheat	17000	20000	13000	1920	1250
Barley	9500	10000	7000	Nil	Nil
Arhar	6000	7000	6000	7600	10150
Moong	2000	2900	1250	650	1260
Naga dal	2800	3440	3140	3150	4320
Beans	1250	2000	1000	1180	2010
Other Kharif Pulses	950	2560	1000	1100	2770
Pea	6200	4930	5440	10500	8790
Lentil	2300	1070	1100	5500	3510
Gram	750	2000	1000	400	470
Other Rabi Pulses	3500	3000	3150	6300	7190
Ground nut	2500	3000	6980	320	960
Soyabeans	35000	36000	48000	32000	30620
Sunflower	5500	6000	570	650	1060
Sesame	4500	5000	250	3750	3460
Niger	1000	760	880	850	560
Rape seed	18000	12800	20490	21180	20650
Linseed	8500	6400	5640	4800	5720
Sugarcane	80000	30000	142100	210880	233850
Cotton	5000	150	150	20	40
Jute	5500	11000	12100	8800	10650
Potato	61000	44050	95000	104000	31420
Tea	290	3020	3450	3340	3140

Statistical Handbook of Nagaland, 2007.

Shifting Cultivation

In the Northeastern India, more than two-thirds of total geographical area is covered by hills. Shifting cultivation (Jhum cultivation) is the common practice in the hills. About 4.43 lakh families solely depend upon shifting cultivation. The practice of jhum has been undergoing rapid changes particularly in the recent times. Jhum cycle declined from 10 to 15 years to 2-3 years. Since the jhum system has a number of merits, declining jhum cycle would have serious adverse implication to the poor. The strategy for Jhum improvisation in tune with socio-cultural milieu would benefit the society. Among the alternative methods of improvement include adoption of improved cultural practice, planting perennial crops, control of soil erosion, encouraging allied agricultural activities.

Crop intensity is an index of agricultural development and is directly related to irrigation facilities. Nagaland is a mountainous state and has red and yellow, deep, acidic and soil with low in fertility. Shifting cultivation (*jhum*) is a common practice in the state and rice is the important crop. The cropping intensity is 110 per cent. Fertilizer use is very low (less than 10kg/ha). Soil erosion is a problem.

Suggested technological interventions made for natural resource management for agriculture in the State are as follows:

- Liming and adequate fertilizer use for higher productivity in Mokokchung and Mon areas.
- 3-tier system as an alternative to shifting cultivation.
- Integrated farming system involving rice, pig and horticulture.
- Vermi composting.

The State has 0.15 million ha under rice cultivation, which covers mainly rain fed areas. The State average productivity is about 1.7 tonnes/ha. The major constraints in production are *jhum* cultivation, acid soils, low coverage of high-yielding varieties, and inadequate availability of seed and other inputs.

The interventions needed for it are:

1. Growing high-yielding varieties.
2. Discouraging *jhum* cultivation and encouraging of improved agricultural practices.
3. Application of lime.

Fruit productivity in Nagaland is comparatively very low (3.7 tonnes/ha) as compared to national average (9.9 tonnes/ha). The State has a potential for increasing fruit production, particularly pineapple with adoption of improved technologies: like, use of varieties Kew and Queen, planting in trenches across the slope in two rows, high density planting of 45,000 plants/ha, induction of uniform flowering with the use of 100 ppm ethephon, and application of nutrients based on tissue analysis, etc.

Animal Husbandry

Animal husbandry is an important component of the agriculture sector. Animal husbandry is a tradition with the Nagas and therefore, rearing of domestic animal such as Cattle, Mithun, Pig and Poultry birds play a significant role in the socio-economic development of the Nagas. Thus, the great responsibility of Veterinary and Animal Husbandry Department lies with matters relating to Livestock and Poultry development, prevention of livestock diseases, Dairy Development, Feed and Fodder Development including livestock statistics of the State. In other words, the Veterinary and Animal Husbandry and Dairying sector also provides gainful self-employment opportunities to the ever-increasing unemployment problems amongst the educated youths of the State.

This climatic condition of Nagaland is quite suitable for livestock rearing and for which rearing of livestock has been an integral part of Naga life from time immemorial and symbolic to the health and wealth of a Naga family.

In order to accelerate livestock industry during the 10th Five Year Plan, the department focused and intensified through appropriate techniques of breeding, feeding, health coverage and production oriented management programme. Table 19.3 gives an account of Livestock availability in Nagaland as per 2003 census.

Table 19.3 : Number of Livestock and Poultry in Nagaland as per 2003 Census

Livestock	*No.*
Cattle	423017
Buffalces	33757
Mithun	40452
Pigs	644214
Sheep	4187
Goat	174929
Rabbit	384085
Horse	893
Mules	13
Dogs	141373
Fowls	2605554
Ducks	116576

Source: Statistical Handbook of Nagaland, 2007.

Forests

The Nagalands flora and fauna vividly illustrates the diverse nature heritage that the North-Eastern region is blessed with. The State of Nagaland is covered by the vegetative growth of the evergreen tropical and sub-tropical forests which occupy 8,62,930 hectares of land in the State. Rare species of trees and plants are found in the forests of Nagaland. The variety of endangered species of animals and birds also make the forest regions of Nagaland their home.

The flora of Nagaland is dominated by the growth of the thick wooded trees like the mahogany and timber. Palm, rattan and bamboo trees are also abundantly found in the forests of the State. The government has reserved a part of the forest region exclusively for the State's inhabitants, who earn their livelihood through trade of the forest products. Most of the dense regions of the forests in Nagaland are impenetrable and remain inaccessible to the people. The interiors of the forests are rich in the fauna of Nagaland. Ferocious animals like the leopards and the bears reside in these interiors. A variety of arboreal monkeys are found in the forests of Nagaland. Elephants, deer, wild oxen, sambar and buffaloes also reside in the wooded forests. The Indian Hornbill is the State bird. But, the forest of Nagaland is receding due to its destruction to facilitate *Jhum* cultivation. The wanton destruction is leading to the gradual depletion of the flora and fauna of Nagaland. Table 19.4 depicts the Forest coverage in Nagaland during 2003-04.

Table 19.4 : Classification of Forest Area in Nagaland 2003-04

(In Hectares)

Particular	*Forest Area*	*% to Total Forest Area*
Reserved Forests	8583	0.99
Purchased Forests	19247	2.23
Protected Forests	50756	5.88
Wild life Sanctuary	22237	2.58
Virgin Non-accessible forest	477827	55.37
Degraded Forests	284280	32.95
Total	862930	100.00

Source: Statistical Handbook of Nagaland, 2007.

Fisheries

Nagaland is endowed with rich and unique natural resources, which provides immense potential for aqua-culture development. In spite of the available resources, aquaculture has not made much impact in the State so far. The meagre production of the State is still far from self-sufficient and this can be attributed to a number of constraints such as land locked hilly terrain, lack of adequate funds, lack of professional support and non-availability of critical inputs.

Of late, there have been certain remarkable changes in the State's fisheries scenario especially during the last plan period wherein local farmers are coming forward to take up aquaculture practices. In spite of the constraints, the department is making serious efforts to assist, guide and educate the people about the importance of fisheries development and sustainable fisheries.

Certain villages/communities are taking steps to conserve their river/stream systems by their own customary law, and today we find many rivers/streams being protected under this law. The numbers of fish farmers are increasing year after year and production has increased considerably. The above given account goes to prove that in spite of major hurdles and constraints, the department has been able to make sufficient progress in achieving its aims and objectives and also induce the rural mass to take up fish culture practice by whatever technical assistance and guidance the department could provide with limited funds. In this regard, the department can very soon boast of bringing a revolution in fish culture in the State by way of transfer of scientific technology through extension service by fishery personnel. Table 19.5 shows the achievement of the Fishery Department during the period from 2001-02 to 2004-05.

Table 19.5 : Achievement of Fishery Department in Nagaland

Particulars	*2001-02*	*2002-03*	*2003-04*	*2004-05*
No. of Fishery Ponds	1560	1176	657	794
Fingerling supplied	500	461	406	440
Production of Fish	5246	5500	4000	4900
Number of Beneficiaries	1125	1135	657	670

Source: Statistical Handbook of Nagaland, 2007.

Conclusion

Thus, to conclude, it can be said that Nagaland is blessed with favourable climate for Agriculture. The soil is fertile and the people are socially and culturally acquainted with agriculture.

Altogether there is a high potential for agricultural growth. Nagaland is known for its unique and quality agricultural output evident from the famous King chilly and the tallest paddy. Although, the emerging evidences do not subscribe to this view point fully, this is mainly due to the trend of urbanization and lack of persistence and determination to promote agriculture. Agriculture is the strength of Nagaland and its economy can be built upon it. Through an all-round effort, agriculture can be developed and thereby Nagaland can be ahead of many other North-Eastern States in the primary sector.

Index